CHAPPELLUNIVERSITY

Troubleshooting with Wireshark®
Locate the Source of Performance Problems

Laura Chappell

Founder, Chappell University™
Founder, Wireshark University™

Always ensure you obtain proper authorization
before you listen to and capture network traffic.

Protocol Analysis Institute, Inc
5339 Prospect Road, # 343
San Jose, CA 95129 USA
www.packet-level.com

Chappell University
info@chappellU.com
www.chappellU.com

To arrange bulk purchase discounts for sales promotions, events, training courses, or other purposes, please contact Chappell University via email (info@wiresharkbook.com), phone (1-408-378-7841), or mail (5339 Prospect Road, #343, San Jose, CA 95129).

Book URL: *www.wiresharkbook.com*
10-digit ISBN: 1-893939-97-9
13-digit ISBN: 978-1-893939-97-4 (Version 1.0b)

Distributed worldwide for Chappell University through Protocol Analysis Institute, Inc. Protocol Analysis Institute, Inc. is the exclusive educational materials developer for Chappell University.

For general information on Chappell University or Protocol Analysis Institute, Inc., including information on corporate licenses, updates, future titles, or courses, contact Protocol Analysis Institute, Inc., at 408/378-7841 or send email to info@wiresharkbook.com.

For authorization to photocopy items for corporate, personal, or educational use, contact Protocol Analysis Institute, Inc., at info@wiresharkbook.com.

Trademarks. All brand names and product names used in this book or mentioned in this course are trade names, service marks, trademarks, or registered trademarks of their respective owners. Wireshark and the "fin" logo are registered trademarks of the Wireshark Foundation.

Limit of Liability/Disclaimer of Warranty. The author and publisher used their best efforts in preparing this book and the related materials used in this book. Protocol Analysis Institute, Inc., Chappell University, and the author(s) make no representations or warranties of merchantability of fitness for a particular purpose. Protocol Analysis Institute, Inc., and Chappell University assume no liability for any damages caused by following the instructions or using the techniques or tools listed in this book or related materials used in this book. Protocol Analysis Institute, Inc., Chappell University, and the author(s) make no representations or warranties that extend beyond the descriptions contained in this paragraph. No warranty may be created or extended by sales representatives or written sales materials. The accuracy or completeness of the information provided herein and the opinions stated herein are not guaranteed or warranted to produce any particular result and the advice and strategies contained herein may not be suitable for every individual. Protocol Analysis Institute, Inc., Chappell University, and author(s) shall not be liable for any loss of profit or any other damages, including without limitation, special, incidental, consequential, or other damages.

Copy Protection. In all cases, reselling or duplication of this book and materials referenced in this book without explicit written authorization is expressly forbidden. We will find you, ya know. So do not steal or plagiarize this book.

Other Books by This Author

Wireshark 101: Essential Skills for Network Analysis
ISBN10: 1-893939-72-3
ISBN13: 978-1-893939-72-1
Series: Wireshark Solutions Series
Book URL: www.wiresharkbook.com

Available in hardcopy and digital format. Visit
www.amazon.com for more details.

**Wireshark Network Analysis: The Official Wireshark
Certified Network Analyst Study Guide – Second Edition**
ISBN10: 1-893939-94-4
ISBN13: 978-1-893939-94-3
Book URL: www.wiresharkbook.com
Related URL: www.wiresharktraining.com

Available in hardcopy and digital format. Visit
www.amazon.com for more details.

**Wireshark Certified Network Analyst
Official Exam Prep Guide – Second Edition**
ISBN10: 1-893939-90-1
ISBN13: 978-1-893939-90-5
Book URL: www.wiresharkbook.com
Related URL: www.wiresharktraining.com

Available in hardcopy and digital format. Visit
www.amazon.com for more details.

Acknowledgments

My sincere thanks go to the **Wireshark Core Developers** who have built Wireshark into an indispensable tool. The current list of core developers can be found at wiki.wireshark.org/Developers.

My heartfelt thanks go to Gerald Combs for creating an amazing tool and leading the development team to implement many impressive enhancements over the years.

Thanks to Joy DeManty for reviewing the book tirelessly and running through all the labs time and time again.

Thanks to Jim Aragon for putting in so much time over the holidays to edit this book. I so appreciate the time and effort you dedicated to improving this title.

Hugs to my kids, Scott and Ginny. Thanks for keeping me laughing through this process.

If I've missed anyone in this acknowledgments section, I sincerely apologize.

Laura Chappell

Dedication

This book is dedicated to C.W. Rogers
with my deepest gratitude for teaching me many moons ago
that technology and training can be entertaining!

Laura

About this Book

This book was designed to teach you the most efficient network analysis and Wireshark techniques necessary to quickly locate the source of network performance problems.

We begin with a brief list of problems that can plague a network. It was a daunting task deciding which issues to cover in this book. We focused on the most common problems and the problems that Wireshark and network analysis are most suited to solve.

Part 1: Preparing for Problems focuses on a basic four-part troubleshooting methodology, crucial Wireshark skills used in troubleshooting, and a comparison of capture techniques. Mastering the fundamental processes and skill set in this part of the book will reduce your overall troubleshooting time.

Part 2: Symptom-Based Troubleshooting is the "heart" of this book. This part delves into the various symptoms that a problematic network may experience and the possible causes of those symptoms. The symptoms are separated into four sections: resolution problems, time-related problems, problems that can be detected with Wireshark's Expert Infos, and application problems. This part of the book is filled with hands-on labs to help locate symptoms as well as details on what causes those types of problems.

It's important to understand that Wireshark can always be used to determine *where* the problem occurred, but it cannot tell you *why* the problem occurred. We will, however, attempt to point you in the right direction regarding the cause of various symptoms.

Part 3: Use Graphs to Detect Problems explains how to use Wireshark's various graphs to build pictures of network performance issues and prioritize your troubleshooting tasks. Although you likely will have found the location of performance problems using the techniques learned in Part 1 and Part 2 of the book, visualization of problems can help when you must explain the issues to others. In addition, this section includes a chapter that explains how to export trace file information to various third-party charting and graphing tools.

Finally, *Part 4: Final Tips for Troubleshooting with Wireshark*, lists some insider tips and techniques for becoming an efficient network analyst. This section deals with challenges such as troubleshooting intermittent problems, sanitizing trace files, detecting WLAN problems, and working with extremely large trace files.

This book can used in conjunction with the *Wireshark 101: Essential Skills for Network Analysis* and *Wireshark Network Analysis: the Official Wireshark Certified Network Analyst Study Guide - Second Edition*.

Who is this Book For?

This book is written for beginner and experienced analysts who need to locate the source of network problems based on network traffic.

This book provides numerous techniques used to identify the symptoms of network problems. In addition, wherever possible we list off the potential cause(s) of these problems.

What Prerequisite Knowledge do I Need?

Before you delve into this book (or network analysis in general), you should have a solid understanding of basic network concepts and TCP/IP fundamentals. For example, you should know the purpose of a switch, a router, and a firewall. You should be familiar with the concepts of Ethernet networking, basic wireless networking, and be comfortable with IP network addressing, as well.

Although this book offers step-by-step instructions on key Wireshark tasks, consider expanding your skill set with *Wireshark 101: Essential Skills for Network Analysis*. If you need more in-depth information on protocols and applications, refer to *Wireshark Network Analysis: The Official Wireshark Certified Network Analyst Study Guide – Second Edition*.

There are a few spots in this book where you will need to access the command prompt to set a path to an application directory or to run basic command-line tools such as *ipconfig/ifconfig*. If you are unfamiliar with these tools, there are plenty of resources on the Internet to show you how to use these tools on various platforms.

In addition, *Appendix C: Network Analyst's Glossary* covers many of the network analysis and networking terms mentioned in the book.

What Versions of Wireshark does this Book Cover?

This book was written using several Wireshark 1.10.x stable release versions and several Wireshark 1.11.x development versions.

Does this Book Explain How to Troubleshoot My Network Applications?

Deciding which applications and networking technologies to cover was a daunting task. We focus on the most common network applications as well as the most common network problems in this book. Rather than cover every application and every network element and create a 5,000-page book, we honed in on the most common applications and elements. The techniques used to locate application delays and errors can be used to identify any application problems.

Where Can I Get the Book Trace Files and Other Supplements?

Your first step should be to download the book trace files and other supplemental files from www.wiresharkbook.com. Click the *Troubleshooting with Wireshark* book link and download the entire set of supplemental files. You should follow along with each of the labs to practice the skills covered in each section.

If you have questions regarding the book or the book web site, please send them to info@wiresharkbook.com.

Where Can I Learn More about Wireshark and Network Analysis?

There are numerous resources available to learn more about network analysis, TCP/IP communications and Wireshark specifically. The following lists some of the recommended resources.

- There are many areas of interest at www.wireshark.org– check out the Wireshark blog and visit the developer area to see what is in the works for the future version(s) of Wireshark.
- Download or watch Laura's free four-part Wireshark Basics course online at the All Access Pass portal (www.lcuportal2.com).
- Learn more analysis skills in the book *Wireshark 101: Essential Skills for Network Analysis* (wiresharkbook.com/wireshark101.html). This book contains 43 labs to teach and reinforce your analysis skills.
- The All Access Pass training subscription offers one-year of online training on Wireshark, TCP/IP communications, troubleshooting, security and more (www.lcuportal2.com).
- "100 Wireshark Tips" (PDF) was compiled after 100 days of new Wireshark tips were tweeted from @laurachappell (www.chappellU.com).
- Sharkfest is the yearly Wireshark User and Developer Conference. Join Gerald Combs and the many of the Wireshark Core Developers at this event (sharkfest.wireshark.org).
- Research analysis or traffic issues or ask your questions at ask.wireshark.org, the Wireshark Q&A Forum.

The Wireshark community is a very active and welcoming community. Do not hesitate to introduce yourself over at ask.wireshark.org or at the Sharkfest User and Developer Conference.

This page intentionally left blank.

Foreword by Gerald Combs

 Stop looking at the wrong packets.

I originally wrote Wireshark as a troubleshooting tool. I was working at an ISP and often had to diagnose and fix network problems. I needed a tool that would let me dig deep into network packets and show me everything it could about every last byte they contained. Other people had the same need and Wireshark quickly gained a large, knowledgeable developer and user community. This community has turned Wireshark into the best tool in the world for protocol analysis and I am grateful to be a part of it.

However, having the packet details is only half the answer for troubleshooting. If you don't have an understanding of what Wireshark is showing you and what those packets mean, it's easy to lose direction. You can end up spending too much time going down dead ends, looking at the wrong packets (i.e. ones that have nothing to do with your problem). In order to find the right packets you need to know how protocols work and what they mean in the context of your particular network. That's where Laura and this book come in. She will show you how to make full use of the information that Wireshark provides and solve real problems on your network.

Troubleshooting is an important skill to master. Aside from the obvious benefit of fixing an immediate problem it has follow-on benefits. Each time you dig down deep into your network, you get more knowledge and insight into its behavior. This can help you resolve problems more quickly the next time they arise and it can help guide the design and implementation of your network in order to avoid problems in the future.

This can also help your career. The Wireshark community is filled with people who have gained the respect of their peers due in no small part to their network troubleshooting skills.

So how do you become a troubleshooting guru? You could learn everything yourself, but that would be silly. Unfortunately I regularly encounter people in this position. They are "the Wireshark guy" or "the Wireshark gal" at their organization and have little to no outside support.

Trying to learn how to diagnose network problems by yourself is a bit like learning dentistry or jet engine repair by yourself. It's certainly possible, but it's not something I would recommend. The formal troubleshooting approach in this book will show you where and how to start looking for network problems.

Stop looking at the wrong packets. Laura can show you how to find the right ones.

Gerald Combs

Creator of Wireshark® (formerly *Ethereal*)

This page intentionally left blank.

Table of Contents

List of Labs

List of Network Problems and Symptoms

LIST OF LABS

This page intentionally left blank.

LIST OF NETWORK PROBLEMS AND SYMPTOMS

In my 20+ years of analyzing network traffic I've accumulated a list of the most common network problems that I encounter. I often share the "Top 10" at conferences and on the All Access Portal (our online training portal).

Since I know many of you hate to wade through non-technical materials in the front of books (even though foundation materials are often necessary to lay the groundwork), I decided to begin this book with a list of the key network problems and symptoms seen in trace files.

In *Part 2: Symptom Based Troubleshooting* you will delve into most of the symptoms contained in this list of problems.

Laura Chappell

Lab 20	TCP connection refused		Zero Window condition	Labs 7, 63-70
Lab 21	application services refused	Server Problem?	DNS error response	Lab 77
Labs 34-36	DNS response delays		HTTP error response	Lab 78
Labs 2, 37-40	HTTP response delays		SMB/SMB2 error response	Lab 79
Labs 41-43	SMB/SMB2 response delays		SIP error response	Lab 80
Lab 88	DHCP response delays	Infrastructure Problem?	delays during a download	Page 110
Page 10	bandwidth throttling		high path latency	Labs 31, 32
Lab 86	queuing traffic		routing loop	Page 8
Page 12	switch loop		lousy routing path	Page 11
Labs 48, 49	dropped packets		excessive broadcasts	Page 13
Lab 60	ACKed unseen segment with SPAN		route resolution failure	Page 97
Page 322	infected host		TCP functionality missing	Lab 9
Lab 15	no WLAN traffic captured		Zero Window condition	Labs 7, 63-69
Lab 18	name resolution failures	Client Problem?	Reused port conflicts	Lab 74, 75
Lab 19	address resolution failures		low packet sizes	Lab 85
Lab 60	faulty capture		WLAN retries and low signal strength	Lab 98
Lab 76	checksum errors		delays before a TLS encrypted alert	Page 108

Each problem listed in this section includes a list of possible symptoms that may be seen in your trace files. Wherever applicable, the symptom defines the Expert Infos Error, Warning or Note indications and/or display filter syntax for the symptom.

 Possible Symptoms

1.   TCP Connection Refused by Server

If everything is configured and running properly, TCP connection refusals should never be seen on a network. This problem is caused when a service is not running on a server or perhaps a firewall is preventing the connection. TCP connection refusals may also be a sign of a TCP port scan to a closed port.

 Possible Symptoms

- Client's SYN followed by Reset (RST)/ACK
- Expert Infos Note: Retransmission (retransmission of SYN packet by client)
- Client SYN followed by an Internet Control Messaging Protocol (ICMP) Type 3/Code 3 (Destination Unreachable/Port Unreachable) response from a host-based firewall (`icmp.type==3 && icmp.code==3`)

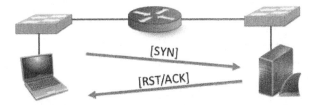

2.   Application Request Refused

Any service refusals should be of concern on your network. In an ideal network environment, clients make requests of servers and servers respond with the required information in a timely manner.

 Possible Symptoms

- Client request followed by an application error response such as an HTTP 404 Reply Code or a DNS Name Error
- Service refusals for applications that run over UDP are indicated by a UDP-based command followed by an ICMP Type 3/Code 3 (Destination Unreachable/Port Unreachable) response (`icmp.type==3 && icmp.code==3`)

3.   Connection Blocked by a Host-Based or Network Firewall

Ideally, hosts wouldn't even attempt to communicate with firewalled resources. Such an attempt could be due to a misconfiguration, malware, malicious user, or other issue.

Possible Symptoms

- No response to a SYN packet
- RST/ACK response to a SYN packet
- No response to a UDP-based application request
- ICMP Type 3/Code 3 response to a TCP SYN packet (`icmp.type==3 && icmp.code==3`)

4.   Slow Application at Server

The good news is that the server did not refuse to provide a desired service. The bad news is that the server is slooooow. This may be due to a lack of processing power at the server, a poorly behaving application, or even, in a multi-tiered architecture, a slow upstream server that actually provides the data (mentioned in *Slow Loading of Remote Content*).

Possible Symptoms

- TCP-based application: Large delay (`tcp.time_delta`) between the server ACK to a client request and the response data
- UDP-based application: Large delay (`frame.time_delta`) between a request and the response data

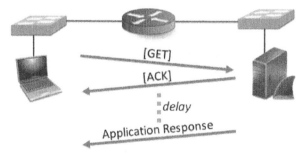

5.   Slow Load of Remote Content

Many networks are designed in a multi-tiered fashion. For example, consider a client that sends a request to Server 1. In a multi-tiered environment, that server may need to obtain information from Servers 2 through 9 before answering the client. Once we identify the delays from the client's perspective, we need to capture this multi-tiered traffic to determine which server is actually responding slowly.

Possible Symptoms

- TCP-based application: Large delay (`tcp.time_delta`) between the server ACK to a client request and the response data
- UDP-based application: Large delay (`frame.time_delta`) between a request and the response data

6.   Server Application Fault

The server is up and running, but not responding to requests. The server responds to a SYN with a SYN/ACK, but when the client makes a request, no response is received. When the TCP Retransmission Time Out (RTO) time is reached, the client retransmits the request. If no ACK is received, the client continues to retransmit the request using an exponential backoff time until it finally gives up and sends a TCP Reset (RST).

Possible Symptoms

- Expert Infos Notes: Retransmission
- Exponentially increasing time values in a `tcp.time_delta` column

7.   Content Redirection

We've all had the experience of driving to a specialty store (such as an office supply store) to buy something only to be told that the store does not have the item in stock. The clerk performs an inventory check and sends us off to another store to get the item. It is inconvenient in our daily lives and, when this behavior is seen in network communications, it can negatively affect network performance. If an application supports redirection (such as HTTP) and the target knows where the information actually resides, it may send you a redirection response.

Possible Symptoms

- In HTTP communications, response codes 300-399 (`http.response.code > 299 && http.response.code < 400`)
- In SIP communications, response codes 300-399 (`sip.Status-Code > 299 && sip.Status-Code < 400`)
- A sudden name resolution process and traffic to another host

8.   TCP Receive Buffer Full

Each side of a TCP connection maintains its own receive buffer area. As data is received, it is placed in the TCP receive buffer area. Applications must reach down into this buffer area to pick up the data fast enough to prevent the buffer from filling up. Each TCP header states the current receive buffer size (in bytes) of the sender in the Window Size field. It is not unusual to see the advertised Window Size value drop as data is received and then increase as an application picks up data from the buffer. When the advertised TCP receive buffer value drops to zero, the data transfer will stop. A low Window Size value can also cause data flow to stop. The only recovery is a Window Update.

Possible Symptoms

- Expert Infos Warnings: Window Full preceding Zero Window
- Unusually high TCP delay (`tcp.time_delta`) before a Window Update and resumption of data flow
- Low TCP calculated window size value (when SYN, FIN and RST bits are 0)

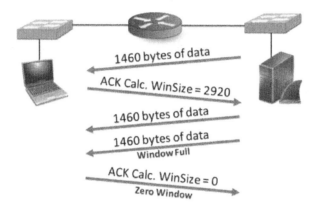

9.   Send Buffer Full

Just as a lack of receive buffer space can slow down a data transfer process, a lack of send buffer space can also negatively impact performance. A limited send buffer space can negatively impact network performance even if the network can handle a high data transfer rate and the receiver has plenty of buffer space. The symptom of a full send buffer is a set of delays in the middle of a data stream transmission with no other logical reason for the delay. The network is healthy, the TCP peer's receive buffer space is adequate, and we do not have a Nagle algorithm/Delayed ACK issue.

Possible Symptoms

- High TCP delay (`tcp.time_delta`) for no apparent reason
- Bytes in Flight column climbs to a specific value and seems to "max out" there

10. Altered TCP Connection Attributes Along a Path

Routers and other interconnecting devices can wreak havoc on a network if they change the attributes of a TCP connection as they forward the traffic. This situation can create some freaky looking trace files and lots of finger pointing.

In essence, if you capture traffic close to the client you can determine the client capabilities based on the TCP options listed in the SYN packets sent from the client. For example, the client may indicate it supports Selective ACK and/or Window Scaling. If an interconnecting device alters the TCP option information before forwarding the SYN packet, the server has a different view of the client's capabilities.

You may blame the server for behaving poorly or not supporting certain TCP options. If you capture traffic at the server, you see the altered traffic and you may blame the client for behaving poorly or being poorly configured. This requires capture on both sides of the interconnecting device to point the finger at the true source of problems—an infrastructure device.

Possible Symptoms

- Low TCP calculated window size (**tcp.window_size**) and significant delays (**tcp.time_delta**) before Window Update packets
- Expert Infos Note: Retransmissions (**tcp.analysis.retransmission**)
- Expert Infos Warning: Window Full (**tcp.analysis.window_full**)
- Excessive Retransmissions after low number of packets lost
- No Left Edge/Right Edge in the second and later Duplicate ACK packets (**tcp.analysis.duplicate_ack && !tcp.options.sack_le && !expert.message == "Duplicate ACK (#1)"**)

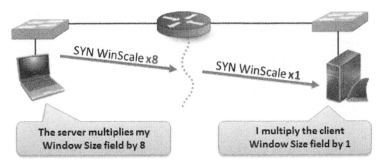

SYN WinScale x8

SYN WinScale x1

The server multiplies my Window Size field by 8

I multiply the client Window Size field by 1

11. Mismatched TCP Parameters across a Proxy Device

Poorly configured or poorly behaving proxy devices may affect performance. This problem could manifest itself in behavior similar to the aforementioned *Altered TCP Connection Attributes Along a Path* except that a proxy box does not forward connection packets – it creates a new connection to the target on behalf of the client. If the connection on one side of the proxy device has a set of connection parameters that do not match the connection parameters offered in the connection on the other side of the proxy device, you may have problems.

The symptoms depend upon which connection characteristics are not established by the proxy. For example, if the connection on the client side of a proxy supports a smaller Window Scale multiplier than the connection on the server side, traffic flowing toward the client may need to be buffered by the proxy device because the target host does not have sufficient receive buffer space.

The symptoms experienced will vary depending on which connection characteristics are mismatched.

Possible Symptoms

- Delays in data forwarded through proxy (proxy queuing)
- Expert Infos Notes: Retransmissions (only on one side of proxy)

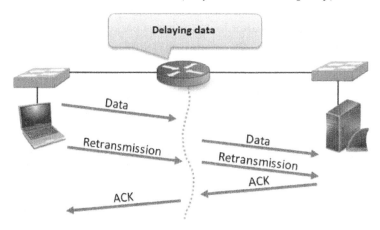

12. Routing Loops

Routing protocols such as OSPF should automatically resolve routing loops. Routing loops occur when a packet is routed back onto a network over and over again.

Possible Symptoms

- Identical packets listed in the Packet List pane, but no TCP Retransmission indications (they are not identical packets — their TTL value decrements)

13. Weak Signal (WLAN)

Wireless signals can only travel a certain distance, as dictated by their transmit signal strength and the effect of interference. If a signal degrades substantially, it may not be interpreted properly when captured. In Wireshark's view, the frame may be tagged as malformed or it may not be defined as a frame at all during the capture process.

Possible Symptoms

- Expert Infos Errors: Malformed Packets
- Low Signal Strength value (`radiotap.dbm_antsignal` or `ppi.80211-common.dbm.antsignal`)
- WLAN Retries (`wlan.fc.retry==1`)
- Expert Infos Notes: TCP Retransmissions

14. Asymmetric Routing

Asymmetric routing is a situation when traffic flowing from Host A to Host B flows along a different path than the traffic flowing from Host B to Host A. This may not cause a problem if each path is healthy and offers the same throughput. If there are devices that must see every packet in order to function, however, this can be a problem.

For example, if proxies are in use the network path must be symmetrical from the client to the proxy host. Another consideration would be an Intrusion Detection System (IDS) box that must see every packet and monitor state information about conversations.

Possible Symptoms

- Expert Infos Warning: ACKed Segment that Wasn't Captured
- Expert Infos Warning: Previous Segment Not Captured

15. Packet Loss

Packet loss typically occurs at an interconnecting device such as a switch, a router, a NAT device, or a network firewall. When a TCP host notices packet loss (based on an unexpected TCP sequence number or no acknowledgment within the Retransmission Time Out), the host begins a recovery process. A UDP-based application must be written to detect packet loss and begin its own recovery process.

If the number of packets dropped is small and the recovery process is quick, the packet loss may go unnoticed. If many sequential packets are lost, however, users will likely feel the impact and complain.

When your trace file indicates packets have been lost, you must move your capture point across interconnecting devices to locate the point where packet loss begins.

Be aware that in some situations Wireshark may trigger a packet loss warning when packets are simply out of order.

Possible Symptoms

- Expert Infos Warning: Previous Segment Not Captured
- Expert Infos Note: Duplicate ACKs
- Expert Infos Note: Fast Retransmission
- Expert Infos Note: Retransmission
- IO Graph: Drops in throughput

16. High Path Latency

A single low speed (high delay) link along a path or the delay between geographically disbursed peers can inject a level of path latency that affects performance.

Possible Symptoms

- Capture at client: Large delays between the outbound SYN and the inbound SYN/ACK of a TCP handshake (**tcp.time_delta**).
- Capture at server: Large delays between the SYN/ACK and the ACK of a TCP handshake (**tcp.time_delta**).

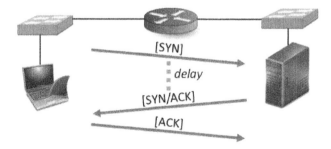

17. Lousy Routing Path

When construction occurs in a major city, traffic is a nightmare as drivers are rerouted along less efficient and less direct routes. This is also true of network traffic. If a target is 10 blocks away and yet for some reason the packets must travel through 17 routers to get there, performance may be unacceptable.

The symptoms are the same as *High Path Latency*.

Possible Symptoms

- Capture at client: Large delays between the outbound SYN and the inbound SYN/ACK of a TCP handshake (`tcp.time_delta`).
- Capture at server: Large delays between the SYN/ACK and the ACK of a TCP handshake (`tcp.time_delta`).

18. Bandwidth Throttling

Transmitting data along a bandwidth throttling link is like driving a car during rush hour. You move along bumper-to-bumper at speeds below your lowest speedometer indication. Bandwidth throttling may be configured for traffic flowing in a particular direction, so a graph of unidirectional traffic can help you spot a limit on throughput ("hitting the ceiling").

Possible Symptom

- IO Graph: "Flat-line ceiling" during a file transfer

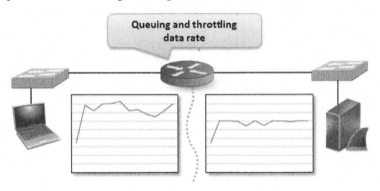

19. Delayed ACKs

Delayed ACK was defined in *RFC 1122*, *"Requirements for Internet Hosts -- Communication Layers"* (Section 4.2.3.2) as a method to "increase efficiency in both the Internet and the hosts by sending fewer than one ACK (acknowledgment) segment per data segment received."

This delay can cause issues for the host that is sending data if it times out waiting for an ACK or it cannot send another data packet until an ACK is received (Nagle algorithm issue).

Hansang Bae recorded a video detailing the issues with the TCP Nagle algorithm and Delayed ACKs. See bit.ly/delayedack.

Possible Symptoms

- 200ms delay before ACK packets (`tcp.time_delta`)
- Delay before transmission of data packet (if Nagle issue) (`tcp.time_delta`)

20. Queued Packets (Overloaded Router)

Everyone hates waiting in a long line. TCP peers and UDP-based applications may detect sudden queue delays and think packets have been lost.

Even a slight queue delay along a path can be felt if you consider that it can take thousands or hundreds of thousands of data packets to download a file. The entire process feels mired in mud. This may be caused by an overloaded router or perhaps prioritization at a router (for example, video streaming first, email traffic last).

Using a throughput testing tool (such as jPerf or iPerf) can help you detect queuing along a path.

Possible Symptoms

- IO Graph: "EKG" pattern (decrease in throughput followed by equal increase in throughput) – consider decreasing X Axis Tick Interval.

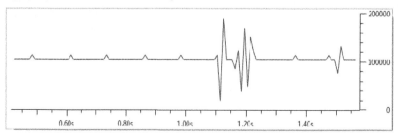

21. Route Redirections

Route redirections should be rare. When a host sends packets to one local router when another local router exists with a preferred path, a route redirection may take place. The receiving router may respond with an ICMP Type 5 (Redirect) packet. This ICMP packet includes the IP address of the recommended router. These ICMP Redirects are considered rare as we often see only one router on the local network.

Possible Symptoms

- ICMP Type 5 packets with either Code 0 (Redirect for Host) or Code 1 (Redirect for Network) indicate route redirection is taking place. (`icmp.type==5`).

22. Broadcast or Multicast Storms

Broadcast and multicast storms should be easy to spot. Simply capture a moment of traffic and look at the target address. Broadcasts are typically not forwarded so you should be capturing on and dealing with hosts on a single network. Multicasts can be forwarded through an internetwork therefore they can cause a greater problem if something goes wrong and they storm the network.

Possible Symptoms

- High rate of packets addressed to the all nets broadcast (255.255.255.255) or the subnet broadcast address.
- High rate of packets addressed to a multicast address (224-239.x.x.x).

23. Switch Loop

A switch loop is immediate death for all devices connected to the problem switches. Since we have protocols to help prevent switching loops (Spanning Tree), this problem should be rare.

Unfortunately, older switches that have not been restarted or rechecked every once in a while may begin to malfunction—if Spanning Tree fails and there is a loop—the network will become overwhelmed with looped packets.

Switch loops are not difficult to detect. The network is flooded with the same packet that is looping endlessly. You only need to capture a few of these packets to know what is going on. You will see duplicate packets appearing over and over again in the trace file.

Possible Symptoms

- High rate of identical packets

24. Virus/Malware on Network Hosts

Virus/malware running on network hosts may affect network traffic rates. For example, when a compromised host begins performing port scans on other network hosts or it begins broadcasting discovery packets, the overhead may be felt. First it will likely be felt by the compromised host—later it may be felt by other network hosts.

The user working on a compromised host may notice performance problems if that host is uploading or downloading files in the background or performing other background tasks.

Having a baseline of normal network traffic can help detect a compromised host.

Possible Symptoms

- Unusual applications or protocols (**Statistics | Protocol Hierarchy**)
- "Data" below IP, TCP or UDP (**Statistics | Protocol Hierarchy**)
- Local broadcasts (potentially discovery processes)
- Suspicious outbound targets
- Unusual internal targets (such as a local client trying to connect to the Accounting server)
- Data transfer during idle times
- High number of service refusals (potential discovery process)

25. Network Name Resolution Problems

When a name resolution query is met with a mind-numbing silence or an error, there is a problem. Since successful completion of this process is imperative to connecting to a target, the user may receive an application error such as "Server not found" as in the case of a DNS Name Error when browsing.

Possible Symptoms

- No responses to a name query
- An error response to a name query (such as a DNS Name Error or Server Error)

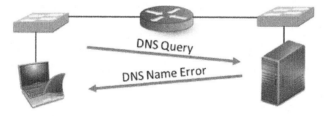

26. Network Address Resolution Problems

Incorrect subnet addressing can cause major performance issues. In some cases, however, our routers hide the problems from us for a while (think Proxy ARP).

In other cases, a client may send packets that are destined to a local device to a router or perform a local-style discovery for a remote device.

Possible Symptoms

- ARP Requests are sent for remote targets
- Traffic destined to local hosts are sent to the router
- Expert Infos Warning: Duplicate IP Address

27. Hardware Address Resolution Problems

The purpose of hardware address resolution is to obtain the MAC address of the local target or local router. Network address resolution problems may cause a host to think local devices are remote (or vice versa). Hardware address resolution problems are local only — you must be capturing on the same network as the faulty host to detect these issues.

Possible Symptoms

- No response to an ARP query for a local host
- No response to an ARP query for a local router

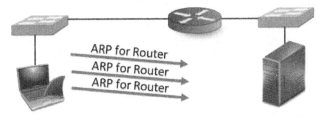

28. No Support for Selective Acknowledgment (SACK)

Selective Acknowledgment (SACK) is an important enhancement to TCP (*RFC 2018, "TCP Selective Acknowledgment Options"*).

When packet loss is detected by a receiving TCP host that supports SACK, that host can acknowledge data received after the missing packet(s). This limits the retransmission to just the missing packet(s).

Without SACK, the recovery process will include retransmissions of the first packet lost and every subsequent data packet regardless of whether those subsequent packets were received successfully.

These extra retransmissions unnecessarily add load to the network links and interconnecting devices and may compound the packet loss problem.

Both sides of a TCP connection must support SACK in order for it to be used.

Possible Symptoms

- No SACK Option in the TCP header of a SYN packet
- No SACK Option in the TCP header of a SYN/ACK packet when there was a SACK Option in the TCP header of a SYN packet
- No SACK Left Edge/Right Edge information in the Duplicate ACK #2 and higher

29. No Support for Window Scaling

Window Scaling (*RFC 1323, "TCP Extensions for High Performance"*) is used to increase the advertised TCP receive buffer size past the 65,535-byte limit caused by the 2-byte Window Size field.

During the TCP handshake, TCP peers indicate that they support Window Scaling and provide a Window Scale Shift Count. This Shift Count is used to determine by how much the Window Size value should be multiplied. Offering a larger Window Size reduces the delays caused by a low window or Zero Window condition.

Both sides of a TCP connection must support Window Scaling in order for it to be used.

Possible Symptoms

- No Window Scaling Option in the TCP header of a SYN packet
- No Window Scaling Option in the TCP header of a SYN/ACK packet when there was a Window Scaling Option in the TCP header of a SYN packet
- Significant delays before a host sends data
- Significant delays before a Window Update
- Expert Infos Warning: Zero Window
- Expert Infos Warning: Window is Full

30. Client Misconfiguration

A misconfigured client may have the wrong DNS address, the wrong router address, incorrect port numbers defined in a *services* file, or other problems.

Usually this type of problem can be detected quickly and a comparison with other client traffic can help pinpoint the misconfiguration.

The symptoms will vary based on the misconfiguration.

Possible Symptoms

- The client sends traffic to the wrong target
- The client receives service refusals or no answer
- Numerous other symptoms may appear depending on the misconfiguration

31. Low Packet Size/Low MTU Size

It's more efficient to go to the store once and buy a dozen eggs than to go to the store 12 times to pick up one egg at a time. Likewise, it is more efficient to send as much data as possible in each packet during a file transfer.

The amount of data that can be carried in a frame is limited by the Maximum Transmission Unit (MTU) setting, the Maximum Segment Size (MSS) setting, or even an inefficient application.

This problem may not be felt in communications that send small files back and forth (such as general email messages), but when the file sizes increase, the performance pain does as well.

Possible Symptoms

- The packet sizes are not optimal during a file transfer (Length column)
- The MSS value defined in the TCP SYN or SYN/ACK packet is illogically small

32. TCP Port Number Reuse

In most cases, port numbers can be reused without any problem as long as the previous TCP connection is terminated. If the previous connection is still valid when a host attempts to reuse a previous port number, you will see a SYN followed by a RST/ACK as the new connection is refused.

Possible Symptoms

- Expert Infos Note: TCP Port Reused
- TCP RST sent in response to a SYN packet to a server port that is known to be open

33. Slow Application

Some applications are just dog-slow. This could be due to poor or bloated coding, internal errors, or even man-made timers defining the application's performance speed. Unless you are the programmer or can reach out to the programmer to get the application fixed/improved, you may need to either live with this problem or find a better application to use.

Other times, the application is not at fault. The system on which the application is installed may be overloaded and short on resources. In this case it is time for a system upgrade.

Possible Symptoms

- Large delay in the **time.delta** or **tcp.time_dela** columns
- Large delay in the application response time value (such as the high **http.time** value)

This is just a short list of things that can go wrong on the network.

In *Part 1: Preparing for Problems*, you will review a four-part troubleshooting methodology and troubleshooting checklist, master key Wireshark troubleshooting tasks and focus on your capture techniques.

In *Part 2: Symptom-Based Troubleshooting*, you will analyze numerous trace files to gather symptoms of performance problems and learn what can cause each of the symptoms.

Part 1: Preparing for Problems

The time and effort you put into preparing to troubleshoot is as important as the time and effort you put into actually sifting through the packets.

You can save yourself many hours of work, frustration, and distraction by employing a basic four-step troubleshooting methodology, using key Wireshark troubleshooting skills, and applying the proper capture techniques.

This page intentionally left blank.

CHAPTER 1: USE EFFICIENT TROUBLESHOOTING METHODS

If you've been working in the world of troubleshooting for a while, you likely have a tried and true method for detecting the causes of network problems.

In this chapter we will focus on a basic four-part methodology for troubleshooting networks based on traffic:

Task 1: Define the problem

Task 2: Collect system, application and path information

Task 3: Capture and analyze packet flows

Task 4: Consider other tools

Chapter 1 Notes

There are certain traffic characteristics that I look for/rule out before diving into packets.

- Make sure the trace file is "good" and packets weren't dropped during the capture process.

- Apply filters to focus on the complaining user's traffic.

- Watch for delays first – Chapter 5 is a great resource for this.

- Find drops in throughput and look for causes. See Chapter 9.

- Watch the TCP connection set up process.

- Look for TCP problems such as packet loss, full buffers and more. Check out Chapter 6 (it's full of TCP details).

- Check for application error responses. Check out Chapter 7.

A Sample Four-Part Analysis Methodology

Let's look at these four elements from a network analyst's perspective:

Task 1: Define the problem

Task 2: Collect system, application and path information

Task 3: Capture and analyze packet flows

Task 4: Consider other tools

Task 1: Define the Problem

"The network is slow" is a common complaint from network users. This vague description will not help you to hone in on the problem.

When a user complains about performance in such a general way, we need to ask some questions to focus and prioritize our troubleshooting tasks.

Here are sample questions that you might ask a network user before capturing or analyzing a single packet.

1. What were you trying to do? (Are you troubleshooting a file upload, file download, login, email send, email receive, database update, or something else? What type of traffic will you be looking for?)
2. What web site/server target were you communicating with? (Do you have an address upon which to filter?)
3. What are the symptoms? (This is my attempt to get past "the network is slow" self-diagnosis often offered. You want to know if this is a problem loading a specific page, running a specific application, or a recurring problem for a specific user.)
4. Did you receive any error message? (The error might tell me the exact problem.)
5. Is this happening all the time? (Can your complaining user reproduce the problem so you can capture the traffic right now, or do you need to start an ongoing capture to catch the issue at some point?)

There are so many questions that one can ask to get a feel for the problem — we just need to get past "the network is slow" generic complaint.

Task 2: Collect System, Application and Path Information

Obtain as much system, network and infrastructure information as possible. This will help put a framework around the tasks at hand.

I've hit a number of problems over the years with various operating systems, applications and interconnecting devices. If I know a certain version of a firewall is causing problems during the TCP handshake, this might be an issue to consider if the customer is using that product.

Here are some sample questions that you might ask a customer about their configuration.

1. What operating system is running on the client/server?
2. What application (and version) is running?
3. Describe the network path that the traffic must traverse.

Sometimes the person you will speak with does not have this information. In that case you might not be talking with the right person or the customer really doesn't know their network.[1]

Task 3: Capture and Analyze Packet Flows

This is the focus of this book. Packet analysis is often referred to as an art form, but if you know how TCP/IP and your applications work, it is more like a game. Anyone can play and the more you practice, the better you will be.

Capture Location Tips

I am a firm believer in capturing as close as possible to the complaining host first if possible. I want to see the traffic from that host's perspective. I want to examine the roundtrip time to the target(s), the TCP handshake establishment process (if used), indications of network problems, background traffic to which the host must listen, and more.

Capturing as close as possible to the complaining host will allow me to focus in on relevant traffic without having to apply a capture filter.[2]

Capture Tool Tips

I also prefer using a tap or dedicated capture device rather than spanning a switch port for the capture process. Why do I avoid spanning switch ports? First, the switch might be part of the problem. Second, switches have enough to do these days—I do not want to burden them further with spanning functions. An oversubscribed switch may not be able to

---

[1]   I had one customer draw a picture of their network with a square in the middle marked as "magic box." That "magic box" was their NAT gateway to the Internet.

[2]   I avoid using capture filters whenever possible. I will explain this a bit further in *Use Capture Filters when Necessary* on page 77.

forward all the traffic and therefore my trace file is not complete[3]. Third, some switches just do not do spanning very well.

On a high traffic network, consider using a command-line capture tool such as *tcpdump* or *dumpcap*. These tools require few resources and can be deployed for remote capture without installing the entire Wireshark application. You can use these streamlined tools for capture and then open the trace files in Wireshark for the analysis process.

Analysis Process Tips

Remember, analysis is more like a game than an art form — practice, practice, practice. Review *Use a Troubleshooting Checklist* on page 27.

Here are some quick tips for analyzing efficiently:

- Know what is "normal." Create baseline trace files of normal communications **before** the problems occur. See *Tips for Faster Problem Detection* on page 331.
- Remove unrelated traffic from view (use an exclusion filter). See *Filter OUT "Normal" Traffic (Exclusion Filters)* on page 51.
- Focus on traffic related to the complaining user's machine (use an inclusion filter and possibly Export Specified Packets to a new trace file). See *Filter on a Host, Subnet or Conversation* on page 42.
- Verify your trace file is usable (no problems during the capture process). See *Verify Trace File Integrity and Basic Communications* on page 27.
- Verify basic host connectivity. See *Verify Trace File Integrity and Basic Communications* on page 27.
- Click your troubleshooting buttons to quickly detect common problems (such as DNS errors, HTTP errors, and SMB errors). We will add many of these buttons in *Part 2: Symptom-Based Troubleshooting*.
- Sort or filter for delays (increase in general or UDP delta times). See *Detect Delays in UDP Conversations* on page 112.
- Examine the Expert Infos errors, warnings and notes. See *Overview of Wireshark's Expert Infos System* on page 153.
- Create a "Golden Graph" to prioritize throughput drops. See *Correlate Drops in Throughput with TCP Problems (the "Golden Graph")* on page 280.

Refer to *Use a Troubleshooting Checklist* on page 27 for a more complete list of analysis tasks.

---

[3] If you have spanned a switch port, watch for "ACKed Unseen Segment" – this can be an indication that the switch is unable to keep up with the spanning functions. For more information, see *ACKed Unseen Segment* on page 165.

Task 4: Consider Other Tools

Wireshark is an amazing packet analysis tool. There are, however, some functions that it does not offer and other functions that it just does not do very well. In some cases you may need to work with another tool once you have hit a Wireshark limitation.

One example of a Wireshark limitation is seen when you work with large trace files. Try to keep your trace files under 100 MB maximum size. Anything larger and Wireshark becomes too slow and at times, unstable. This problem is worse when you add coloring rules, columns and additional protocol processing requests to Wireshark.

The following list includes some tools to consider when analyzing trace files:

- Cascade Pilot® (architected by Loris Degioanni[4] and available at www.riverbed.com) was designed to work with very large trace files. Cascade Pilot offers numerous Views that you can apply to trace files to visualize traffic characteristics. You can simply click and drag across the timeline to export a subset of interesting traffic to Wireshark for further analysis. Cascade Pilot also includes an impressive reporting feature. A sample analysis report from Pilot is included in this book's supplement file set. See *Open Large Trace Files in Cascade Pilot* on page 316.
- TraceWrangler (created by Jasper Bongertz and available at www.tracewrangler.com) was designed to anonymize and edit trace files. Demonstrated at Sharkfest 2013, TraceWrangler is now de facto trace file editing tool. See *Use TraceWrangler* on page 330.
- For WLAN analysis on a Windows host, the AirPcap adapters (www.riverbed.com) are must-have tools. These USB adapters (and their specialized drivers) were created to capture all WLAN traffic (including Management and Control frames), capture the true 802.11 header and prepend either a Radiotap or PPI header to the trace files to offer additional analysis capabilities. See *Tips for Detecting WLAN Problems* on page 325.
- Also for WLAN analysis, the Wi-Spy and Chanalyzer products from MetaGeek (www.metageek.net) are required tools. See *Tips for Detecting WLAN Problems* on page 325.

Visit www.wiresharkbook.com/resources.html for a list of other tools I use in my analysis processes.

---

[4]   Loris Degioanni is the creator of WinPcap and a brilliant product architect. We sat for many hours going over the function and interface for Pilot. As network traffic, network files and network speeds increased, so did the size of my trace files. I use Pilot to perform my initial assessment of large trace files and then export just the portions of interest to Wireshark for further analysis.

Use a Troubleshooting Checklist

I have a basic troubleshooting checklist (albeit in my head) that I run through each time I open a trace file. The order in which I go through the checklist may change depending on the troubleshooting issue (UDP-based application troubleshooting vs. TCP-based application troubleshooting for example).

Consider expanding this checklist to suit your needs.

A PDF version of this checklist is available with the book supplements at www.wiresharkbook.com/troubleshooting.html.

Verify Trace File Integrity and Basic Communications

☐ Look for ACKed Unseen Segment (`tcp.analysis.ack_lost_segment` filter) [Switch oversubscribed?] See *What Causes ACKed Unseen Segment?* on page 191.

☐ Verify traffic from the complaining user's machine is visible. If not…
   - o Ensure the host is running.
   - o Test the host's connectivity (Can it communicate with another host?).
   - o Recheck capture location and process.
   - o Consider a resolution problem.

☐ Verify resolution process completion
   - o DNS queries/successful responses (consider cache use).
   - o ARP requests/responses (consider cache use).

Focus on Complaining User's Traffic

☐ Filter **on** related traffic (such as `tcp.port==80 && ip.addr==10.2.2.2`).

☐ Filter **out** unrelated traffic (such as `!ip.addr==239.0.0.0/8` or perhaps `!bootp`).

☐ Export related traffic to a separate trace file (**File | Export Specified Packets**).

Detect and Prioritize Delays

☐ Sort and identify high delta times (**Edit | Preferences | Columns | Add | Delta time displayed**).

☐ Sort and identify high TCP delta times (`tcp.time_delta` column).
   - o If Expert Infos items are seen, examine the Errors, Warnings and Notes listings.
   - o Consider "acceptable delays" (such as delays before TCP FIN or RST packets). See *Do not Focus on "Normal" or Acceptable Delays* on page 107.

☐ Measure path latency (Round Trip Time) using delta times in TCP handshake (see *Wireshark Lab 31: Obtain the Round Trip Time (RTT) Using the TCP Handshake* on page 128).

     o Capturing at client: measure delta from TCP SYN to SYN/ACK

     o Capturing at server: measure delta from SYN/ACK to ACK

     o Capturing in the infrastructure: measure delta from SYN to ACK[5]

☐ Measure server response time

     o TCP-based application: measure from request to response, not request to ACK.

     o Use Wireshark's response time function if possible (such as `dns.time`, `smb.time`, and `http.time`). For example, see *Identify High DNS Response Time* on page 135.

☐ Measure client latency

     o How long did it take for the client to make the next request?

     o Consider "acceptable delays" (such as a delay before an HTTP GET). See *Do not Focus on "Normal" or Acceptable Delays* on page 107.

Look for Throughput Issues

☐ Build the Golden Graph (IO Graph with "Bad TCP" on Graph 2). See *Correlate Drops in Throughput with TCP Problems (the "Golden Graph")* on page 280.

☐ Click on low throughput points to jump to problem spots in the trace file.

☐ Look at traffic characteristics at low throughput points.

☐ Consider using an Advanced IO Graph to detect delays (such as `tcp.time_delta`). See *Graph High Delta Times (UDP-Based Application)* on page 285 and *Graph High TCP Delta Time (TCP-Based Application)* on page 286.

Check Miscellaneous Traffic Characteristics

☐ Check packet sizes during file transfer (Length column).

☐ Check IP DSCP for prioritization.

☐ Check 802.11 Retry bit setting (`wlan.fc.retry == 1`).

☐ Check for ICMP messages.

☐ Check for IP fragmentation.

---

[5] This trick was brought up by Jasper Bongertz at the Sharkfest conference.

TCP-Based Application: Determine TCP Connection Issues/Capabilities

☐ Look for unsuccessful TCP handshakes.
- o SYN, no answer (connection blocked, packet loss)
- o SYN, RST/ACK (connection refused)

☐ Examine the TCP handshake Options area.
- o Check MSS values
- o Check for Window Scaling and Scale Factor
- o Check for Selective ACK (SACK)
- o Check for TCP Timestamps (especially on high-speed links)

TCP-Based Application: Identify TCP Issues

☐ Launch the Expert Infos window.
- o Consider number of errors, warnings and notes
- o Consider impact of each item

☐ Check the Calculated window size field values (`tcp.window_size`).

☐ Examine unexpected TCP RSTs.

UDP-Based Application: Identify Communication Issues

☐ Look for unsuccessful requests.
- o Request, no answer

☐ Look for repeated requests.

Spot Application Errors

☐ Filter for application error response codes (such as `sip.Status-Code >= 400`)

This page intentionally left blank.

CHAPTER 2: MASTER THESE KEY WIRESHARK TROUBLESHOOTING TASKS

Become comfortable with the troubleshooting tasks in this chapter. You will use them repeatedly to find the cause of poorly performing networks.

In addition, consider mastering the tasks covered in *Wireshark 101: Essential Skills for Network Analysis*. That book includes another set of 43 hands-on labs to enhance your network analysis skills.

Chapter 2 Notes

These are skills I use almost every time I capture traffic or open a trace file that's been sent in.

- Create and use a customized profile with settings that speed up the process of finding problems.

- Add columns to the Packet List pane.

- Change the Time column to see delays faster.

- Filter on a host address, subnet, conversation, port, field existence or field value.

- Use Wireshark's Expert Infos to spot problems in a trace file.

- Extract individual conversations.

- Create graphs to identify sudden drops in the throughput rate.

- Build coloring rules to call attention to problems in the trace file.

Create a Troubleshooting Profile

With the exception of a few default coloring rules and expert notifications, Wireshark is not customized to be used for in-depth troubleshooting. Wireshark is a piece of clay. You can mold it into an ideal troubleshooting tool with very little effort.

Appendix A provides step-by-step instructions on creating a troubleshooting profile. You do not have to be a Wireshark wizard to perform these steps. You just need to set aside about 15 minutes to go through the customization process.

If you do not have time to build a custom profile, Appendix A also includes step-by-step instructions to import a troubleshooting profile that is part of this book's supplement set.

Until you create a new profile, you are working in Wireshark's *Default* profile. The profile you are working in is shown in the right side column of the Status Bar.

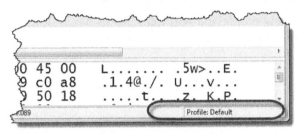

Wireshark Lab 1: Create Your Troubleshooting Profile

You can create profiles to customize Wireshark with buttons, colors, and more. You can create separate profiles for different needs. For example, perhaps you want to make a VoIP profile, a WLAN profile, and a general troubleshooting profile. You can quickly switch between profiles depending on your needs.

In this lab we will build our *Troubleshooting Book Profile* and customize this profile in various labs in this book.

Step 1:   Right-click the **Profile** column on the Status Bar.

Step 2:   In the Configuration Profile window, select **New**.

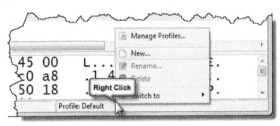

Step 3:   Click the **arrow** in the **Create from** area, expand the **Global section** and select **Classic**. This profile uses the most vibrant colors.

Step 4:   Enter **Troubleshooting Book Profile** in the Profile Name area. Click **OK**.

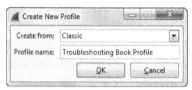

Once you create your new profile, the Wireshark Status Bar indicates that you are working in the **Troubleshooting Book Profile**, as shown below.

You will add capabilities and customization to your new **Troubleshooting Book Profile** as you follow along with the labs in this book.

Remember that you can also jump to *Do It Yourself: Build Your New Troubleshooting Profile* on page 339 and learn to build a complete troubleshooting profile yourself.

If you'd like to download/import a predefined profile for immediate use, see *Import Laura's Troubleshooting Profile* on page 337.

Enhance the Packet List Pane Columns

By default, the Packet List pane contains No. (number), Time, Source, Destination, Protocol, Length, and Info columns.

You can add columns to display additional information about packets to speed up your analysis process. In the example below we have added five columns to display the time between packets in each TCP conversation:

- TCP delta (**tcp.time_delta**) indicates the time from the end of one packet in a TCP conversation to the end of the next packet in that same TCP conversation.
- DNS Delta (**dns.time**) indicates the time between DNS requests and DNS responses.
- HTTP Delta (**http.time**) indicates the time between HTTP requests and HTTP responses.
- Stream Index (**tcp.stream**) indicates the TCP conversation number.
- WinSize (**tcp.window_size**) indicates the Calculated TCP Window Size.

All of these columns were added using the right-click method, which is the fastest way to add new columns.

In the next lab (and in many of the labs in this book), you will add key columns to the Packet List pane and sort the columns to find problems in the trace file.

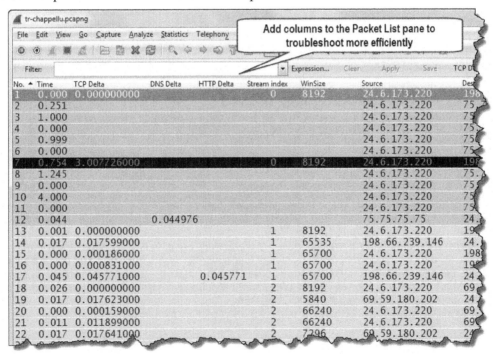

Wireshark Lab 2: Add and Use a Custom Column to Locate HTTP Delays

This trace file contains traffic to/from a user's machine that is checking for Windows updates as well as virus detection file updates.

Step 1:   Open **tr-httpdelta.pcapng**.

Step 2:   Packets 1-3 are TCP handshake packets. Packet 4 is an HTTP GET request for a file called *minitri.flg*. Packet 5 is an ACK for the GET request. Packet 6 is the HTTP 200 OK Response.

Select **Packet 6** in the Packet List pane and then, in the Packet Details pane, click the ⊞ button in front of **Hypertext Transfer Protocol** to expand the section.

```
⊞ Frame 6: 317 bytes on wire (2536 bits), 317 b                    n int
⊞ Ethernet II, Src: Cadant_31:bb:c1 (00:01:5c:3  Packet Details Pane  bf:
⊞ Internet Protocol Version 4, Src: 96.17.148.1                    .6.1
⊞ Transmission Control Protocol, Src Port: http (80), Dst Port: 52382 (52382)
⊟ Hypertext Transfer Protocol
  ⊟ HTTP/1.1 200 OK\r\n
    ⊞ [Expert Info (Chat/Sequence): HTTP/1.1 200 OK\r\n]
      Request Version: HTTP/1.1
      Status Code: 200
      Response Phrase: OK
    Server: Apache\r\n
    ETag: "7215ee9c7d9dc229d2921a40e899ec5f:1197576108"\r\n
    Last-Modified: Fri, 29 Jul 2005 20:24:32 GMT\r\n
    Accept-Ranges: bytes\r\n
  ⊞ Content-Length: 1\r\n
    Content-Type: text/plain\r\n
    Date: Thu, 19 Jul 2012 18:34:45 GMT\r\n
    Connection: keep-alive\r\n
    \r\n
    [HTTP response 1/2]
    [Time since request: 0.019036000 seconds]
    [Request in frame: 4]
    [Next request in frame: 7]
    [Next response in frame: 15]
```

> Click the ⊞ to expand sections or right-click on a line and select Expand Subtrees

Many of the trace files used in this book will indicate they contain bad IP checksums if you have Wireshark's IP checksum validation feature enabled (which is the default setting). The packets appear with a black background and red foreground in the Packet List pane and a red highlight appears on the Internet Protocol line in the Packet Details pane. In this trace file, and many others, Wireshark is capturing traffic on a host that supports "task offloading." The checksum is calculated after Wireshark obtains a copy of the outgoing packets. To remove these false "bad checksum" indications, you will disable checksum validation in Wireshark Lab 10: Use Expert Infos to Identify Network Problems (starting on page 56)

Step 3:   Scroll to the bottom of the HTTP section and right-click on the **[Time since request: 0.019036000 seconds]** line. Select **Apply as Column**.

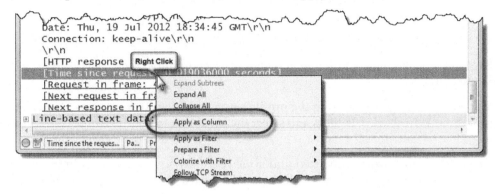

Step 4:   Wireshark places the new Time Since Request column to the left of the Info column.

Right-click on this new column heading and select **Edit Column Details**. Enter **HTTP Delta** in the Title area. Click **OK**.

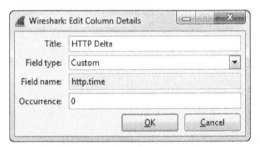

Step 5:   Click twice on your new **HTTP Delta** column header to sort the column data from high to low. Wireshark indicates there is a 2.807332 second delay before one of the HTTP 200 OK responses (Packet 49).

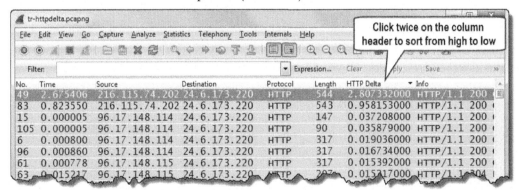

Step 6:   Since you won't be using this column again for a bit, right-click on your **HTTP Delta** column heading and select **Hide Column**. To restore this hidden column at any time, right-click on any column header, select **Displayed Columns** and select the column to restore.

Adding/hiding columns is a task that you may perform multiple times when working on a single trace file.

Profile column settings are saved in the profile's *preferences* file. To locate this file, select **Help | About Wireshark | Folders** and select the hyperlink to your personal configuration folder.

The profile's column settings are listed under the *User Interface: Columns* heading. The column names are followed by their value variable (such as *%t* for the Time column value and *%s* for Source column value). Custom columns are preceded by *%Cus:*.

```
####### User Interface: Columns ########

# Packet list hidden columns
# List all columns to hide in the packet list.
gui.column.hidden: %Cus:http.time:0:R

# Packet list column format
# Each pair of strings consists of a column title and its format
gui.column.format:
        "No.",   "%m",
        "Time",  "%t",
        "Source", "%s",
        "Destination",  "%d",
        "Protocol",  "%p",
        "Length",  "%L",
        "HTTP Delta",
        "Info",  "%i"
```

Change the Time Column Setting

Packets are time stamped at the moment they are captured[6]. By default, Wireshark sets the Time column to Seconds Since Beginning of Capture. In addition, the resolution is set to nanoseconds regardless of whether the packet timestamps contain that level of precision.

Wireshark Lab 3: Set the Time Column to Detect Path Latency

This trace file contains a web browsing session and was captured at the client. We will alter the default Time column setting to measure the time between the first two packets of the TCP handshake (the TCP SYN packet and the SYN/ACK packet).

Step 1:   Open **tr-australia.pcapng**.

The default Time column is set to Seconds Since Beginning of Capture and Automatic precision. We will change this column setting so we can quickly measure the delta time between displayed packets.

Use this delta time to obtain a snapshot of the round trip time between a client and as server. If you capture at the client, measure the delta time between the SYN and SYN/ACK, as shown in the following image.

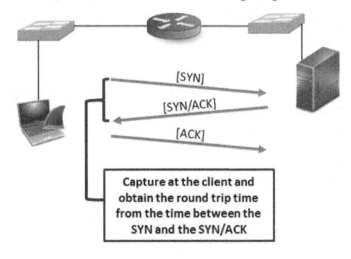

---

[6]   To be more precise, packets are time stamped at the end of the packet receipt process.

If you capture at the server, obtain the round trip time from the time between the SYN/ACK and ACK, as shown in the following image.

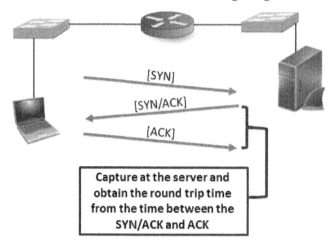

Step 2:   This trace file begins with a DNS query and response. The TCP connection establishment begins in Packet 3. Select **View | Time Display Format | Seconds Since Previous Displayed Packet**.

Step 3:   To change the precision, select **View | Time Display Format | Milliseconds: 0.123**.

Now we can look at the time from the SYN (Packet 3) to the SYN/ACK (Packet 4) to get a snapshot of the round trip time to the server. It appears the round trip time is 192 milliseconds (ms).

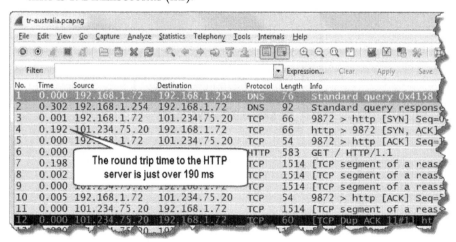

Is 192 ms a good or bad round trip time? The answer depends on what is normal round trip time for that path. If the round trip time is usually 43 ms, this is a large round trip time.

What can you do about large round trip times? If the delay is incurred within your network infrastructure, perhaps there is a reason. For example, a firewall with an exorbitant number of rules can affect network response times. If the delay is incurred outside your network infrastructure (such as along a path through the Internet), there is not much you can do.

In this same trace file we can also look at the time from the DNS request to the DNS response to determine the DNS response time (302 ms), however Wireshark has as DNS response time field (**dns.time**).

We will add a column for Wireshark's DNS response time value in *Identify High DNS Response Time* on page 135.

Filter on a Host, Subnet or Conversation

If you capture traffic at the server or inside the network infrastructure, your trace file may contain conversations between many hosts on the network. If you are interested in the traffic between a specific client and server, you can apply a display filter based on a host address, a subnet address or a conversation.

Filtering based on addresses is a skill that you will use quite often. In the next lab you will first examine Wireshark's address resolution details and then filter on a subnet address used by cnn.com.

Wireshark Lab 4: Extract and Save a Single Conversation

Step 1:   Open **tr-cnn.pcapng**.

Step 2:   This trace file contains numerous conversations. We are going to extract the conversations between the local client and cnn.com servers.

Let's begin by looking at the name resolution information that Wireshark extracted from the trace file.

Select **Statistics | Show Address Resolution**. We can see the servers in the cnn.com domain all begin with 157.166. Click **OK** to close the Address Resolution window.

Step 3:   In the display filter area, enter `ip.addr==157.166.0.0/16`. Click **Apply**. The Status Bar indicates that 360 packets match your filter. This filter is ideal if you want to focus on all conversations to and from the cnn.com servers.

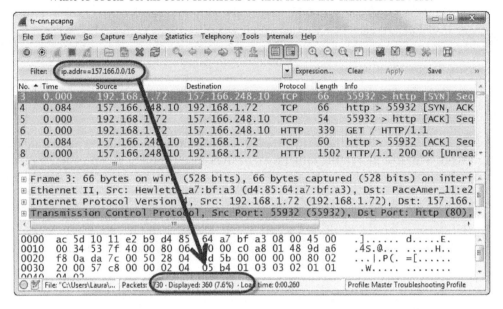

Step 4:   Select **File | Export Specified Packets**. The **Displayed** radio button is selected by default, as shown below. Name your file **tr-cnntraffic.pcapng**. Click **Save**.

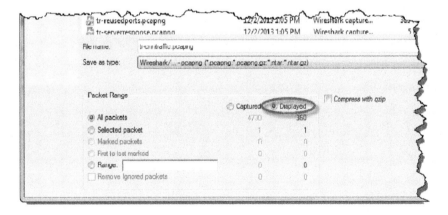

Step 5:   We will continue working in **tr-cnn.pcapng**. Next we will use the right-click method to apply a display filter to a single conversation.

Right-click on **Packet 3** in the Packet List pane and select **Conversation Filter | TCP**. Fifty-five packets should match this filter.

Step 6:   Select **File | Export Specified Packets**. Name your file **tr-cnnconv1.pcapng**. Click **Save**.

Step 7:   Click the **Clear** button to remove your display filter.

Oftentimes it is easier to save the traffic from an interesting conversation to a separate trace file and work with just that traffic rather than analyze a larger file with unrelated traffic and potential distractions.

Filter on an Application Based on Port Number

There are two ways to define a display filter on an application in a trace file — you can filter based on the application name (if known to Wireshark) or the port number in use.

If an application is UDP-based and Wireshark offers a filter based on the application name, you can simply filter based on that application name. For example, the filter **tftp** works fine for viewing all TFTP traffic.

If the application is TCP-based, you should use a display filter based on the port number in order to view the TCP overhead (such as the TCP handshake, ACKs and connection tear down) as well as the application traffic. For example, the filter **tcp.port==21** would display the FTP command channel traffic, including the TCP handshake, ACKs, and the TCP connection teardown packets.

Wireshark Lab 5: Filter Traffic Based on a Port Number

This trace file contains traffic from two hosts that are using FTP to download a file called *OOo_3.3.0_Linux_x86_langpack-rpm_en-US.tar.gz*. We will use a port-based filter to view the FTP data transfer connection established by 192.168.1.119.

Step 1:   Open **tr-twohosts.pcapng**.

Step 2:   First, let's filter on all traffic to and from 192.168.1.119. Enter **ip.addr==192.168.1.119** in the display filter area and click **Apply**.

Look for the response to the PASV command (Packet 3,959). Expand the File Transfer Protocol (FTP) section in the Packet Details pane to see the port number that the server will be listening on for the FTP data channel (port 39,757).

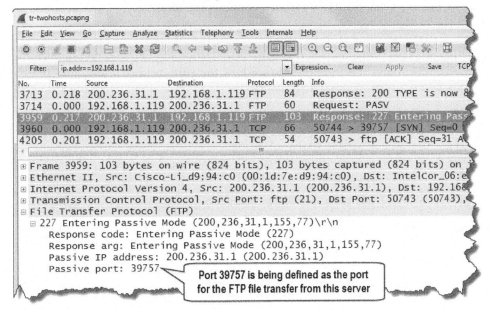

Step 3:   Replace your address display filter with `tcp.port==39757`. Click **Apply**. The
Status Bar indicates that 28,020 packets match this filter.

Notice that you are able to analyze the FTP data channel traffic and the TCP
handshake, ACKs, and the TCP connection teardown packets using a port-based
filter.

Let's contrast this with a display filter based on an application name.

Step 4:   Replace your TCP port filter with `ftp-data` and click **Apply**. Notice that you
don't see the TCP handshake, ACKs, or the connection teardown packets.

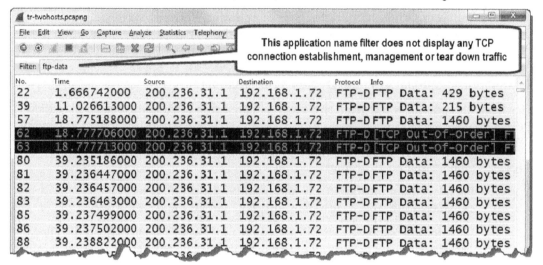

Step 5:   Click the **Clear** button to remove your display filter.

Do not filter out TCP problems when you are troubleshooting network communications of
TCP-based applications. It is important to see how the application's underlying TCP
connection was established as well as maintained.

Since UDP-based applications do not have any transport layer overhead (such as
connection establishment and tear down traffic), you can use an application name display
filter and see all traffic related to that application.

Filter on Field Existence or a Field Value

There will be many times when you want to identify packets that contain a specific field or a specific field value.

For example, the display filter **http.request.method** can be used to view all HTTP client request packets based on the existence of the **http.request.method** field. This field is only used in HTTP requests.

The display filter **dns.flags.rcode > 0** can be used to identify DNS error responses based on the value contained in the **dns.flags.rcode** field. The **dns.flags.rcode** field must exist in the displayed packets and the value in that field must be greater than 0.

If you know the field name in which you are interested, you can simply type it into the display filter area.

Alternately, if you have a packet that contains that field you can right-click on the field and select Apply as Filter (place in the display filter area and apply immediately) or Prepare a Filter (place in the display filter input field only, but do not apply). You may want to use Prepare a Filter to check the filter syntax first, edit the filter, or add to the filter to create a compound filter with more than one condition. The right-click method will always create a filter based on the field value in the packet.

Wireshark Lab 6: Filter on the HTTP Request Method Field To View Client Requests

HTTP clients send commands such as GET and POST in the HTTP Request Method field. We will create a filter to display all packets that contain this field.

Step 1:   Open **tr-winsize.pcapng**.

Step 2:   Right-click on the **Hypertext Transfer Protocol** section in the Packet Details pane in **Packet 4** and select **Expand Subtrees**. When you click on the **Request Method: GET** line, the Status Bar provides the name of this field — **http.request.method**.

Step 3:   Type **http.request.method** in the display filter area and click **Apply**.

One packet matches the filter. This quick filter method can be used when you are interested in determining how many HTTP requests were sent to a server. You can expand this filter to include an IP address to focus on requests to or from a single source, if desired. For example, **ip.addr==10.1.1.1 && http.request.method** would display all HTTP requests to or from 10.1.1.1. If 10.1.1.1 is a client, you would only see HTTP requests sent *from* this host.

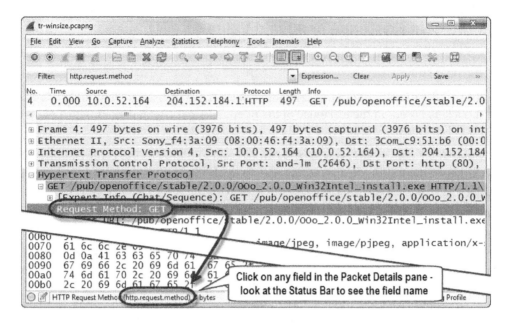

Step 4:   Click the **Clear** button to remove your display filter.

Wireshark Lab 7: Filter on the Calculated Window Size Field to Locate Buffer Problems

Every TCP packet sent by a host includes information about that host's available receive buffer space in the Window Size field. This Window Size field value may be multiplied by a scaling factor if Window Scaling is in use.

Read RFC 1323, "TCP Extensions for High Performance to learn more about TCP Window Scaling as well as Protection Against Wrapped Sequence Numbers (PAWS)". Since Window Scaling problems are not uncommon, this is time well spent.

If the advertised buffer space drops to zero, the host cannot accept any more data – a Zero Window condition has occurred. In some situations even a low Window Size value can stop a TCP peer from transmitting data.

Step 1:   Open **tr-winsize.pcapng** again if you closed it after the last lab.

Step 2:   Expand any **TCP header** in the Packet Details pane. Right-click on the **Calculated window size** field and select **Prepare a Filter | Selected**.

Step 3:   Change the display filter value to `tcp.window_size < 1000` and click **Apply**. Your filter displays Packet 374 when the client is advertising a 536-byte receive buffer area. This value will stop the TCP peer from transmitting data if it has more than 536 bytes of data queued up to transmit.

Let's see if this low Window Size value is affecting the file transfer process.

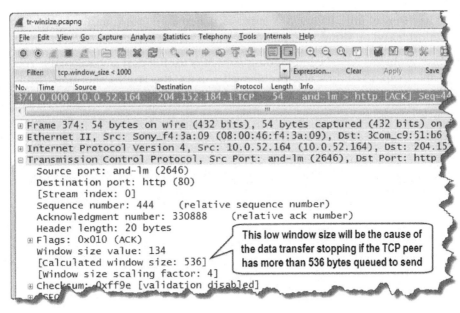

Step 4:   Click **Clear** to remove your filter.

Notice the delay before the Window Update packet in this trace file (Packet 375). Essentially, the server could not transmit the full-sized packet because the client only had 536 bytes of buffer space available.

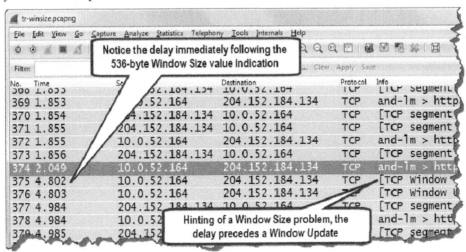

The server had to wait until the client's buffer size increased (the Window Update packet). For more information on Window Updates, see *Window Update* on page 218.

Window Size problems have been plaguing networks for the past several years. You will always be able to spot Window Size problems if you use the Troubleshooting Checklist— see *TCP-Based Application: Identify TCP Issues* on page 29.

Filter OUT "Normal" Traffic (Exclusion Filters)

You may want to filter *out* good traffic to focus on anomalies. To filter out traffic based on an application name, simply precede the application display filter name with an exclamation point (!).

For example, to remove ARP from view, use **!arp**.

There are two methods you can use to exclude traffic based on a field value. One method uses the **!** or **not** operator with **==** or **eq**. The other uses the **!=** or **ne** operator.

Each of these methods is used in the examples below.

```
!ip.addr==10.10.10.10
http.request.method != "GET"
```

When to Use ! and == and When to Use ! =

Use the first method (**!**/**not** with **==**/**eq**)when you filter on a field name that matches <u>two fields</u> such as **ip.addr**, **tcp.port**, or **udp.port**.

Use the second method (!=) when you refer to a field name that only matches <u>one field</u> such as **dns.flags.rcode** or **tcp.dstport**.

Correct Display Filter	Incorrect Display Filter
!ip.addr==10.1.1.1	ip.addr != 10.1.1.1
!tcp.port==21	tcp.port != 21
!udp.port==53	udp.port != 53
dns.flags.rcode!=0	!dns.flags.rcode==0
tcp.dstport!=80	!tcp.dstport==80

Just keep this the rule in mind—if the field name can match more than one field in a packet, avoid **!=**.

Wireshark Lab 8: Filter Out Applications and Protocols

In this lab you will remove a set of applications and protocols from view. We know that this network supports ARP, DNS, DHCP, and a number of TCP-based file transfer applications. We will filter these from view to determine what other traffic is seen on this network.

Step 1:   Open **tr-general.pcapng**.

Step 2:   In the display filter area, type **!tcp && !arp** and click **Apply**.

```
0010   00 8a 43 b7 00 00 80 11  34 bc c0 a8 01 48 ff ff
0020   ff ff 44 5c 44 5c 00 76  c2 77 7b 22 68 6f 73 74
0030   5f 69 6e 74 22 3a 20 33  36 34 32 35 36 33 30 37
```
File: "C:\Users\Laura\... | Packets: 1067 | Displayed: 40 (3.7%) | Load time: 0:00.042

Step 3:   There are 40 packets that match this filter. Now expand your filter to remove DNS and DHCP from view (add **&& !dns && !bootp**[7]) (Don't forget to clear your filter when you are finished reviewing the results of this lab step.)

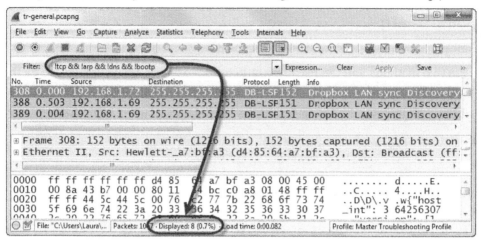

Eight packets are displayed. The displayed packets indicate there are two hosts running Dropbox on the network. Both hosts are sending Dropbox LAN sync Discovery Protocol packets to the broadcast address (255.255.255.255).

This process of filtering out traffic is especially useful when you are analyzing traffic during idle time—when no user is at the keyboard. The traffic indicates background processes that run without user interaction. This is a great baseline to create. For more information on creating baselines, see *Tips for Faster Problem Detection* on page 331.

---

[7]   Since DHCP is based on BOOTP (Bootstrap Protocol), the display filter syntax is **bootp**, not **dhcp**. DHCPv6 traffic does not have a dependency on BOOTP so you can filter DHCPv6 traffic using simply **dhcpv6**.

Create Filter Expression Buttons

Filter Expression buttons are based on display filters. These buttons can be created and used to quickly apply display filters to your traffic to identify common network problems.

In the next lab you will create a button to quickly identify TCP SYN or SYN/ACK packets that are missing either the SACK option or the Window Scaling option.

These are two options that enhance TCP's performance by reducing the number of retransmissions after packet loss (SACK) and increasing the advertised receive buffer space above the 65,535 byte value (Window Scaling).

Wireshark Lab 9: Create a Button to Detect Missing TCP Functionality

We can create a button to quickly identify TCP handshake packets that do not offer Selective Acknowledgment (SACK) or Window Scaling functionality by combining an inclusion filter for the SYN bit set to 1 with an exclusion filter for the SACK and Window Scaling options.

Step 1:   Open **tr-smbjoindomain.pcapng**.

Step 2:   Packet 11 is the first SYN packet in the trace file. Right-click on the TCP header of this packet and select **Expand Subtrees**. We will build the filter first and then turn the filter into a filter expression button.

Right-click on the **SYN: Set** line and select **Prepare a Filter | Selected**. Wireshark places the first part of the filter in the display filter area.

Filter: tcp.flags.syn == 1

Step 3:   Scroll down to the TCP Options area. Click on the **TCP SACK Permitted Option: True** line. Notice the syntax for this field is listed in the Status Bar area —
`tcp.options.sack_perm`.

We are interested in TCP handshake packets that do not contain this value. Expand your filter by typing `&& !tcp.options.sack_perm`.

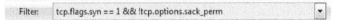

Filter: tcp.flags.syn == 1 && !tcp.options.sack_perm

Step 4:   Let's just type the last portion of the filter — we want to know if the Window Scaling multiplier is missing in these SYN packets.

Add `|| ! tcp.options.wscale.multiplier` and put parentheses around the options, as shown below.

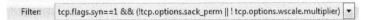

Filter: tcp.flags.syn==1 && (!tcp.options.sack_perm || ! tcp.options.wscale.multiplier)

Step 5:   Click the **Save** button and name your new button **TCP-HS** and click **OK**.

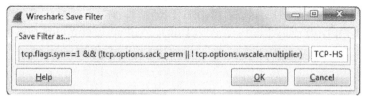

Step 6:   Click your new **TCP-HS** button.

Thirty-eight packets match the TCP-HS button filter. The connections established by these packets will not support all the desired TCP functions. (Don't forget to clear your filter when you are finished reviewing the results of this lab step.)

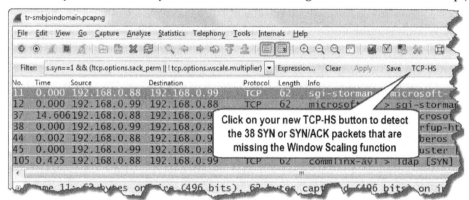

If you need to edit, reorder or delete Filter Expression buttons, select **Edit | Preferences | Filter Expressions**.

*Always use parentheses to group filters when you are combining **&&** and **||** in your filter. Leaving these parentheses out may give you unexpected results because logical OR is evaluated before logical AND[8].*

*As recently as Wireshark 1.10.x, the filter **tcp.port==80 || dns && ip.src==192.168.1.72** would be interpreted as **(tcp.port==80 || dns) && ip.src==192.168.1.72**.*

*If you were actually interested in all TCP port 80 traffic and any DNS traffic from 192.168.1.72, you must put in parentheses to indicate that. The filter would be **tcp.port==80 || (dns && ip.src==192.168.1.72)**.*

Try this yourself on tr-general.pcapng. Compare the results of these three display filters:

```
tcp.port==80 || dns && ip.src==192.168.1.72        = ___ packets
tcp.port==80 || (dns && ip.src==192.168.1.72)      = ___ packets
(tcp.port==80 || dns) && ip.src==192.168.1.72      = ___ packets
```

You should find that the first and last filters display 195 packets while the middle filter displays 417 packets.

---

[8]   This may change in later versions of Wireshark since many people assume the logical AND would be evaluated before the logical OR.

Launch and Navigate Through the Expert Infos

Wireshark's Expert Infos can help you quickly detect network problems as well as obtain basic information about network communications and view/jump to packet comments.

The Expert Infos definitions are contained in the dissectors. For example, the TCP dissector (*packet-tcp.c*) defines the characteristics of TCP Retransmissions, Out-of-Order packets, and Zero Window conditions. For details on how Wireshark defines the TCP packets, see *Overview of Wireshark's Expert Infos System* on page 153.

Wireshark Lab 10: Use Expert Infos to Identify Network Problems

In this lab you will launch the Expert Infos window to identify network problems detected by Wireshark.

Step 1:   Open **tr-twohosts.pcapng**.

Step 2:   Click the **Expert Infos** button in the bottom left corner of the Status Bar.

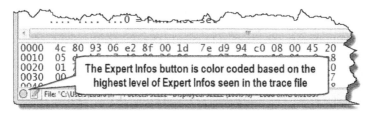

The Expert Infos window is divided into six tabs:

Errors: Checksum errors, dissector failures
Warnings: Potential problems detected
Notes: Symptoms of problems; typically recovery processes
Chats: TCP connection overhead (handshake, Window updates, disconnects)
Details: Summary of Errors, Warnings, Notes and Chats
Packet Comments: List of all packet comments in the trace file

Step 3:   If IPv4 checksum validation is enabled you will see 6,767 IPv4 Bad Checksum Expert Infos Errors[9]. If IPv4 checksum validation is disabled (the recommended setting), there are no Expert Infos Errors in this trace file. To disable IPv4 checksum validation, toggle back to Wireshark, right-click on the **Internet Protocol Version 4** line in the Packet Details Pane, select **Protocol Preferences** and toggle off the *Validate IPv4 checksum if possible* setting. Toggle back to the **Expert Infos** window.

Click the **Warnings** tab.

Click the ⊞ in front of each section to view the packets that are tagged with a particular Expert Infos indication. Click on a packet to jump to that location in the trace file.

There are 456 instances of possible packet loss in this trace file. Since packet loss impacts throughput, this is likely causing some performance problems. For more details on packet loss, see *Previous Segment Not Captured* on page 154.

Out-of-order packets may not be causing a noticeable delay in communications. See *Out-of-Order Packets* on page 174 for more details.

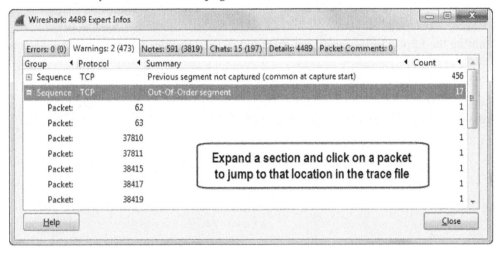

Step 4:   Click the **Notes** tab. Duplicate ACKs are sent by a receiver to request a missing packet. As you scroll through this list you will notice that the receiver sent 589 Duplicate ACKs to recover a missing packet. The high rate of Duplicate ACKs may be caused by a very high latency path or a brief connection outage.

For more information on analyzing Duplicate ACKs, see *Duplicate ACKs* on page 166.

---

[9]   These IPv4 Bad Checksum indications are a result of capturing on a host (192.168.1.72) that is using task offload. The IPv4 checksums are calculated on the network interface card, after Wireshark has obtained a copy.

Click the **Count** column heading twice to sort from high to low and you will
notice there are over 1,000 Retransmissions in this trace file. Certainly packet loss
(and the resulting retransmissions) appears to be plaguing this communication.

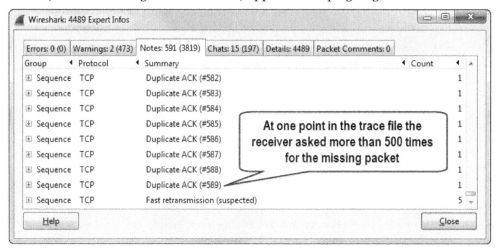

Step 5:   Click **Close** to shut down the Expert Infos window.

Examining the Expert Infos window is included in the Troubleshooting Checklist section
entitled *TCP-Based Application: Identify TCP Issues* on page 29. The Expert Infos window
offers a quick way to locate and jump to communication problems in the trace file.

In *Part 2: Symptom-Based Troubleshooting* you will create numerous filters and filter
expression buttons based on these Expert Infos items.

Change Dissector Behavior (Preference Settings)

Some of Wireshark's predefined preference settings are not ideal for troubleshooting. For example, the *Allow subdissector to reassemble TCP streams* preference is enabled by default, but there are many times when you will want this disabled—such as when you are measuring HTTP Response Times (`http.time`).

Many labs in this book refer to TCP preference settings that should be changed to troubleshoot more efficiently. In the next lab you will compare results when the *Allow subdissector to reassemble TCP streams* preference setting is enabled and disabled. You will use the right-click method to quickly change this TCP preference.

Wireshark Lab 11: Change the TCP Dissector Reassembly Setting to Properly Measure HTTP Response Times

In this lab you will examine the effect the *Allow subdissector to reassemble TCP streams* preference setting has on the traffic display in the Packet List pane. You will also see how this setting affects the `http.time` value which is used to measure HTTP response time.

Step 1:   Open **tr-youtubebad.pcapng**. At the start of this trace file we see a TCP handshake (Packets 1-3). Packet 4 is an HTTP GET request from the client. Packet 5 is the ACK from the server and Packet 6 is the HTTP 200 OK response from the server.

Unfortunately, you cannot see the Response Code in the Info column for Packet 6 because the *Allow subdissector to reassemble TCP streams* preference setting is enabled. The Response Code is visible on Packet 29,259—the packet containing the last bytes of the requested item.

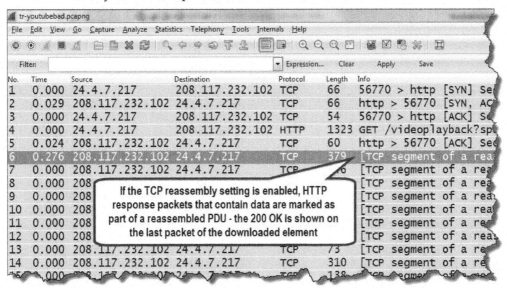

Step 2:   In the Packet Detail pane of **Packet 4**, right-click the **Hypertext Transfer Protocol** heading and select **Expand Subtrees**.

A hyperlink to the response packet is located at the bottom of the HTTP section. Double-click the **hyperlink** to jump to **Packet 29,259**.

```
Frame 4: 1323 bytes on wire (10584 bits), 1323 bytes captured (10584 bit
Ethernet II, Src: Hewlett-_a7:bf:a3 (d4:85:64:a7:bf:a3), Dst: Cadant_31:
Internet Protocol Version 4, Src: 24.4.7.217 (24.4.7.217), Dst: 208.117
Transmission Control Protocol, Src Port: 56770 (56770), Dst Port: http
Hypertext Transfer Protocol
  [truncated] GET /videoplayback?sparams=id%2Cexpire%2Cip%2Cipbits%2Citag
    [[truncated] Expert Info (Chat/Sequence): GET /videoplayback?sparams=
      [Message [truncated]: GET /videoplayback?sparams=id%2Cexpire%2Cip%2
      [Severity level: Chat]
      [Group: Sequence]
    Request Method: GET
    Request URI [truncated]: /videoplayback?sparams=id%2Cexpire%2Cip%2Ci
    Request Version: HTTP/1.1
  Host: v16.lscache8.c.youtube.com\r\n
  User-Agent: Mozilla/5.0 (windows; U; Windows NT 6.1; en-US; rv:1.9.2.15
  Accept: text/html,application/xhtml+xml,application/xml;q=0.9,*/*;q=0.
  Accept-Language: en-us,en;q=0.5\r\n
  Accept-Encoding: gzip,deflate\r\n
  Accept-Charset: ISO-8859-1,utf-8;q=0.7,*;q=0.7\r\n
  Keep-Alive: 115\r\n
  Connection: keep-alive\r\n
  [truncated] Cookie: VISITOR_INFO1_LIVE=xU-BqDEfmck; use_hitbox=72c46ff
  \r\n
  [Full request URI [truncated]: http://v16.lscache8.c.youtube.com/video
  [HTTP request 1/1]
  [Response in frame: 29259]
```

Use the hyperlink to quickly jump to the response packet

Step 3:   Scroll to the bottom of the HTTP header in Packet 29,259. The Time Since Request (**http.time**) field indicates the HTTP response time was over 276 seconds.

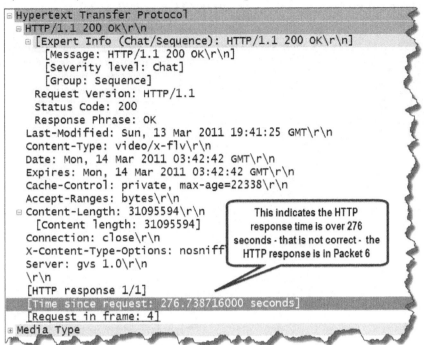

This is not correct. The HTTP response time is measured from the HTTP request packet to the HTTP response packet that contains the 200 OK response. Wireshark, however, marks the last packet of the download as the response packet when the *Allow subdissector to reassemble TCP streams* preference setting is enabled.

Step 4:   Let's find the actual HTTP response time.

In the Packet Details pane of any packet, right-click the **TCP header**, select **Protocol Preferences** and toggle off the *Allow subdissector to reassemble TCP streams* preference setting.

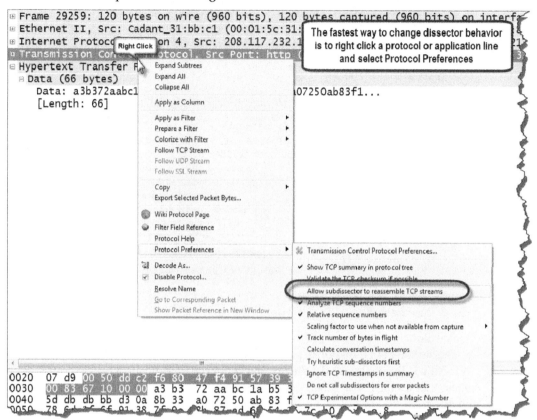

Step 5:   Now click the **Go to First Packet** button 📌. Notice we see that Packet 6 actually contains the 200 OK response.

Examine the HTTP response time value in Packet 6. It is just over 300 ms.

This is quite a difference from the 276 seconds we found earlier when the *Allow subdissector to reassemble TCP streams* preference setting was enabled.

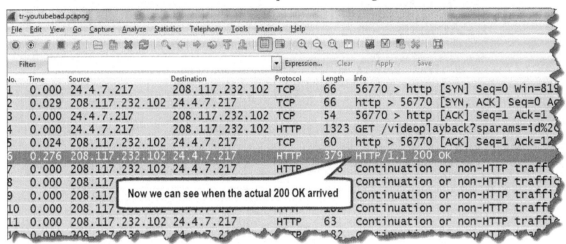

This is one of the most frustrating settings in Wireshark. You will probably want to keep this setting disabled for most of your analysis work. If you plan to export HTTP or SMB objects, however, you must enable that TCP preference setting before selecting **File | Export Objects**.

```
⊞ Frame 6: 379 bytes on wire (3032 bits), 379 bytes captured (3032 bits) on
⊞ Ethernet II, Src: Cadant_31:bb:c1 (00:01:5c:31:bb:c1), Dst: Hewlett-_a7:b
⊞ Internet Protocol Version 4, Src: 208.117.232.102 (208.117.232.102), Dst:
⊞ Transmission Control Protocol, Src Port: http (80), Dst Port: 56770 (5677
⊟ Hypertext Transfer Protocol
  ⊟ HTTP/1.1 200 OK\r\n
     ⊟ [Expert Info (Chat/Sequence): HTTP/1.1 200 OK\r\n]
          [Message: HTTP/1.1 200 OK\r\n]
          [Severity level: Chat]
          [Group: Sequence]
       Request Version: HTTP/1.1
       Status Code: 200
       Response Phrase: OK
    Last-Modified: Sun, 13 Mar 2011 19:41:25 GMT\r\n
    Content-Type: video/x-flv\r\n
    Date: Mon, 14 Mar 2011 03:42:42 GMT\r\n
    Expires: Mon, 14 Mar 2011 03:42:42 GMT\r\n
    Cache-Control: private, max-age=22338\r\n
    Accept-Ranges: bytes\r\n
  ⊟ Content-Length: 31095594\r\n
       [Content length: 31095594]
    Connection: close\r\n
    X-Content-Type-Options: nosniff\r\n
    Server: gvs 1.0\r\n
    \r\n
    [HTTP response 1/1]
    [Time since request: 0.301284000 seconds]
    [Request in frame: 4]
```

> The HTTP response time was actually just over 301 ms

It is important to learn which Wireshark preferences can be changed and how preference settings affect your view of the packets. The best way to identify the preference settings available is to right-click on a protocol in the Packet Details pane and select **Protocol Preferences**.

Next we will count conversations and determine the top talker in a trace file.

Find the Top Talkers

Use the Conversations window to determine the most active conversation based on hardware address, network address, or even the port numbers in use. You can use right-click functionality to filter on a conversation, find a packet in a conversation or even temporarily color a conversation.

Wireshark Lab 12: Find the Most Active Conversation (Byte Count)

In this lab you will use the Conversations window to determine the top talkers based on count of bytes transmitted or received.

Step 1:   Open **tr-general.pcapng**.

Step 2:   Select **Statistics | Conversations**. The tabs indicate the number of each type of conversation seen in the trace file.

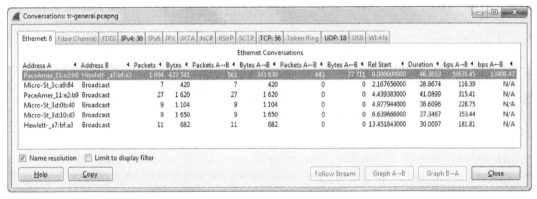

Step 3:   We are interested in the most active TCP conversation (in bytes) in this trace file. Click the **TCP** tab and then click the **Bytes** column heading twice to sort from high to low.

The most active conversation is between 192.168.1.72 on port 32313 and 192.87.106.229 on port 80 (listed as *http*).

Step 4:   Right-click on this **top conversation** and select **Apply as Filter | Selected A ⟷ B**. Wireshark applies the filter and displays the 123 packets of this conversation.

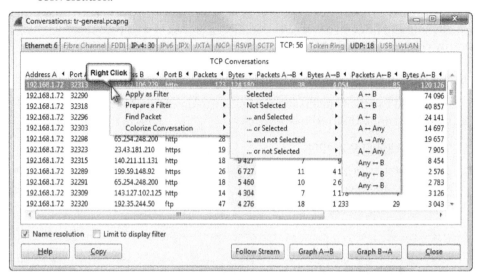

Step 5:   When you are done, click **Clear** to remove your display filter, toggle back to the Conversations window and click **Close**.

This is a good skill to master. When you are confronted with a very large trace file filled with hundreds or even thousands of conversations, use the Conversations window to identify the active applications and hosts and rapidly build filters to focus on specific conversation traffic.

Build a Basic IO Graph

The basic IO Graph can be used to view throughput levels for all traffic in a trace file or plot a subset of traffic (based on display filters). When performance issues arise, consider building an IO Graph to identify any sudden drops in throughput. If there are numerous drops in throughput, the IO Graph can help you prioritize your troubleshooting tasks.

Wireshark Lab 13: Quickly Spot a Throughput Problem in an IO Graph

This trace file contains a single TCP conversation. An HTTP client is downloading a large file from a web server.

Step 1:   Open **tr-winsize.pcapng**.

Step 2:   Select **Statistics | IO Graph**. By default, Wireshark displays the packets per second rate (packet per tick with a default tick rate of one second).

There are two problem points in this download process. The first problem appears to be more significant than the second problem, but both should be investigated.

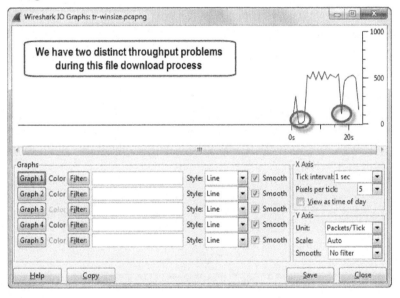

Step 3:   Click on the **first drop in throughput** in the graph. Wireshark jumps to that point in the trace file so we can investigate the problem further.

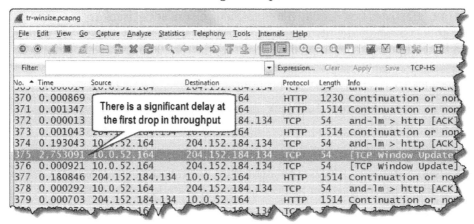

If your Time column is set to *Seconds Since Previous Displayed Packet* (**View | Time Display Format**), you will see a delay of over 2.75 seconds in the trace file. You set this in *Wireshark Lab 3: Time column value in Set the Time Column to Detect Path Latency* on page 39.

Packet 375 is marked as a TCP Window Update packet. This indicates that the delay may have something to do with the Window Size value advertised by the client (10.0.52.164). See *Graph Window Size Problems* on page 291 for more information about this problem.

Step 4:   Toggle back to the IO Graph. Click on the **second problem point** in the graph. Toggle back to Wireshark to see what is happening at this point in the file download process.

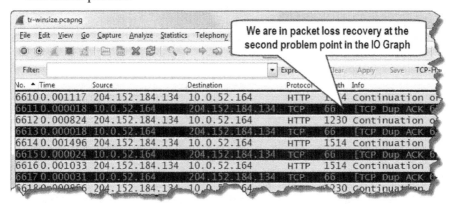

The client appears to be in the middle of a packet loss recovery process. For more information about this process, see *Duplicate ACKs* on page 166. (Don't forget to toggle back to the IO Graph and click **Close**.)

Add a Coloring Rule

Coloring rules can be used to quickly identify packets in the Packet List pane. Wireshark includes a set of default coloring rules. You can edit, import, export, and temporarily disable coloring rules if desired.

Coloring rules are saved in a text file called *colorfilters* in your personal configuration folder. You can locate this folder by selecting **Help | About Wireshark | Folders**.

Wireshark does not have an Expert Infos warning about DNS Errors so in the next lab you will create a "butt-ugly" coloring rule to highlight these DNS errors. In *Detect DNS Errors* on page 237 you will create a filter expression button to detect these errors as well.

Wireshark Lab 14: Build a Coloring Rule to Highlight DNS Errors

Step 1: Open **tr-chappellu.pcapng**.

Step 2: First let's just apply a filter for all DNS traffic. Type **dns** in the display filter area and click **Apply**.

Forty-three packets should match your filter.

You may notice right away that we have some DNS problems. The client asks two DNS servers (75.75.75.75 and 75.75.76.76) to resolve www.chappellU.com nine times before receiving an answer (Packet 12). Unfortunately, we can't create a coloring rule for these repeated requests, which would be denoted by repeated use of the same Transaction ID in multiple DNS requests.

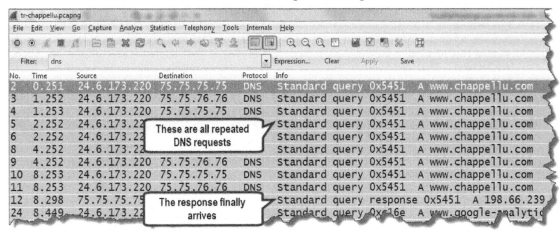

Step 3:   Right-click on the **Domain Name System (query)** section in the Packet Details
window of Packet 12. Select **Expand Subtrees**.

Notice the Reply Code field inside the Flags section. When this field contains a 0,
the DNS response was successful. If this field contains any other value, the
response indicates there is as DNS error.

We will use this information to create our "butt-ugly" coloring rule.

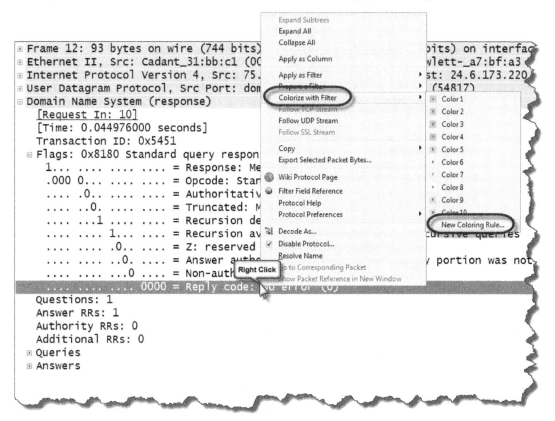

Step 4:   Right-click on the Reply Code field and select **Colorize with Filter | New
Coloring Rule**.

Step 5: Enter **DNS Errors** as the name of your new coloring rule.

Change the String value to **dns.flags.rcode > 0**[10].

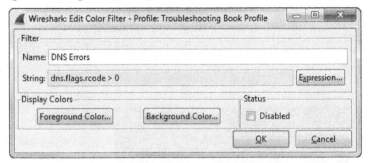

Step 6: Click the **Background Color** button and type **orange** in the Color Name field. When you tab away from the Color Name field, Wireshark changes the word "orange" to the hex value #FFA500 and shows the new color in the color preview area. Click **OK** to close the background color window and click **OK** to close the Edit Color Filter window.

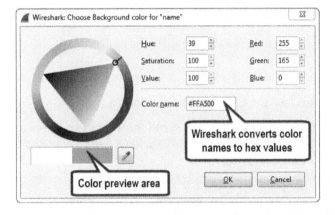

---

[10] You could also use the filter **dns.flags.rcode != 0**, but Wireshark will turn the background yellow to indicate that use of the **!=** operator may yield unexpected results. In this case, since there is only one dns.flags.rcode field in the packet, the use of **!=** is acceptable however. To avoid the yellow background, we decided to use **dns.flags.rcode > 0** and avoid the use of **!=** altogether.

Your new coloring rule appears at the top of the list of color filters. Packets are processed in order through this list. Typically, DNS packets match the UDP coloring rule (as noted in the Frame section of the packets).

Now, DNS errors will appear with an orange background.

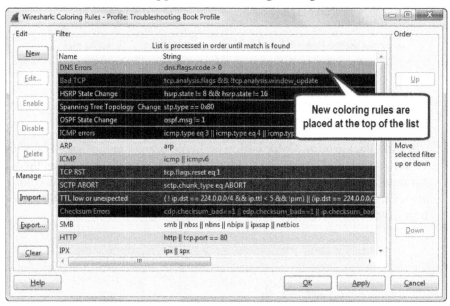

Step 7:   Click **OK** to close the Coloring Rules window.

Step 8:   With your **dns** filter still in place, scroll through the packets to see if you notice the two DNS errors in the trace file. Packet 83 and Packet 84 should appear with your new orange coloring rule.

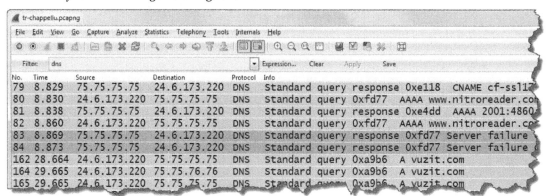

Step 9:   Expand the **Frame** section in the Packet Details pane of Packet 83. You will see
           your Coloring Rule Name and Coloring Rule String listed in this area. Don't
           forget to clear your display filter when you are finished reviewing the results of
           this lab step.

```
⊟ Frame 83: 400 bytes on wire (3200 bits), 400 bytes captured (3200 bits)
    Interface id: 0
    Encapsulation type: Ethernet (1)
    Arrival Time: Oct 24, 2012 15:13:37.608733000 Pacific Daylight Time
    [Time shift for this packet: 0.000000000 seconds]
    Epoch Time: 1351116817.608733000 seconds
    [Time delta from previous captured frame: 0.008743000 seconds]
    [Time delta from previous displayed frame: 0.008743000 seconds]
    [Time since reference or first frame: 8.869124000 seconds]
    Frame Number: 83
    Frame Length: 400 bytes (3200 bits)
    Capture Length: 400 bytes (3200 bits)
    [Frame is marked: False]
    [Frame is ignored: False]
    [Protocols in frame: eth:ip:udp:dns]
    [Coloring Rule Name: DNS Errors]
    [Coloring Rule String: dns.flags.rcode > 0]
⊞ Ethernet II, Src: Cadant_31:bb:c1 (00:01:5c:31:bb:c1), Dst: Hewlett-_a
⊞ Internet Protocol Version 4, Src: 75.75.75.75 (75.75.75.75), Dst: 24.6
⊞ User Datagram Protocol, Src Port: domain (53), Dst Port: 56007 (56007)
⊟ Domain Name System (response)
    [Request In: 82]
```

> The coloring rule applied to packets is shown in the Frame section of each packet

Step 10:   (Optional) To disable this coloring rule, click the **Coloring Rules** button 🖼 on
           the Main Toolbar, select your **DNS Errors** coloring rule and click **Disable**.
           Wireshark places a line through the disabled coloring rule and does not apply it
           to the traffic.

           Click **OK** to close the Coloring Rules window.

Coloring rules can help call attention to specific traffic. Filter expression buttons are a faster
way to detect these problems, however. Through the rest of this book we will create
buttons to quickly detect problems rather than create coloring rules.

This page intentionally left blank.

CHAPTER 3: USE THE RIGHT CAPTURE TECHNIQUE

Capturing the traffic properly is a key step in locating the cause of network performance problems.

Consider the following when validating your trace files before analysis:

- Consider the capture location when you must obtain round trip times.
- Packets dropped during the capture process can lead you to incorrect analysis of the network problems. Be wary of oversubscribing switches.
- WLAN traffic can be tricky to catch — you must catch Management, Control and Data traffic as well as 802.11 headers.
- Wireshark may crash or perform too slowly on large trace files — try to keep your trace files below 100 MB. Use *Editcap* to split large files into file sets when necessary.
- Use capture filters sparingly. Use display filters liberally.

Chapter 3 Notes

There are lots of options available for capturing traffic. Determine the best option depending on who is complaining and the network type.

- Choose to start capturing near a client, near a server or inside the infrastructure.

- Consider using a Tap, switch port spanning or run Wireshark on the target.

- Capture to file sets when working on high traffic links.

- Make sure you capture control, management and data frames on WLAN networks, as well as 802.11 headers. Prepend Radiotap or PPI headers if possible.

- Use capture filters (only when absolutely necessary).

Tips on Choosing a Capture Location

Capturing at the correct location can save you time and reduce distractions when you are troubleshooting performance problems.

When you capture close to the complaining user, you obtain the traffic from that user's perspective. You can determine the round trip time to the server(s), identify the packet loss rate, and spot any error responses sent to the client.

Advantages of capturing close to the complaining user:

- Obtain round trip times to targets from the local host's perspective.
- Obtain service response times from the local host's perspective (such as HTTP, DNS and SMB response times).
- Obtain TCP handshake configurations based on the local host's perspective.
- Determine if the client is witnessing packet loss, out-of-order packets or other TCP errors.
- Avoid capturing unrelated traffic to and from other hosts on the network.

If you cannot capture at the client, consider capturing at the server side of the communication. You can still obtain round trip times on TCP-based applications and service response times. You will also be able to see the TCP handshake characteristics.

If you capture near a busy server, however, you may need to apply a capture filter to focus on the traffic to and from the complaining user's machine. Refer to *Use Capture Filters when Necessary* on page 88.

Capture Options for a Switched Network

These days, almost all network clients are connected to the network through a switch. Switches only forward four types of packets by default:

- Broadcast
- Multicast[11]
- Traffic to your hardware address
- Traffic to an unknown hardware address[12]

Because of this, when you connect a system running Wireshark directly to a switch port, you can't listen to other users' traffic, as shown in the next image.

In order to capture the traffic between the client and the upstream switch (and ultimately a remote host), you need to either (a) install Wireshark or another capture tool on the user's machine, (b) make the switch send a copy of the traffic down your analyzer port, or (c) tap in and obtain a copy of the traffic between the client and the switch.

Install Wireshark (or Other Capture Tool) on the User's Machine

This is a great option – if you can do it. It's great because you can get all the traffic from the user's perspective (the most important perspective after all). There are some negatives here, however. We really do not want Fred (our "user from hell") to even know about Wireshark. We'd prefer not to field questions such as "hey – what's ICMP?"

---

[11] Switches will forward multicast traffic out all ports unless the switch (a) is configured to block multicast forwarding, (b) detects a multicast flood and is configured to block this flood, or (c) uses Internet Group Management Protocol (IGMP) snooping and determines that a switch port does not have a member of a specific multicast group attached.

[12] Traffic to an "unknown hardware address" should not be seen on a network because we have a protocol (ARP) which is used to resolve local hardware addresses.

Switch Port Spanning

If you can't install a packet capture tool on the user's system, often the only other option may be to make the switch send a copy of the traffic down your analyzer port (aka "spanning"). If the switch supports spanning, you can configure the switch to send a copy of the traffic from the user's switch port down your analyzer switch port, as shown below.

Switch port spanning is a simple option if it is available. Unfortunately, not all switches support this feature and it really isn't the best option. If there are corrupt frames traveling from the user's host, those corrupt frames won't be forwarded down the spanned port by the switch.

Be careful not to "oversubscribe" your switch port when performing switch port spanning. Switch port oversubscription occurs when you span a level of traffic that cannot "fit" down the pipe to your Wireshark system. The switch will drop the excess packets and your trace file will be incomplete. (You may see "ACKed Unseen Segment" in the Expert Infos window.) Consider what would happen if you connect Wireshark to a 1 Gbit switch port and span the full-duplex traffic on another 1 Gbit switch port (transmit + receive traffic = 2 Gbit rate) of a server. Your Wireshark connection to the switch can only handle a 1 Gbit traffic rate. The switch will drop any packets over that limit.

Use a Test Access Port ("Tap")

This is where a TAP ("Test Access Port" - simply referred to as "tap") comes in handy. A tap is a simple device that copies all the traffic flowing through it (including those corrupt packets) out to a monitor port.

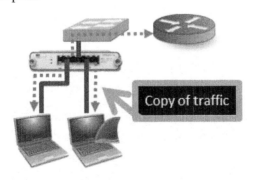

Taps are fabulous! You should know how to "slap a tap" on the network quickly and have some taps in place in the server room.[13] There are several variations of taps on the market. Look for an "aggregating tap"[14] that combines the traffic flowing in both directions on a full-duplex network down a single cable to Wireshark.

The Final Choice – a Hub

Hubs are half-duplex devices (think of a one-lane road). When you only have a hub available, you'll be turning that full-duplex link between the user's system and switch into a half-duplex link. The users will probably not even notice—their network communications are lousy anyway.[15]

---

[13] It is a blessing when a customer has a tap in place on a server when I need to look at that side of the communications.

[14] I would never consider purchasing a non-aggregating tap that requires two capture devices to be attached for capture. This configuration relies on the timestamp accuracy of those two devices and reassembling a bi-directional stream almost never looks correct.

[15] We keep a set of hubs in the office since they are pretty difficult to find. You can still find some hubs on eBay—consider buying one just in case.

Capture on High Traffic Rate Links

If you must capture inside an infrastructure on a high traffic rate link, do not capture with Wireshark.

First of all, Wireshark is a GUI tool — it doesn't have capture capabilities. Wireshark calls on *dumpcap* to perform the capture. If you are running a capture from Wireshark you are watching a graphical interface tool as it receives packets from *dumpcap*. Wireshark may not be able to keep up on a busy link.

Stop capturing if you see the label "Dropped:" in the Status Bar. This is an indication that packets have been dropped by Wireshark, likely because Wireshark cannot keep up with the traffic rate.

There are several capture methods that should be considered when you work on high traffic rate links:

- Consider capturing at the client first if possible. The traffic rate is unlikely to oversubscribe the switch and you may obtain enough information to know what the problem is or where to capture next.
- Capture using command-line "capture only" tools such as *dumpcap* or *tcpdump*. The capture tool *dumpcap* is included in the Wireshark program file directory during installation. Select **Help | About Wireshark | Folders** to locate your Wireshark program file directory.
- Use *Editcap* to split the large capture file into file sets. Use *capinfos <file name>* first to determine the current file size, number of packets and number of seconds in the file as Editcap can only split a file based on number of packets and seconds. Estimate the packets or seconds count to try and limit file sizes to 100 MB if possible.
- If you have a large trace file, but you do not want to split it, use Cascade Pilot to open and analyze the file. Isolate the traffic of interest and then export that subset to Wireshark for further analysis.
- Use a capture device that is designed for high performance networks, such as the Cascade Shark Appliance® (pictured below).[16]

---

[16] During Sharkfest 2013, the Wireshark web site was hit with a DoS attack. Since a new version of Wireshark was releasing that morning, the regular traffic to the Wireshark site was high as well. Gerald Combs had a Cascade Shark Appliance in place to capture all traffic to and from the server. This is an ideal use of the Cascade Shark Appliance!

Consider Your Wireless Capture Options

There are several options available for capturing WLAN traffic. First try to capture traffic on your native wireless adapter. If your adapter's WLAN capture capabilities are limited, consider other options as listed in this section.

Determine Your Native Adapter Capabilities

You are in luck if your native WLAN adapter can capture the WLAN Management and Control traffic and pass up the 802.11 headers. If your native adapter can capture in Monitor Mode, you can see traffic from any network as well.

Wireshark Lab 15: Test Your WLAN Native Adapter Capture Capabilities

Step 1:   Launch Wireshark and click the **Interface List** ⊙ button on the Main Toolbar.

	Device	Description	IP	Packets	Packets/s	
☑	Wireless Network Connection	Microsoft	fe80::407b:3720:1fbf:93a0	1630	1	Details
☐	Local Area Connection	Atheros L1C PCI-E Ethernet Controller	fe80::f829:1573:5f6e:15c5	0	0	Details

Step 2:   Select the checkbox in front of your WLAN adapter and click **Start**.

Step 3:   Toggle over to a browser window and visit www.wireshark.org. Toggle back to Wireshark and examine the packets you captured. If your native adapter is suitable for network capture, you should see some WLAN management and Control traffic (such as Beacon packets and Probe Request/Probe Response packets).

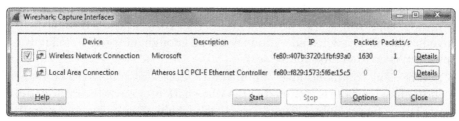

```
⊞ Frame 4599: 148 bytes on wire (1184 bits), 148 bytes captured (1184 bits)
⊞ Radiotap Header v0, Length 20
□ IEEE 802.11 Probe Request, Flags: ........C
    Type/Subtype: Probe Request (0x04)
  ⊞ Frame Control Field: 0x4000
    .000 0000 0000 0000 = Duration: 0 microse
    Receiver address: Broadcast (ff:ff:ff:ff:ff:ff)
    Destination address: Broadcast (ff:ff:ff:ff:ff:ff)
    Transmitter address: Apple_98:26:c0 (60:fa:cd:98:26:c0)
    Source address: Apple_98:26:c0 (60:fa:cd:98:26:c0)
    BSS Id: Broadcast (ff:ff:ff:ff:ff:ff)
    Fragment number: 0
    Sequence number: 478
  ⊞ Frame check sequence: 0x09e00bbe [correct]
⊞ IEEE 802.11 wireless LAN management frame
```

> You want to capture WLAN Management, Control and Data frames

In addition, when you look at the data packets you should see an 802.11 header on the data packets. You will be missing some important information if your adapter strips off the 802.11 header. Wireshark will apply an Ethernet header.

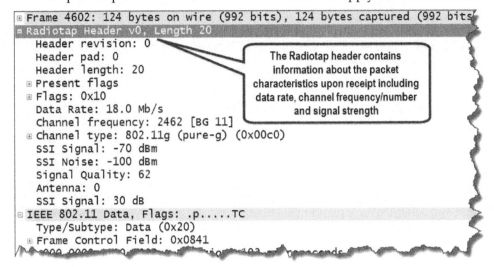

```
⊞ Frame 4602: 124 bytes on wire (992 bits), 124 bytes captured (992 bits
⊟ Radiotap Header v0, Length 20
    Header revision: 0
    Header pad: 0
    Header length: 20
  ⊞ Present flags
  ⊞ Flags: 0x10
    Data Rate: 18.0 Mb/s
    Channel frequency: 2462 [BG 11]
  ⊞ Channel type: 802.11g (pure-g) (0x00c0)
    SSI Signal: -70 dBm
    SSI Noise: -100 dBm
    Signal Quality: 62
    Antenna: 0
    SSI Signal: 30 dB
⊟ IEEE 802.11 Data, Flags: .p.....TC
    Type/Subtype: Data (0x20)
  ⊞ Frame Control Field: 0x0841
```

The Radiotap header contains information about the packet characteristics upon receipt including data rate, channel frequency/number and signal strength

If you do not see these traffic types or characteristics, consider another solution for WLAN capture. Visit wiki.wireshark.org/CaptureSetup/WLAN for additional options for WLAN capture.

Step 4:   Click the **Stop Capture** button on the Main Toolbar.

Consider the AirPcap Adapter

AirPcap adapters were designed for WLAN capture on a Windows host. These USB adapters run in Monitor Mode. Since the adapter does not join any WLAN, it cannot be used to communicate on the WLAN—it is used for capture only.

The adapter can capture all WLAN Management, Control and Data frames. In addition, the driver can apply a Radiotap or PPI header to the traffic. If you connect multiple AirPcap adapters to your system, you can configure each adapter to listen to a different channel and capture all traffic simultaneously using the AirPcap aggregating driver.

When you use an AirPcap adapter, select **View | Wireless Toolbar** to configure the adapter from within Wireshark. The AirPcap includes an AirPcap Control Panel that can be used to configure the adapters as well.

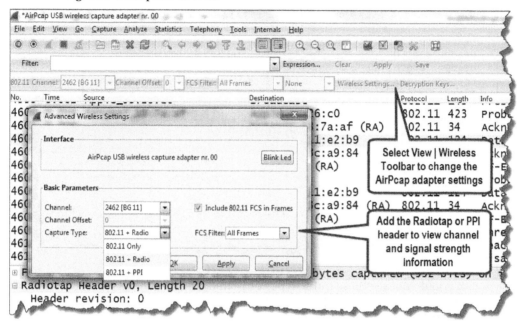

These AirPcap adapters are worth the price if you work on WLANs because you can't troubleshoot what you can't see. For more information about the AirPcap adapters, visit www.riverbed.com. Also see *Tips for Detecting WLAN Problems* on page 325.

Capture to a File Set in High Traffic Rate Situations

Capturing to file sets is an important task when you are working in high traffic situations or trying to capture an intermittent problem. (See also *Tips for Locating the Cause of Intermittent Problems* on page 324.) Ideally, try to keep your file sizes to 100 MB maximum.

File sets are groups of trace files that are linked based on their file name. For example, the following three files would be considered part of a file set:

- sw1-slowftpup_00001_20131222102734.pcapng
- sw1-slowftpup_00002_20131222103004.pcapng
- sw1-slowftpup_00003_201312221 03259.pcapng

The file names are created using a stem, file number, date and time stamp, and extension.

stem   file number   date/time stamp   extension

To work quickly with file sets, use **File | File Set | List files**. In the next lab you will configure Wireshark to capture to a file set and then open and work with that file set.

Wireshark Lab 16: Capture and Work with File Sets

In this lab we will capture to file sets and use an autostop condition to only capture three files. If you do not define an autostop condition, consider defining a ring buffer value. For more information, see *Tips for Locating the Cause of Intermittent Problems* on page 324.

Step 1:   Click the **Capture Options** button ⊙ on the Main Toolbar.

Step 2:   In the Capture Options window, set the following:

> Enter a **path and file name** for your file set.
> Enable **Use Multiple Files**.
> Set **Next file every 1 Minute(s)**.
> Set **Stop capture after 3 Files**.

Click **Start**.

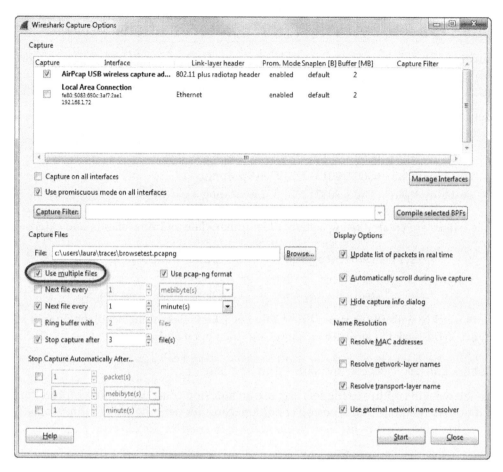

Step 3:   Open a browser and visit several web sites.

Browse for at least **3 minutes** and toggle back to Wireshark. Your capture process will automatically stop after 3 minutes. The third file will be displayed in Wireshark.

Step 4:   To move from one file to the next file in a file set, select **File | File Set | List Files**, select a file in the list and Wireshark will load that file. When you are finished navigating through files, click **Close** on the File Set window.

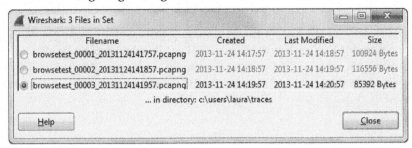

You can quickly locate specific packets in the file set by applying a display filter to one of the files and then clicking subsequent files in the file list. The display filter will remain in place as you open each file.

To learn how to use the ring buffer function, see *Tips for Locating the Cause of Intermittent Problems* on page 324.

Use Capture Filters when Necessary

Capture filters can reduce the traffic that you must look through. If applied too broadly, however, capture filters can exclude the problem indications from the trace file.

For example, let's consider the task of troubleshooting slow web browsing sessions. If you apply a capture filter for traffic on port 80, you will not see the DNS name resolution processes preceding the various TCP connections to the web sites. What if the DNS resolution process was the problem? You would miss it because you have filtered the DNS traffic from view.

Use capture filters sparingly—use display filters liberally.

Wireshark Lab 17: Create and Apply a MAC Address Filter

In the following lab, you will create and use a capture filter based on your own MAC address. This will enable you to see all of the traffic to or from your machine regardless of the protocols or port numbers in use.

Step 1:   Obtain the MAC address of your host using either *ipconfig* or *ifconfig*[17].

Step 2:   Click the **Capture Options** button 🞉 on the Main Toolbar.

Step 3:   Enter **ether host** xx:xx:xx:xx:xx:xx (replacing the x indications with your MAC address).

Make sure you uncheck **Use multiple files**. Click **Start**.

If this is a filter you might apply again, click the **Capture Filter** button. Click **New** and name your filter *MyMac* and click **OK**. If you want to apply this capture filter in the future, just click the **Capture Filter** button again and select your filter from the list.

---

[17]   If you are not familiar with these tools, search online for *ipconfig* or *ifconfig* to locate resources that provide step-by-step instructions on accessing the command prompt and running these tools.

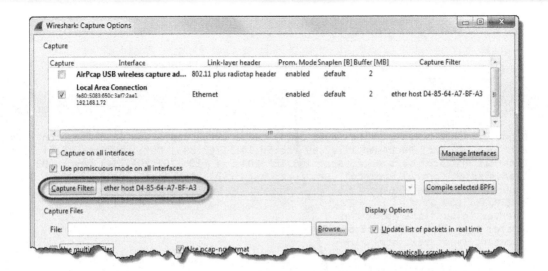

Step 4:   Toggle to or open a browser window and visit www.wireshark.org.

Step 5:   Toggle back to Wireshark and click the **Stop Capture** button ■ on the Main Toolbar.

Step 6:   Your trace file should contain the HTTP traffic from your browsing session to www.wireshark.org.

Just for fun, enter `frame contains "X-Slogan"` in the display filter area and click **Apply**. Expand the **Hypertext Transfer Protocol** section in the Packet Details pane and look for the X-Slogan line.[18]

---

[18]   The X-Slogan value changes often so consider capturing the traffic again to see other X-Slogan values.

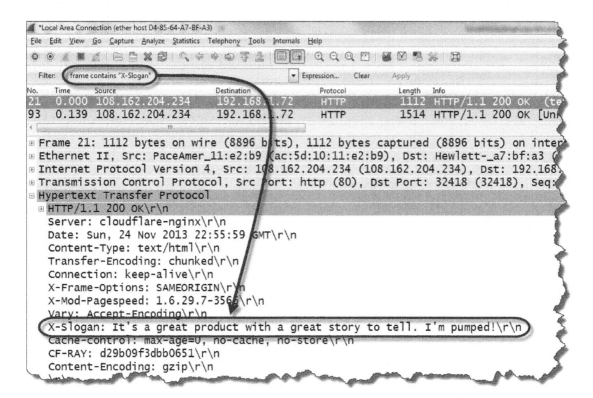

Wireshark will use the same capture filter the next time you begin a capture unless you explicitly remove the capture filter. Don't forget to clear your display filter when you are finished reviewing the results of this lab step.

The most commonly used capture filters are based on addresses, application names, and port number. To learn more about Wireshark capture filtering, visit wiki.wireshark.org/CaptureFilters.

Part 2: Symptom-Based Troubleshooting

When outlining this book, my natural tendency was to write down all the problems and expand upon the issues that make those problems happen. In the real world, however, we do not know the problem—we are able to see only symptoms in the trace files. We must work our way from these symptoms towards possible causes.

Now is probably a good time to reiterate: Wireshark can always tell *where* the problem occurred, but it cannot tell you *why* the problem occurred.

For example, you can determine that a switch along a path is dropping packets with Wireshark. You cannot determine why that switch is dropping packets with Wireshark.

If your role is to capture and analyze traffic only, it is important to work with the client, server or infrastructure team members as they investigate the cause for network problems. Capture the traffic after each fix is applied to verify the problem has been resolved.

If your role is to capture and analyze traffic, and you are responsible for the network clients, servers, and network infrastructure, you will need to take traces before and after you test any fixes applied to network hosts, protocols, or applications. These new trace files can be used to verify fixes and they can also function as your new baseline traces.

In this part of the book, we will look at many common symptoms of network problems and try to trace back to the possible causes of those problems. Oftentimes there are numerous possible causes that need to be ruled out by capturing additional network trace files or performing other network tests.

We will go as far as we can go based on the symptoms in network traffic.

This page intentionally left blank.

CHAPTER 4: RESOLUTION PROBLEMS

The first step of any analysis process is to verify that the hosts are able to communicate and you can see their traffic in the trace file.

There is no use looking into TCP, UDP, or even application problems if the host isn't communicating on the network.

There are several reasons why a host may not communicate. We will start by looking at client issues and then move to server issues in this section.

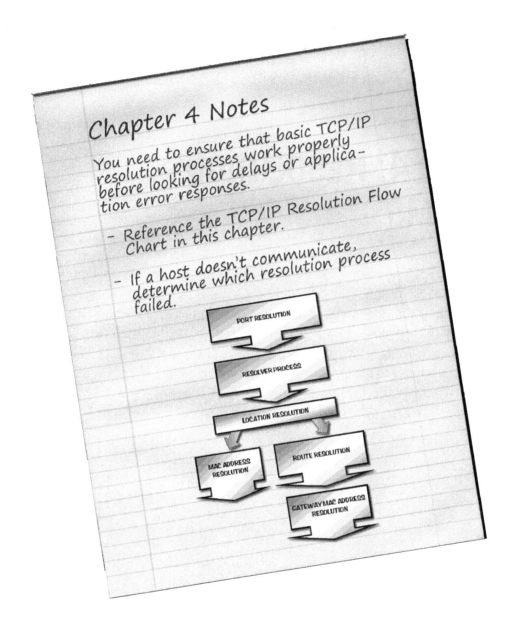

Chapter 4 Notes

You need to ensure that basic TCP/IP resolution processes work properly before looking for delays or application error responses.

- Reference the TCP/IP Resolution Flow Chart in this chapter.

- If a host doesn't communicate, determine which resolution process failed.

Silence is NOT Golden: Verify the Target Host Traffic

If you can't see traffic to or from the complaining user's machine, you can't troubleshoot their traffic-based issues. First you need to ensure your capture process is correct before looking at that client's machine to try and figure out why it is silent. Also consider the TCP/IP resolution process to determine where the problem may reside.

Check Your Capture Process

First, you must rule out any problems with your capturing device and process. If you do not see any traffic, something may have gone wrong during the capture process.

Consider the following possible problems:

- Wireshark had a capture filter in place and the complaining user's traffic did not match the capture filter.
- If you are using a tap, perhaps the user's network cable isn't plugged into the tap.
- If you are capturing on a WLAN, maybe you are capturing on the wrong channel.
- You have lots of traffic in the trace file and you've just missed the packets to/from the host of interest.
- If you are spanning a switch port, perhaps the switch is not spanning the traffic down your analyzer port.

If you captured a lot of traffic, you can use a display filter to determine if your trace file contains traffic to/from the complaining user's machine.

- Example MAC address display filter: `eth.addr==d4:85:64:a7:bf:a3`
- Example IPv4 address display filter: `ip.addr==192.168.1.72`
- Example IPv6 address display filter: `ipv6.addr==2002:1806:addc::1806:addc`

If you are certain your capture process is functioning properly, it's time to start looking at the resolution process.

Consider the TCP/IP Resolution Flow Chart

Consider the resolution flow chart that follows as we walk through several potential problems. All applications must go through this basic resolution process to build the packet to communicate with another host on a TCP/IP network.

(TX) This symbol indicates that the process may generate traffic on the network.

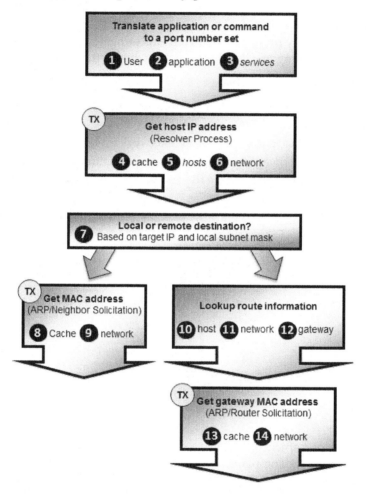

Let's do a quick review of what must take place before a client can even send that TCP handshake packet onto the network.

Port Resolution

➊ The user may specify the port number (such as http://www.chappellU.com:81).

➋ The application may have the port number defined in the code.

➌ The application may consult the local *services* file to determine the port number.

Name Resolution

➍ Examine local cache to locate the information.

➎ Look for the information in a local *hosts* file.

➏ Send a name resolution request on the network (a DNS Query, for example)

Location Resolution - Local or Remote

➐ Compare target address to local host subnet mask.

MAC Address Resolution - Local Target

➑ Examine local cache to locate the target MAC address.

➒ Send an ARP Request (IPv4) or Neighbor Solicitation (IPv6).

Route Resolution

➓ Examine local cache to locate the best route for the target host.

⑪ Examine local cache to locate the best route for the target network.

⑫ Look for a default gateway in the local configuration.

MAC Address Resolution - Remote Target

⑬ Examine local cache to locate the target MAC address.

⑭ Send an ARP Request (IPv4) or Router Solicitation (IPv6).

Resolution Problems Can Cause a Silent Client

If you are absolutely certain your capture technique is correct, you need to figure out why a host isn't communicating. One possibility is that one of the TCP/IP resolution processes failed. For example, if a client can't resolve the port information, that client can't move on to the name resolution process. It is done.

Name Resolution Problems

If a client does not know the IP address of a target (either in cache or a local hosts file), the client can send a DNS query to obtain this information.

If the client doesn't know of a DNS server to ask, the client can't send out a DNS query. The resolution process ends there.

If a client sends a DNS query and does not get a response or receives an error in the DNS response, the client can't talk to the target.

Route Resolution Problems

If a client doesn't know of a route to the host or network and does not have a gateway (router) to get off the local network, it won't send any packets to the remote target. Some hosts will send ICMP Router Solicitation messages to locate a router. Hopefully a local router is configured to send out ICMP Router Advertisements so the client can discover the router.

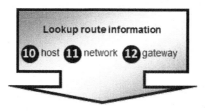

MAC Address Resolution Problems

A client may also go silent if it cannot resolve the MAC address of a local target or local router. We will look at this symptom in *Wireshark Lab 19: Find Local Address Resolution Problems*.

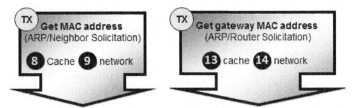

If a client does not communicate, the first step is to examine that client's network configuration. In the next two labs we will identify symptoms indicating problems with these network configurations.

Wireshark Lab 18: Identify a Name Resolution Problem

When network names are used to access hosts (such as www.wireshark.org), the name resolution process must complete successfully in order to move on to determine if the target is local or remote.

In this lab we will quickly identify name resolution problems. Later in this book you will make a filter expression button to detect these problems quickly.

Step 1:   Open **tr-nameresolution.pcapng**.

Step 2:   Type **dns** in the display filter area and click **Apply**.

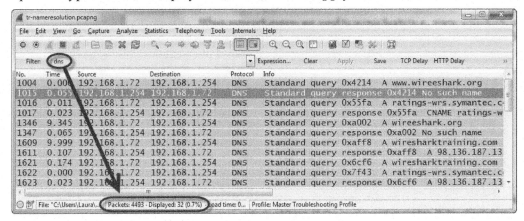

If you look on the Status Bar you'll see that 32 packets match this filter. That's a manageable number of packets to look through.

Focusing on the Info column you can see a number of No Such Name responses indicating the name resolution process failed. This can be due to DNS issues or user issues (such as typing the wrong URL, as we see in this trace file). In *Wireshark Lab 14: Build a Coloring Rule to Highlight DNS Errors* on page 69 you created a coloring rule to highlight DNS errors. Later in this book, you will create a filter expression button to display only these error responses. Don't forget to clear your display filter when you are finished reviewing the results of this lab step.

Wireshark Lab 19: Find Local Address Resolution Problems

Before a client can send a packet to a local target or a local router, it must obtain the MAC (Media Access Control) address of that local target or router. If the client does not have the MAC address information in cache, the client sends out either an Address Resolution Protocol (ARP) request on an IPv4 network, or an ICMP Neighbor Solicitation or ICMP Router Solicitation on an IPv6 network.

If no response is received when trying to acquire the local target's MAC address, the client is done. It cannot send out a packet to the target.

Step 1:   Open **tr-localresolution.pcapng**.

Step 2:   Scroll through this trace file. Look at the ARP requests sent to discover the MAC address of 192.168.1.45.

There are no responses.

Without a successful MAC address resolution process, 192.168.1.72 will not be able to communicate with 192.168.1.45.

Based on this ARP traffic we cannot tell what application 192.168.1.72 is running to communicate with 192.168.1.45. All we know is that the hardware address of 192.168.1.45 was not resolved. Maybe 192.168.1.45 is not currently up. Maybe that is the wrong IP address. We can't tell just from looking at these packets.

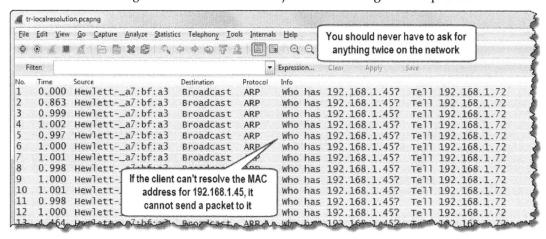

Next we will look at the potential issues the network might be facing when we do not see a server response.

Analyze a Lack of Server Responses

Once you verify that the client is communicating on the network, you must look for the server response. There is no reason to troubleshoot latency, buffer size issues or other problems if the server is simply not responding to the client.

Wireshark Lab 20: No Response to TCP Connection Request

There are several reasons why a server may not respond to a TCP connection attempt.

The TCP handshake request packet (SYN) may not arrive at the server. Maybe the SYN packet was lost, or a firewall along the path dropped the SYN packet, or a host-based firewall on the server blocked access to the port.

Alternately, the response (SYN/ACK) may not arrive at the client. Perhaps the SYN/ACK packet was lost along the path or a firewall along the path blocked the SYN/ACK to prevent the handshake from completing.

If you capture close to the client and do not see the SYN/ACK, consider capturing close to the server to determine if the SYN/ACK was actually sent. If the SYN/ACK was sent, you can now conclude that an interconnecting device along the path has dropped the packet. Continue moving your capture point closer to the client until you see the point where the SYN/ACKs are being dropped.

Step 1:   Open **tr-noserver.pcapng**.

Step 2:   Scroll through this trace file. This trace file only contains only SYN packets from 192.168.1.72 to 192.168.1.66. None of the SYN packets have received SYN/ACK responses.

Expand the TCP header in Packet 1. Right-click on the **[Stream index: 0]** line and select **Apply as Column**. Wireshark assigns each unique connection attempt a separate TCP stream based on the source/destination addresses and source/destination port numbers.

There are six separate connections that the client attempts in the trace file (TCP Stream Index 0 through TCP Stream Index 5).

Step 3:   Right-click on the TCP **Source Port** field in any packet and select **Apply as Column**.

You can now see that the client has set up numerous ports for these connections. The client ports are not contiguous, however. This could be because the client is establishing other connections to other devices and those packets were not captured in this trace file.

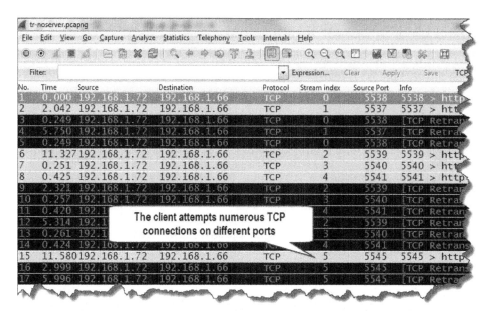

Step 4:   Some of these SYN packets match the HTTP coloring rule while others match the Bad TCP coloring rule because the SYN packets are Retransmissions.

Wireshark tracks each connection attempt and can automatically determine which SYN packets are Retransmissions.

You can see the TCP backoff process if you have set the Time column to Seconds Since Previous Displayed Packet.

Right-click on the **Source Port** column heading and select **Hide Column**. If you want to view this column again later, just right-click on any column heading, select Displayed Columns and select the column from the list.

You can still face server response issues after a successful TCP handshake. We will look at that issue in the next Wireshark lab.

Wireshark Lab 21: No Response to Service Request

In this lab you will extract a single conversation to analyze traffic to a server that is not responding to service requests.

Step 1:   Open **tr-serverresponse.pcapng**.

Step 2:   Scroll through this trace file to get familiar with the traffic pattern. The Stream Index column can help you differentiate the separate connections between 24.6.173.220 and 50.62.146.230.

Let's extract just one of the conversations using the right-click method.

Right-click on **Packet 1** in the Packet List pane and select **Conversation Filter | TCP**.

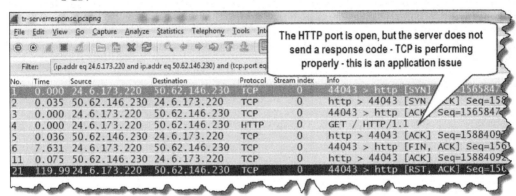

Let's analyze this conversation.

1.   In Packets 1-3 we see the TCP handshake completes successfully.

2.   In Packet 4, the client requests "/" (the default file from the web site's root directory).

3.   Packet 5 is an acknowledgment from the server. This packet contains acknowledgment number 288, indicating the server has received every sequence number up to 287, and it expects sequence number 288 next. So it appears the server did receive the request.

4.   Instead of sending back the requested default page or perhaps a redirection, however, the server goes quiet.

5.   TCP doesn't retransmit the GET request because the client received an ACK for that request.

6. The client's browser appears to time out and sends a FIN/ACK after almost 8 seconds. The client is done sending information to the server and it begins an implied connection termination. The client is in FIN-WAIT-1 state at this time.[19]

7. The server sends an ACK. The client is now in FIN-WAIT-2 state. We would expect to see the server send a FIN to begin closing its side of the connection, but it does not.

8. The client waits almost 120 seconds before giving up on the connection altogether by sending a RST/ACK.

Each of the connections goes through the same pattern. This is not just a temporary "glitch" in network communications or a one-time problem with the service running on the server.

TCP appears to be functioning properly in this trace file. The symptoms indicate the application has failed at the server side.

---

[19] For more information on FIN wait states, see RFC 793, "Transmission Control Protocol" (Section 3.5. Closing a Connection).

Chapter 5: Troubleshoot with Time

"Time is money." - Benjamin Franklin

You must always keep an eye on the time values in the trace file. You may find a poorly-behaving application that requests the same item over and over again before giving up and moving on to another request. The traffic will look ugly and you may rush to judgment and declare this the likely cause of performance problems.

Before pointing the finger[20], look at the amount of time wasted by this application to determine whether it really had an impact on performance. If the entire ugly process wasted 2 ms it is doubtful that this is the cause of the user's complaints.

There are two basic types of delays in traffic:

- delays that **do not** matter (do not affect the end user experience)
- delays that **do** matter (delays that cause the phone to ring in the IT department)

This chapter will differentiate between these two types of delays first and then provide numerous methods to detect delays in UDP-based and TCP-based traffic, path delays, application delays, client delays and server delays.

---

[20] I've always told people, the only finger that matters in the world of finger-pointing during network problems is the finger of the protocol analyst. The packets never lie.

Chapter 5 Notes

When users complain that the "network is slow," I watch for delays in the trace file. I always keep in mind that some delays are OK.

- Make sure you know which delays are "normal" – don't spend time troubleshooting those delays.

- Add and sort delta time columns to find delays quickly.

- Enable TCP's Calculate Conversation Timestamp setting to see TCP conversation delta times.

- Add columns based on Wireshark's response time fields (such as http.time and dns.time).

Do not Focus on "Normal" or Acceptable Delays

It may sound strange, but some delays should be ignored in your trace files. For example, a delay before a TCP RST packet would likely not be felt by the end user. Most likely the user toggled to another window and the application eventually terminated the connection to the server. This is transparent to the user and no cause for alarm.

The following section describes numerous delays that may be considered "normal" and acceptable delays.

Delays before DNS Queries

DNS Queries are often triggered by a user submitting a request to go to a target. For example, when you browse a web page, you enter the URL and then press Enter. This will trigger a DNS query (if you do not have the IP address in cache or a local *hosts* file). When the user sees an interesting link on the web page and clicks on it, this may again trigger a DNS Query. Both queries would have preceding delays caused by the user deciding what page they want to visit next.

The image below shows two sudden increases in time in **tr-delays.pcapng**. The delay before Packet 29 is caused by an eventual time out of a connection. The delay before Packet 32 (a DNS query) is because the user didn't click on a hyperlink on www.wireshark.org right away.

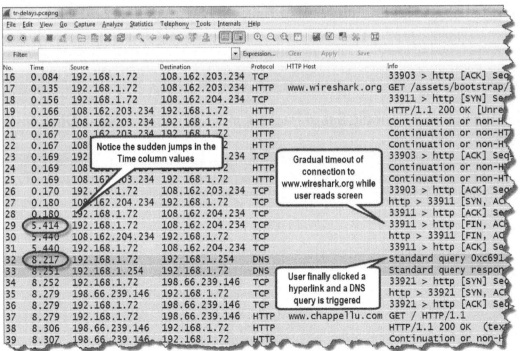

Delays before TCP FIN or Reset Packets

An application may eventually send TCP FIN or RST packets to close the connection after waiting a specified amount of time or upon completion of some task. The user won't even know the connection is being terminated.

Delays before a Client Sends a Request to a Server

In many cases, an application requires user interaction, such as filling out a form and pressing the Submit button, or clicking the next link on a web page. We only focus on the client delays if user interaction has no bearing on the client request rate.

Delays before Keep-Alive or Zero Window Probes

These two packet types, Keep-Alives and Zero Window Probes, are sent during a Zero Window situation to determine if more buffer space is available at the target. The Zero Window situation is the problem, not the Keep-Alives and Zero Window Probes. These symptoms indicate a receive buffer problem. For more information, see *Keep Alive and Keep Alive ACK* on page 195 and *Zero Window Probe and Zero Window Probe ACK* on page 215.

Hosts may also send Keep-Alives periodically to maintain a TCP connection. These packets may have large delays preceding them, but the delays are not noticeable since the user is not actively working in that application.

Delays before TLS Encrypted Alert Followed by a TCP FIN or RST

When an application sends a TLS Encrypted Alert to eventually close an encrypted connection, we can't see the Close command. If an encrypted alert packet arrives just before a FIN or RST process, we must assume it is simply the Close command. An application activity time out eventually triggers the FIN or RST to be sent.

Delays before a Periodic Set of Packets in a Connection that is Otherwise Idle

Applications can define their own keep-alive processes as well. They may not use TCP's Keep-Alive packet structure. The applications may define their own keep alive packet types to keep the connection active. The process is transparent to the end user.

Watch for the Delays that DO Matter

It is important to recognize delays that do affect the end user experience. It is also important to realize that the term "slow" is relative. In some situations a 2 second delay goes unnoticed by an end user while in other situations a 200 ms delay is felt.

Knowing what "normal" delay times are on your network will help you identify unusually high delay times.

The following is a list of delays that should be examined and their potential causes.

Delays before a Server Responds with a SYN/ACK

If you capture traffic at the client, the time between the SYN and SYN/ACK in the TCP handshake can be used to determine the round trip time between the hosts. It is only a snapshot of the round trip time, however. A large delay before the SYN/ACK is an indication of a high round trip time between the hosts.

For more details on calculating round trip times when capturing at the client, go through the labs in *Detect Delays in TCP Conversations* (starting on page 119).

Delays before a Client Completes the 3-Way TCP Handshake

If you capture traffic at the server, the time between the SYN/ACK and the client's ACK to finish the TCP handshake can be used to determine the round trip time between the hosts. Again this is only a snapshot of the round trip time, however. A large delay between the SYN/ACK and the final ACK of the TCP handshake is an indication of a high round trip time between the hosts.

For more details on calculating round trip times when capturing at the server, go through the labs in *Detect Delays in TCP Conversations* (starting on page 119).

Delays before a Server Sends a Response

If a trace indicates a server quickly sent an ACK to a client's request, but then there is a long delay before the server response, we point the finger at the server. The server is slow to respond to the request. This is not a path latency issue—the ACK arrived in a timely manner. We need to consider why a server might be slow. Perhaps that server must ask another server for information (such as in a tiered architecture). Perhaps that server is low on processing power and can't keep up with the current number of requests. Perhaps that server is under attack.

In **tr-http-pcaprnet101.pcapng**, we see the client's GET request (GET /home) in packet 18 followed by the server ACK (within 17 ms). Then we see a delay of almost 1.8 seconds before the requested data begins flowing towards the server. The trace was taken at the client. The round trip time between the hosts is acceptable, but the server response time is not.

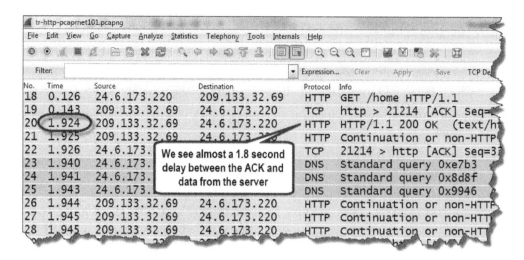

Delays before the Next Packet in a Data Stream

We hope to see continuous data flow during a file download or file upload process. Sudden delays in the middle of the data stream may indicate that either the sender became busy with other processing, or a tiered configuration is in place and is injecting time delays — alternately consider that a device along the path may be buffering the data for higher priority traffic.

This situation could also be caused by a lack of receive buffer space at a receiver. If the receiver does not have sufficient receive buffer space, the sender must wait for a Window Update before continuing the data transmission.

Hansang Bae showed how the Nagle algorithm and delayed ACKs can cause sudden delays in the middle of a data stream as well. See the video at bit.ly/delayedack.

Delays before an ACK from a TCP peer

Delays before transmitted data is ACKed may be caused by path latency or the Delayed ACK function. Since Delayed ACK timers are often set at 200 ms, that is a good time value to look at when trying to detect if Delayed ACK is in use.

Delays before a Window Update

If you see large delays before a Window Update, pay close attention to the Calculated window size field (`tcp.window_size`) in packets. If the Window Size advertised is too small to fit a full-sized data segment, the peer must wait for a Window Update before sending a packet. There is no Expert Infos warning for this "low window size" problem, so be watchful for small Calculated window size field values.

In this next section, we examine the various Wireshark time measurements for UDP and TCP traffic.

- Delta time (**frame.time_delta**)
- Delta displayed time (**frame.time_delta_displayed** and Delta time displayed)
- TCP delta time (**tcp.time_delta**)

In addition, we look at several application response time measurements that are used in troubleshooting.

- DNS response time (**dns.time**)
- HTTP response time (**http.time**)
- SMB response time (**smb.time**)

Detect Delays in UDP Conversations

Display Filter Value

```
frame.time_delta
frame.time_delta_displayed
```
Delta time displayed (predefined column)

User Datagram Protocol (UDP) is a connectionless transport protocol with a very simple 8-byte header. Unlike TCP, UDP has no sequencing or acknowledgement capability. To detect delays in a UDP conversation, we can use two time fields—`frame.time_delta` and `frame.time_delta_displayed`.[21]

Wireshark offers application response time measurements for several applications that can run over UDP, such as DNS (`dns.time`). If available, use these response time measurements to identify slow responses.

UDP Delay Detection Methods

Since UDP is not connection-oriented, we measure delays between requests and responses. In the upcoming labs you will examine UDP conversation statistics and two time field columns to detect delays in all UDP-based applications.

Wireshark Lab 22: Obtain UDP Conversation Statistics and Filter on a UDP Conversation

Use the Conversations window to obtain basic UDP conversation statistics such as packet rate, bits-per-second rate and conversation duration.

Step 1:   Open **tr-voip-extensions.pcapng**.

Step 2:   Select **Statistics | Conversation**.

Step 3:   Click the **UDP** tab. If you prefer seeing port numbers rather than port names, uncheck the **Name Resolution** option.

Step 4:   To sort UDP conversations based on traffic flowing from Address A/Port A to Address B/Port B, click twice on the **bps A——▸B** column heading. The conversation between 192.168.5.11/port 25436 and 192.158.5.10/port 8000 is listed first.

Step 5:   This conversation also appears to be the most active UDP conversation based on the Bytes column value. Right-click on this conversation line and choose **Apply as Filter | Selected | A◄——▸B**.

---

[21]   Because of a Wireshark 1.10.x bug in calculating the `frame.time_delta_displayed` value when listed in a column, we will create our delta displayed time column using the Preferences window and the predefined *Delta time displayed* column.

Before using **frame.time_delta_displayed**, *filter on a UDP conversation so you have a "displayed" set. Before using* **frame.time_delta**, *consider filtering on a UDP conversation and saving the conversation in a separate trace file. Interwoven UDP conversations will make it more difficult to locate delays in a single conversation.*

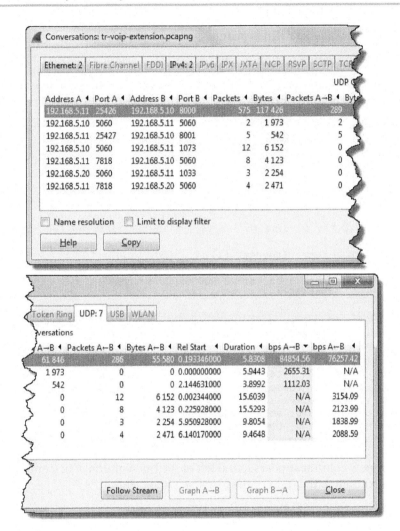

Step 6:   Select **File | Export Specified Packets** and name your new file **udpconv1.pcapng**. Clear your display filter and close the Conversations window when you are done.

Filtering on and exporting a conversation to a separate trace file can help remove unrelated traffic from view. When you open the new single-conversation trace file, Wireshark's statistics only relate to that traffic set, often making it easier to identify performance issues.

Wireshark Lab 23: Add/Sort a Delta Time Column

The default Time column setting is Seconds Since Beginning of Capture. It is usually easier to spot delays when a time column displays delta times. Sorting on a delta time column from high to low displays the largest delays in the trace file. In this lab you will create a **frame.time_delta** column to indicate the arrival time from the end of one packet to the end of the next to locate high delta times.

Step 1:   Open **tr-malaysianairlines.pcapng**.

Step 2:   Expand the **Frame** section of any packet.

Step 3:   Right-click on the **Time delta from previous captured frame** line and select **Apply as Column**. You have now created a **frame.time_delta** column.

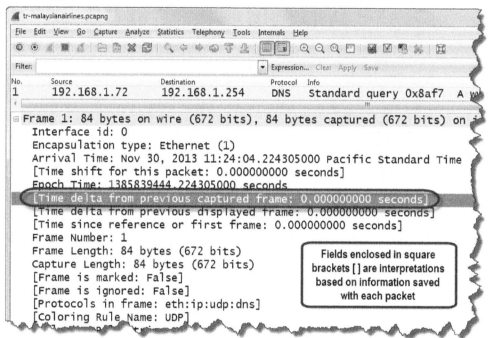

Step 4:   Your new column appears to the left of the Info column. Click and drag your new column to the right of the existing **Time** column.

Step 5:   The column name can be shortened by right-clicking on the column heading and selecting **Edit Column Details**. Consider changing the Title to **Delta**. Click **OK**.

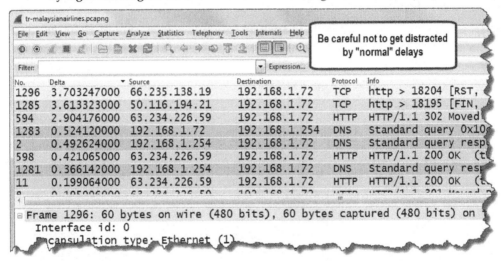

Step 6:   Click your new **Delta** column heading twice to sort from high to low. If necessary, click the **Go To First Packet** button 🔝 to jump to the top of the sorted list. The packets with the largest delays between them are located at the top of the list. (Note: In the image below, we have hidden the Time and Length columns by right-clicking on those columns and selecting **Hide Column**.)

There are numerous "normal" delays in this trace file. We do not care about the delays before DNS queries, TCP RST packets, or TCP FIN packets. We do care about delays before DNS and HTTP responses.

In the next lab, you will apply a display filter and use **frame.time_delta_displayed** to locate delays in the DNS responses.

Click the Resize All Columns 🔲 button to quickly reset column widths after creating a column.

Wireshark Lab 24: Add/Sort a Delta Displayed Time Column

When you apply a filter, you can use a Delta Displayed time column to identify delays between displayed packets. In the previous step-by-step lab, we saw DNS and HTTP packets in the trace file. Now we will create another new time column to show the delta times of DNS traffic only.

In Wireshark 1.10.x, there is a bug in the `frame.time_delta_displayed` calculation. To avoid this bug, we will add our delta displayed time column using Wireshark's Preferences window and the *Delta time displayed* predefined column.

Step 1:   Open **tr-malaysianairlines.pcapng**. If this file is still open from the previous lab, click the **No.** column heading once to sort by frame number.

Step 2:   Click the **Preferences** button on the Main Toolbar and then select **Columns**.

Step 3:   Click the **Add** button. In the drop-down Field Type list, select *Delta time displayed*. Click on the column name and change the value from New Column to **Delta Displayed**.

Step 4:   Click and drag your **Delta Displayed** column above the Source column. Click **OK**. You can right click on your new column heading to set left alignment, if desired.

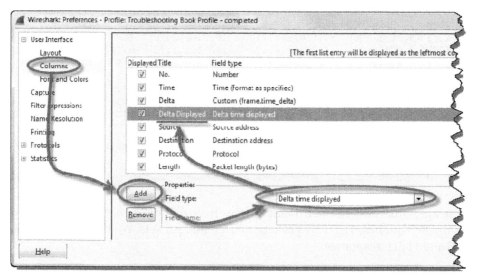

> When the `frame.time_delta_displayed` calculation bug is fixed, you will be able to simply right click on the *Time delta from previous displayed frame* line in a packet Frame section and select *Apply as Column*.

Step 5:   Now let's apply a filter for DNS traffic. In the display filter area, enter **dns** and click **Apply**.

Step 6:   Click twice on your new **Delta Displayed** column to sort from high to low. We do not care about delays before DNS queries, but we do care about delays before DNS query responses.

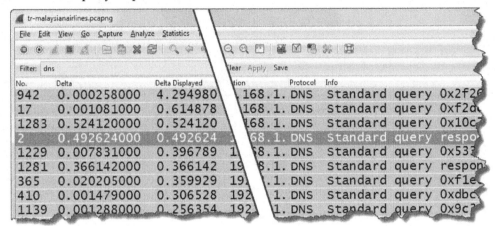

There are two DNS responses that are particularly "slow" in the trace file—Packet 2 and Packet 1,281. The delays may be caused when the local DNS server performs recursive queries to obtain the data because it does not have these names in its cache.

In the next lab we will graph UDP delays using a `frame.time_delta_displayed` filter value.

Wireshark Lab 25: Graph UDP Delays

You can use Wireshark's Advanced IO Graph with a filter and a reference to the maximum `frame.time_delta_displayed` value to create a picture of delays in a trace file.

Step 1:   Open **tr-queuing.pcapng**.

Step 2:   Select **Statistics | IO Graph**.

Step 3:   In the **Y Axis Unit** area, select **Advanced...**

Step 4:   This trace file contains less than 2 seconds of traffic. In the X Axis **Tick Interval** area, select **0.01 sec**.

Step 5:   Select the **MAX(*)** Graph 1 Calc option and enter `frame.time_delta_displayed` in the Calc area.

Step 6:   Click the **Graph 1** button to graph your results.

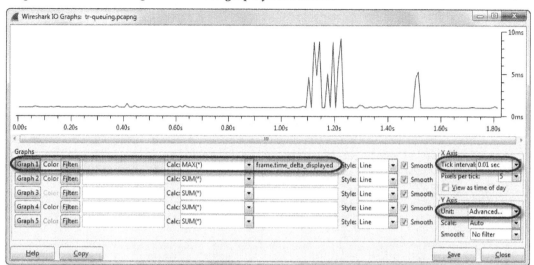

At approximately 1.2 seconds into the trace file, you can see a sudden increase in the delta time. When you click on these points in the graph, Wireshark jumps to that point in the trace file. This enables you to do additional analysis on the trace file.

If you work on a trace file that contains TCP-based traffic, enter **udp** in the Graph 1 filter area before you click the Graph 1 button.

Don't forget to close the IO Graph when you are finished.

Detect Delays in TCP Conversations

Display Filter Value

`tcp.time_delta`

Transmission Control Protocol (TCP) is connection-oriented and offers sequencing and acknowledgement capability. Wireshark numbers each separate TCP conversation with a TCP Stream Index (`tcp.stream`) value starting with 0. In the image below, the packet is part of the first TCP conversation seen in the trace file.

```
⊞ Frame 1: 863 bytes on wire (6904 bits), 863 bytes captured (6904 bit
⊞ Ethernet II, Src: Hewlett-_a7:bf:a3 (d4:85:64:a7:bf:a3), Dst: Cada
⊞ Internet Protocol Version 4, Src: 24.6.173.220 (24.6.173.220), Dst:
⊟ Transmission Control Protocol, Src Port: 7439 (7439), Dst Port: htt
    Source port: 7439 (7439)
    Destination port: http (80)
    [Stream index: 0]
    Sequence number:        (relative sequence number)
```

A "stream" is basically a TCP conversation. In TCP communications, we can look for delays within a specific TCP stream. First we need to enable Wireshark to track time within separate TCP conversations.

TCP Preference: *Calculate Conversation Timestamps*

Wireshark has several TCP preference settings that can be used to quickly detect problems in TCP-based communications. One of these preference settings is *Calculate conversation timestamps*.

You can change TCP preferences by right-clicking on a TCP header in the Packet Details pane or clicking the **Preferences** button ![icon], expanding **Protocols** and choosing **TCP**.

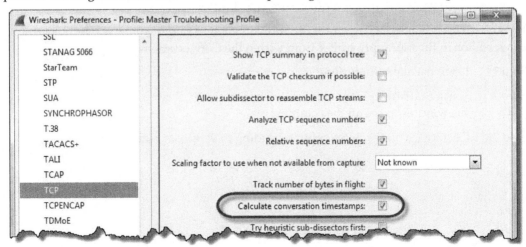

After you enable the *Calculate conversation timestamp* preference setting, two additional time fields will be visible at the end of the TCP header:

- Time since first frame in this TCP stream (`tcp.time_relative`)
- Time since previous frame in this TCP stream (`tcp.time_delta`)

```
⊞ Frame 1: 863 bytes on wire (6904 bits), 863 bytes captured (6904 bits) on inte
⊞ Ethernet II, Src: Hewlett-_a7:bf:a3 (d4:85:64:a7:bf:a3), Dst: Cadant_31:bb:c1
⊞ Internet Protocol Version 4, Src: 24.6.173.220 (24.6.173.220), Dst: 74.125.224
⊟ Transmission Control Protocol, Src Port: 7439 (7439), Dst Port: http (80), Seq
     Source port: 7439 (7439)
     Destination port: http (80)
     [Stream index: 0]
     Sequence number: 1    (relative sequence number)
     [Next sequence number: 810    (relative sequence number)]
     Acknowledgment number: 1    (relative ack number)
     Header length: 20 bytes
  ⊞ Flags: 0x018 (PSH, ACK)
     Window size value: 16391
     [Calculated window size: 16391]
     [Window size scaling factor: -1 (unknown)]
  ⊞ Checksum: 0xf434 [validation disabled]
  ⊞ [SEQ/ACK analysis]
  ⊟ [Timestamps]
        [Time since first frame in this TCP stream: 0.000000000 seconds]
        [Time since previous frame in this TCP stream: 0.000000000 seconds]
⊞ Hypertext Transfer Protocol
```

Between these two time settings, the `tcp.time_delta` is the most useful for troubleshooting. Unlike the basic delta time value, this time value tracks the time from the end of one packet in a TCP conversation (aka "stream") to the end of the next packet in that same TCP conversation.

First we will obtain TCP conversation statistics and filter on a TCP conversation using the `tcp.stream` field.

Wireshark Lab 26: Obtain TCP Conversation Statistics

If you have been handed a large trace file and you want to find the most active TCP conversation in the file, apply a filter from within the Conversations window.

Step 1:   Open **tr-chappellu.pcapng**.

Step 2:   Select **Statistics | Conversations** and click the **TCP** tab. You may need to expand the window to see all the columns.

Step 3:   Click twice on the **Bytes** column heading to sort from high to low.

Step 4:   Right-click on the top entry and select **Apply as Filter | Selected | A ←→ B.**

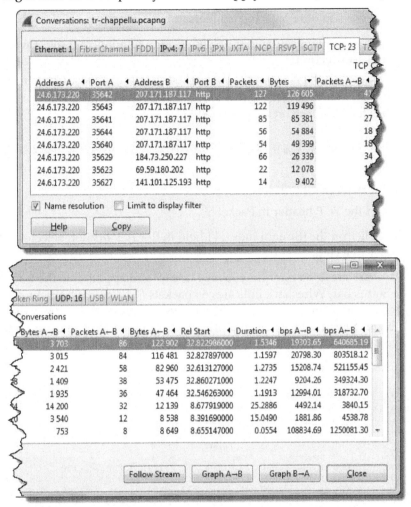

Wireshark creates a filter based on the source/destination address and source/destination port fields.

Step 5:   Click **Clear** to remove your filter when you are finished.

If you are working with a trace file that has many TCP conversations in it, you can use this method to find the most active conversation and quickly apply a filter on that conversation. This is one way of filtering on a TCP conversation. In the next lab you will filter on a conversation using the **tcp.stream** field.

Wireshark Lab 27: Filter on a TCP Conversation Using the Stream Index Field

There are several ways to filter on a TCP conversation.

- Right-click on a conversation in the Conversation window and select **Apply as Filter | Selected | [direction]**.
- Right-click on a TCP packet in the Packet List pane and choose **Conversation Filter | TCP**.
- Apply a filter using `tcp.stream==[number]`

In this lab we will practice using the right-click method to create a filter based on the `tcp.stream` field.

Step 1:   Open **tr-chappellu.pcapng**.

Step 2:   Expand the **TCP header** in Packet 59.

Step 3:   Right-click on the **[Stream index: 7]** field in the TCP header. Select **Apply as Filter | Selected**.

Wireshark creates a filter for `tcp.stream==7` and applies it to the trace file. On the Status Bar, Wireshark indicates 66 packets (9.1% of the traffic) match this filter. If you want to save this TCP conversation as a separate trace file, select **File | Export Specified Packets** and provide a file name. Wireshark automatically saves just the displayed packets.

Step 4:   Click **Clear** to remove your filter when you are finished.

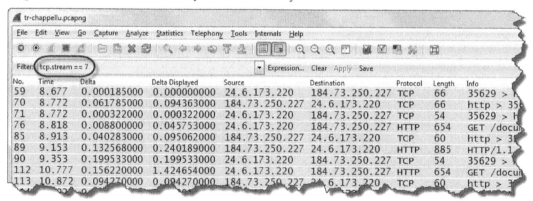

Wireshark Lab 28: Add a TCP Stream Index Column

Your trace files may contain numerous TCP conversations. Creating a column based on the TCP Stream Index value can help differentiate these conversations.

Step 1:   Open **tr-chappellu.pcapng**.

Step 2:   If you hid your TCP Stream index column (created in *Wireshark Lab 20: No Response to TCP Connection Request* on page 101), right-click on any column, select **Displayed Columns** and select your **Stream index** column.

Step 3:   Click on your **Stream index** column once to sort the trace file by conversations. If you jump to the end of this trace file you can quickly determine that there are 23 TCP conversations (remember that Wireshark starts counting TCP streams at 0).

Wireshark Lab 29: Add/Sort a TCP Delta Time Column

You must enable the TCP *Calculate conversation timestamp* preference in order to add the `tcp.time_delta` column (see *TCP Preference: Calculate Conversation Timestamps* on page 119). This column will display the time from the end of one packet in a TCP stream to the end of the next packet in that same TCP stream.

No matter how intertwined various TCP conversations are, this `tcp.time_delta` column can be used to locate delays within a conversation.

Step 1:   Open **tr-chappellu.pcapng**.

Step 2:   Fully expand the **TCP header** in Packet 1. Right click anywhere on the TCP header, select **Protocol Preferences** and ensure that *Calculate conversation timestamps* is enabled.

Step 3:   At the end of the TCP header, locate and right-click on the **Time since previous frame in this TCP stream** field (under the [Timestamps] section). Select **Apply as Column**.

Step 4:   Your new column appears to the left of the Info column. Click and drag your new column to the right of the existing **Delta Displayed** column.

Step 5:   The column name can be shortened by right-clicking on the column heading and selecting **Edit Column Details**. Consider changing the Title to **TCP Delta**. Click **OK**.

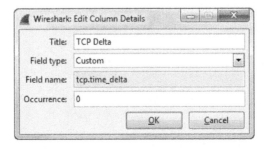

Step 6:   Click your new **TCP Delta** column heading twice to sort from high to low. The packets with the largest delays before them in a TCP conversation appear at the top of the list.

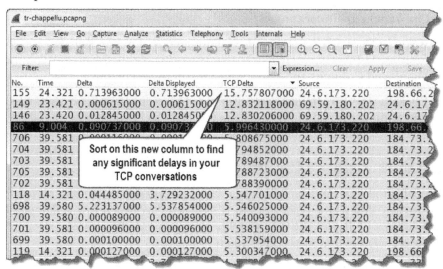

Since we do not have a display filter applied, the time values in the Delta and Delta Displayed columns are the same.

Step 7:   Scroll through the packets to determine where delays are incurred in this communication. You will see numerous delays before TCP FIN packets, but those are delays that the user will not notice. There are numerous delays before retransmissions. It appears some of the TCP connection attempts are unsuccessful.

In addition, there are quite a few HTTP responses that have one-half second delays before them. These delays will add up and be felt by the user.

Remember, there are certain delays that are considered "normal" or are not noticeable. Refer to *Do not Focus on "Normal" or Acceptable Delays* on page 107.

The TCP Delta column is a key column to add when troubleshooting TCP-based applications. It's one of the first steps I use when locating the cause of poor performance of a TCP-based applications on a network.

Wireshark Lab 30: Add a "TCP Delay" Button

You sorted your new **tcp.time_delta** column to find the highest delays in TCP conversations. Let's become more efficient at locating delays by creating a "TCP Delay" button (filter expression button).

When clicked, this button will display TCP packets that are preceded by a noticeable delay (you will need to adjust the time to match your needs). We will ignore packets that we know are often preceded by delays, but are "normal" or not noticeable.

Step 1:   Open **tr-chappellu.pcapng**.

Step 2:   In the display filter area, enter the following filter:

> **tcp.time_delta > 1**

Step 3:   Click the **Save** button on the display filter toolbar. Enter **TCP Delay** as the label when prompted. Click **OK** to save your new button.

Create a filter expression button for every network problem that you want to locate in a trace file. In the labs in this book you will create buttons for various delays and error responses. These filter expression buttons are maintained in the profile's preferences file. The preferences file is just a text file and can be edited with a text editor.

Step 4:   Click your new **TCP Delay** button. Thirty-seven packets should match your filter. Notice that we have numerous TCP FIN packets in the list. This is one of the delays that we do not care about—the delay is transparent to the user.

```
Stream index  Info
     0    [TCP Retransmission] 35621 > http [SYN] Seq=0 Win=8192 Len=0 MSS=1460 W
     0    [TCP Retransmission] 35621 > http [SYN] Seq=0 Win=8192 Len=0 MSS=1460 S
     2    GET /pdf2html/view_online.php?url=http%3A%2F%2Fwww.chappellu.com%2Ffile
     3    GET /pdf2html/vuzit.php HTTP/1.1
     4    GET /legacy/graphics/promo/reader_2_728x90.png HTTP/1.1
     7    GET /documents.json?key=b8411b64-c2e5-335f-894d-f984bc98b9b5&url=http%3
     7    GET /documents.json?key=b8411b64-c2e5-335f-894d-f984bc98b9b5&url=http%3
     6    35628 > http [FIN, ACK] Seq=1 Ack=1 Win=65700 Len=0
     0    35621 > http [FIN, ACK] Seq=1 Ack=1 Win=64240 Len=0
     7    GET /documents.json?key=b8411b64-c2e5-335f-894d-f984bc98b9b5&url=http%3
     7    [TCP Retransmission] GET /documents.json?key=b8411b64-c2e5-335f-894d-f9
     7    [TCP Retransmission] GET /documents.json?key=b8411b64-c2e5-335f-894d-f9
     3    http > 35625 [FIN, ACK] Seq=4849 Ack=1553 Win=8960 Len=0
     2    http > 35623 [FIN, ACK] Seq=7861 Ack=2989 Win=12032 Len=0
     1    35622 > http [FIN, ACK] Seq=410 Ack=370 Win=65328 Len=0
     7    GET /documents.json?key=b8411b64-c2e5-335f-894d-f984bc98b9b5&url=http%3
     7    [TCP Retransmission] GET /documents.json?key=b8411b64-c2e5-335f-894d-f9
     8    [TCP Retransmission] 35630 > http [SYN] Seq=0 Win=8192 Len=0 MSS=1460 W
     8    http > 35630 [SYN, ACK] Seq=0 Ack=1 Win=5840 Len=0 MSS=1460 SACK_PERM=1
     9    [TCP Retransmission] 35631 > http [SYN] Seq=0 Win=8192 Len=0 MSS=1460 W
    11    [TCP Retransmission] 35633 > http [SYN] Seq=0 Win=8192 Len=0 MSS=1460 W
    12    [TCP Retransmission] 35634 > http [SYN] Seq=0 Win=8192 Len=0 MSS=1460 W
    13    [TCP Retransmission] 35635 > http [SYN] Seq=0 Win=8192 Len=0 MSS=1460 W
    10    [TCP Retransmission] 35632 > http [SYN] Seq=0 Win=8192 Len=0 MSS=1460 W
    17    [TCP Retransmission] 35639 > http [SYN] Seq=0 Win=8192 Len=0 MSS=1460 W
    14    [TCP Retransmission] 35636 > http [SYN] Seq=0 Win=8192 Len=0 MSS=1460 W
    15    [TCP Retransmission] 35637 > http [SYN] Seq=0 Win=8192 Len=0 MSS=1460 W
    16    [TCP Retransmission] 35638 > http [SYN] Seq=0 Win=8192 Len=0 MSS=1460 W
    17    35639 > http [FIN, ACK] Seq=1 Ack=1 Win=65700 Len=0
    16    35638 > http [FIN, ACK] Seq=1 Ack=1 Win=65700 Len=0
    15    35637 > http [FIN, ACK] Seq=1 Ack=1 Win=65700 Len=0
    14    35636 > http [FIN, ACK] Seq=1 Ack=1 Win=65700 Len=0
    13    35635 > http [FIN, ACK] Seq=1 Ack=1 Win=65700 Len=0
    12    35634 > http [FIN, ACK] Seq=1 Ack=1 Win=65700 Len=0
    11    35633 > http [FIN, ACK] Seq=1 Ack=1 Win=65700 Len=0
    10    35632 > http [FIN, ACK] Seq=1 Ack=1 Win=65700 Len=0
     9    35631 > http [FIN, ACK] Seq=1 Ack=1 Win=65700 Len=0
```

Step 5:   Select **Edit | Preferences | Filter Expressions** or click the **Edit Preferences** button on the Main Toolbar. Change your TCP Delay filter expression button to the focus on packets that do not have the FIN or RST bit set:

`tcp.time_delta > 1 && tcp.flags.fin==0 && tcp.flags.reset==0`

Click **OK** to save your edited filter expression button[22].

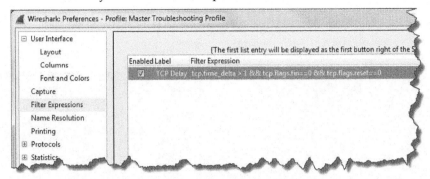

Step 6:   Click your **TCP Delay** button again. Only 23 packets should be displayed. You
have removed the TCP FIN and RST packets.

You might consider removing HTTP GET requests from your TCP Delay button
because often the delay is caused by a user who has not clicked on the next link
on a web site. To remove these GET requests, add the following string to the end
of your filter:

`&& !http.request.method=="GET"`

After adding this string, your final filter expression button should contain the
following:

`tcp.time_delta > 1 && tcp.flags.fin==0 && tcp.flags.reset==0`
`&& !http.request.method=="GET"`

Remember to clear your display filter when you are finished reviewing the
results of this lab step.

The highest TCP Delta delay appears to be just under 6 seconds. It is a SYN retransmission
packet. In fact there are 12 SYN retransmissions between the client and 184.73.250.227.
There is one SYN/ACK from that server that is displayed because the RTT is 1.28957
seconds.

*In this trace file, there are several delays before GET requests that are marked with the Bad TCP
coloring rule because the packets are Retransmissions. If you exclude these GET requests from
view, you will not see that there is a problem with these packets. Don't worry—you would have
detected these retransmissions when you checked the Expert Infos Errors, Warnings and Notes
as listed in the Troubleshooting Checklist.*

---

[22]   If Wireshark does not save your edits, click somewhere in a blank area of the Filter Expressions editing area
before clicking OK. This takes Wireshark out of editing mode and allows you to save your changes.

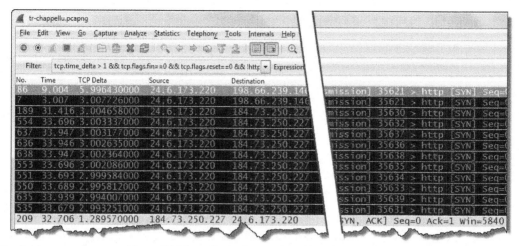

In the image above we have hidden the Delta and Delta Displayed columns.

As you analyze more trace files, consider fine-tuning this TCP Delay filter expression button to remove false positives from other "normal" or unnoticeable delays.

In this book we will repeatedly hide and display this column to find the cause of poor performance on the network.

Wireshark Lab 31: Obtain the Round Trip Time (RTT) Using the TCP Handshake

It's important to determine if path latency is the reason for poor performance. For example, if everything else is functioning properly in a TCP conversation, but the Round Trip Time (RTT) is extremely high, the file transfer process will likely appear very slow.

You can get a glimpse of the RTT by looking at the `tcp.time_delta` value of TCP handshake packets.

For example, if you are capturing at the client, look at the `tcp.time_delta` value between the client's TCP SYN packet and the server's TCP SYN/ACK response.

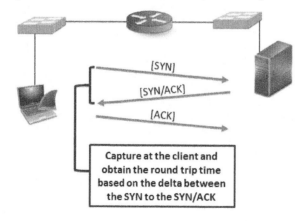

If you are capturing at the server, look at the `tcp.time_delta` value between the server's TCP SYN/ACK packet and the client's TCP ACK response.

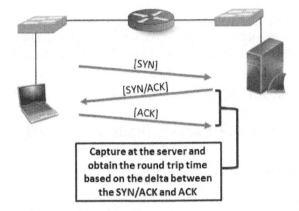

If you are capturing inside the infrastructure, add up the delta time between the TCP SYN and ACK packets of the handshake.

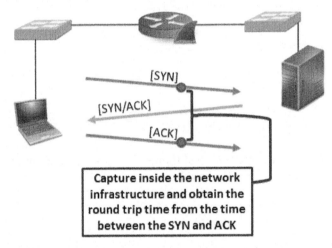

You can create filters and filter expression buttons for these packets to make this process easier.

Filter for SYN and SYN/ACK Packets (Packet 1 and 2 of the TCP Handshake)

This is a very simple filter and filter expression button to build. Essentially it is based on the TCP SYN bit set to 1.

```
tcp.flags.syn==1
```

That's the only filter you need to capture the first two packets of the TCP handshake.

Step 1:   Open **tr-cnn.pcapng**.

Step 2:   Enter `tcp.flags.syn==1` in the display filter area and click **Apply**.

Step 3:   Click your **TCP Delta** column heading twice to sort from high to low. We are interested in the delays preceding SYN/ACK packets. Three packets are marked as Retransmissions so we know there are connection establishment problems. We can also get a glimpse at the RTT values to various servers in this trace file.

Remember to clear your display filter when you are finished with this lab.

Filter for SYN/ACK and ACK Packets (Packet 2 and 3 of the TCP Handshake)

The SYN/ACK packet is easy to locate with a display filter, but the ACK (third packet of the handshake) is a bit trickier.

To detect the second packet of the handshake, the SYN/ACK packet, we can filter on the following:

> `(tcp.flags.syn==1 && tcp.flags.ack==1)`[23]

Detecting the third packet of the handshake is difficult. The following are possible characteristics of the third packet of the handshake.

- `tcp.seq==1`   (Required) TCP Seq. Number 1 (Relative Seq. Number)
- `tcp.ack==1`   (Required) TCP Ack. Number 1 (Relative Ack. Number)
- `tcp.len > 0`   (Optional) data in the third packet of the handshake
- `tcp.push==1`   (Optional) PUSH bit set

The best we can do is "cast a wide net" and then either ignore (or perhaps remove) false positives from view. Let's begin with the following filter to try and capture the third packet of the handshake:

> `(tcp.seq==1 && tcp.ack==1)`

When we add this to the filter for the SYN/ACK packet, we have the following:

> `(tcp.flags.syn==1 && tcp.flags.ack==1) || (tcp.seq==1 && tcp.ack==1)`

Filter for SYN and ACK Packets (Packet 1 and 3 of the TCP Handshake)

Putting together what we've already done, we can filter on the following:

> `(tcp.flags.syn==1) || (tcp.seq==1 && tcp.ack==1)`

---

[23] I've placed parentheses around this entire string because I will add it to another display filter string in just a moment.

Wireshark Lab 32: Obtain RTT using Display Filters

Let's test the filter for the first two packets of the TCP handshake and then test our filter for the last two packets of the TCP handshake.

Step 1:   Open **tr-chappellu.pcapng**.

Step 2:   In the display filter area, enter the filter `tcp.flags.syn==1` and click **Apply**.

Fifty-eight packets match this filter. The first two packets are sent from the client port 35,621. Packet 3 and Packet 4 are the first two packets of a new TCP connection. The TCP Delta column indicates the time from the TCP SYN from port 35,622 and the SYN/ACK to that same port, RTT is about 17 ms.

Although this trace file was captured at the client, we will use it to practice locating the second and third packet of the TCP handshake. These are the packets we would use to determine RTT when capturing at the server.

Step 3:   In the display filter area, enter the following filter:

```
(tcp.flags.syn==1 && tcp.flags.ack==1) || (tcp.seq==1 &&
tcp.ack==1)
```

Click **Apply** and examine the results. Sixty-nine packets match this filter. There are several packets that are not of interest to us, however.

For example, Packets 14 and 15 are the second and third packets of the TCP handshake, but Packet 16 is the first HTTP command sent after the handshake. Our filter is displaying this packet because the Relative sequence number value is 1 and the Relative Acknowledgment Number value is 1. We can add `&&` `tcp.len==0` to our filter to remove these packets from view.

Packets 698 through 706 are FIN packets. These FIN packets are also being displayed because of the Relative Sequence Number and Relative Acknowledgment Number values. We can add `&& tcp.flags.fin==0` to remove these packets from view.

Step 4:   Enhance your filter with these two additional conditions:

```
(tcp.flags.syn==1 && tcp.flags.ack==1) || (tcp.seq==1 &&
tcp.ack==1) && tcp.len==0 && tcp.flags.fin==0
```

Click **Apply**. Now you should see only the SYN/ACK and ACK packets of the handshakes in the trace file. Your TCP Delta column illustrates the time between each of these packets in each of the TCP conversations.

Step 5:   Click **Clear** to remove your filter before continuing.

Consider saving two filter expression buttons — one for the first two packets of the handshake and another for the second and third packet of the handshake. Name these buttons **TCP HS1-2** and **TCP HS2-3**. These two filter expression buttons can be used to quickly identify high path latency.

Next we will create an Advanced IO Graph to detect TCP delays in a trace file.

Wireshark Lab 33: Graph TCP Delays

You can use Wireshark's Advanced IO Graph to graph the maximum `tcp.time_delta` value to locate TCP conversation delays in a trace file.

Step 1:   Open **tr-chappellu.pcapng**.

Step 2:   Select **Statistics | IO Graph**.

Step 3:   In the Y Axis **Unit** area, select **Advanced...**

Step 4:   Select the **MAX(*)** Graph 1 Calc option and enter `tcp.time_delta` in the Calc area. We will first work without a filter at this time.

Step 5:   Click the **Graph 1** button to graph your results.

The graph indicates that there is a spike in the RTT values around 25 seconds into the trace file.

Click on this high point in the graph and Wireshark will jump to that packet in the main Wireshark window. Notice the value in the TCP Delta column—15.757807 seconds.

If you look at that packet (Packet 155), this is a TCP FIN packet. That is not a delay we care about. To make this graph more usable, we will add a filter to remove acceptable delays from view.

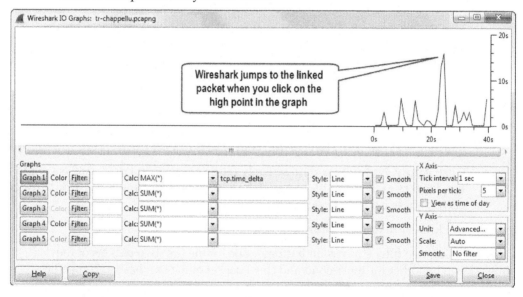

Step 6:   In the Filter area of Graph 1, enter the following filter:

```
tcp.time_delta > 1 && tcp.flags.fin==0 && tcp.flags.reset==0 &&
!http.request.method=="GET"
```

This is the same display filter you created in *Wireshark Lab 30: Add a "TCP Delay" Button*.

You will need to click the **Graph 1** button again to enable the graph to use this filter.

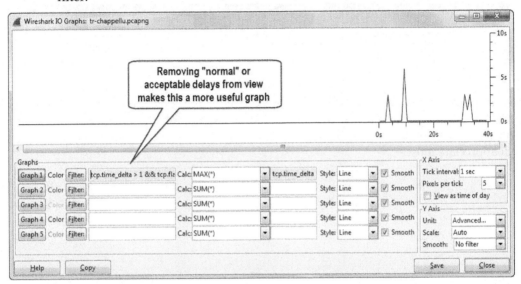

The new graph highlights fewer problems because we've removed many false positives from view. When we click on the largest delay point in this graph, Wireshark jumps to Packet 86. (Remember to toggle back to your IO Graph to close it once you have finished this lab.)

*If you see different results when creating this graph, check to ensure your TCP Calculate conversation timestamps preference setting is **enabled** (see TCP Preference: Calculate Conversation Timestamps on page 119). Also ensure your TCP Allow subdissector to reassemble TCP streams preference setting is **disabled** (see Wireshark Lab 11: Change the TCP Dissector Reassembly Setting to Properly Measure HTTP Response Times on page 59).*

This packet is a TCP SYN retransmission packet that arrived almost 6 seconds after the previous packet in this TCP stream (which would also be a TCP SYN packet). We can see the indication of a connection request that is not receiving responses.

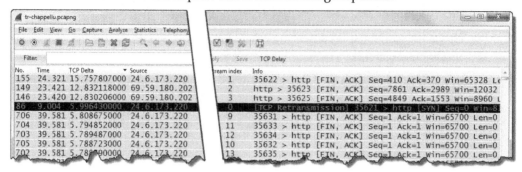

Always consider time when you are troubleshooting network performance. A 20 ms delay probably isn't going to be felt by the end user. A 20 second delay is going to be felt. Try to prioritize your troubleshooting to eradicate the biggest delays first. That's what the users will appreciate most.[24]

---

24   Although they probably won't thank you. Sigh.

Identify High DNS Response Time

Display Filter Value

`dns.time`

Domain Name Service (DNS) is most often used to resolve a network name (such as www.wireshark.org) to a network address (IPv4 or IPv6).

Many applications, such as HTTP, can trigger DNS queries when a user (or a web page element) refers to a network name while running the application.

DNS is a request/response protocol which can run over UDP or TCP. Typically, standard name queries run over UDP while zone transfers run over TCP.

Wireshark Lab 34: Add/Sort a `dns.time` Column to Find DNS Response Times

We will use the same steps that we used to create and sort the TCP Delta column to create and sort a **dns.time** column.

Step 1:   Open **tr-dns-slow.pcapng**.

Step 2:   The **dns.time** field exists only in DNS response packets. The first DNS response packet is Packet 3 (Standard Query Response). We will use this packet to create a **dns.time** column.

Expand the **Domain Name System (response)** section of Packet 3.

Step 3:   Right-click on the **[Time: 0.107083000 seconds]** line and click **Apply as Column**. The new **dns.time** column appears with the label *Time*.

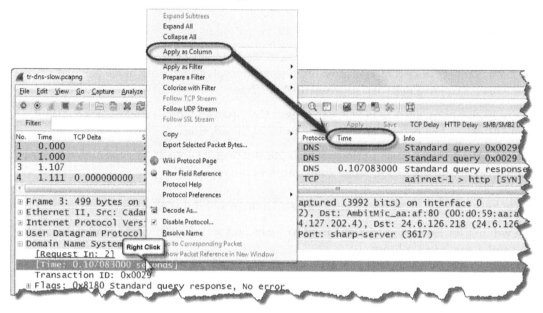

Step 4:   Your new column appears to the left of the Info column. Click and drag your new column to the right of the existing **TCP Delta** column.

Step 5:   Rename your new column by right-clicking on the column heading and selecting **Edit Column Details**. Consider changing the Title to **DNS Delta**. Click **OK**.

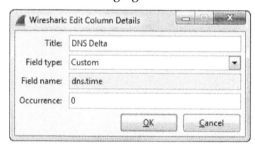

Step 6:   Click your new **DNS Delta** column heading twice to sort from high to low. The DNS response packets with the largest delays preceding them appear at the top of the list.

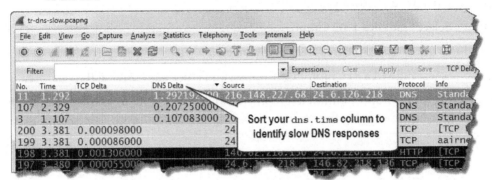

In this trace file, Packet 11 has a significant delay preceding it—almost 1.3 seconds.

Again, Wireshark can always point to *where* the problem occurred, but it cannot always tell us *why* the problem has occurred. We'd have to do more research on that DNS server to find out why it is slow.

Wireshark Lab 35: Create a Button to Detect High DNS Response Times

In this lab we will create a button to detect DNS response times larger than 1 second.

Step 1:   Open **tr-dns-slow.pcapng**.

Step 2:   Type `dns.time > 1` in the display filter area and click **Save**.

Step 3:   Name your button **DNS Delay** and click **OK**.

Step 4:   Click your new **DNS Delay** button. Packet 11 is the only packet that matched your filter. It worked! You quickly found the largest DNS delay time. Remember to clear your display filter when you are done examining your results.

Remember that you can adjust these delay values as you see fit. For example, if your typical DNS response times are less than 20 ms, you might consider setting this button value at 100 ms.

Wireshark Lab 36: Graph DNS Response Times

We will create a graph to highlight DNS delays in the trace file.

Step 1:   Open **tr-dns-slow.pcapng**.

Step 2:   Select **Statistics | IO Graph**.

Step 3:   In the **Y Axis Unit** area, select **Advanced...**

Step 4:   Select the **MAX(*)** Graph 1 Calc option and enter `dns.time` in the Calc area.

Step 5:   Click the **Graph 1** button to graph your results. Close your graph when you have finished examining the results.

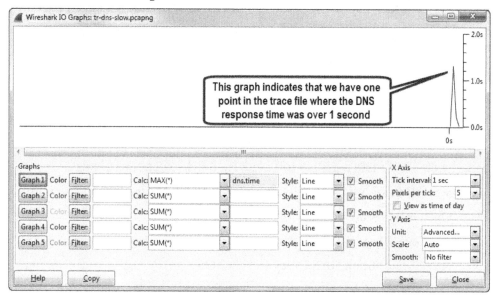

Once again, this is a graph that you may never need to build — you can detect delays more quickly by sorting your `dns.time` column.

Identify High HTTP Response Time

Display Filter Value

`http.time`

High HTTP response times may be seen when a web server becomes overloaded with connection or service requests or needs to consult another server before answering client requests.

When we measure HTTP response time, we look at the delta time between a service request (such as an HTTP GET request) and the response (such as an HTTP 200 OK). The HTTP response time field is called `http.time`.

Wireshark's *Allow subdissector to reassemble TCP streams* preference setting can change the results you receive when evaluating HTTP response times.

If you enable *Allow subdissector to reassemble TCP streams* (which is the default as of Wireshark 1.10), Wireshark will measure the time from the HTTP Request to the final data packet of the response. If you are actually interested in the amount of time it took to download an element, you want this TCP preference setting enabled. If you want to know how quickly the server responded to the request, disable this setting.

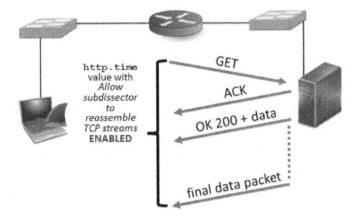

If you disable *Allow subdissector to reassemble TCP streams*, Wireshark will measure the time from the HTTP Request and the actual response packet.

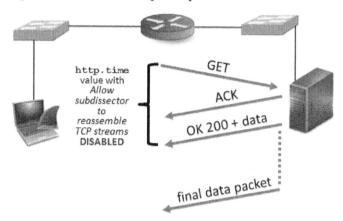

You can use two methods to change this TCP preference setting—the right-click method and the Preferences window method. We will examine both methods in this lab.

Wireshark Lab 37: Disable the *Allow Subdissector to Reassemble TCP Streams* Preference Setting

You may have already disabled this setting in Wireshark Lab 11. If so, you can breeze through this lab. We **must** include a review of how to disable this setting as it affects Wireshark's HTTP response time calculations.

Step 1:   Open **tr-http-pcaprnet101.pcapng**.

Step 2:   To set this preference using the right-click method, right-click on the **TCP header** in the Packet Details of Packet 5 in this trace file. Select **Protocol Preferences** and uncheck *Allow subdissector to reassemble TCP streams*.

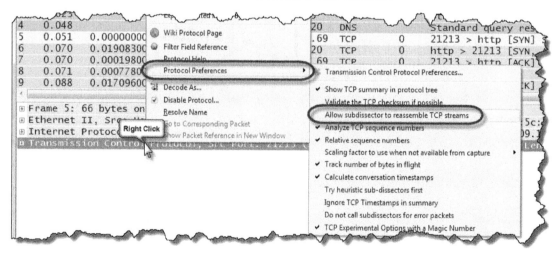

Step 3:   We will use the Preferences window method to verify our new setting. Select
Edit | Preferences | (+) Protocols | TCP.

Alternately, click the **Edit Preferences** button on the Main Toolbar and then
select **(+) Protocols | TCP**.

You can verify that you already disabled this setting in Step 2.

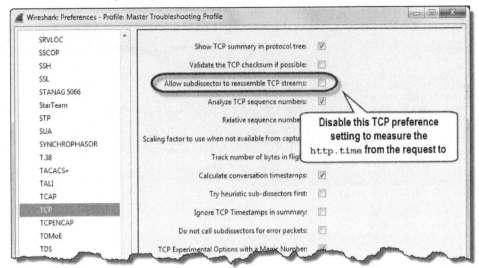

I always disable the Allow subdissector to reassemble TCP streams *preference setting when I create a new profile. I only enable this setting when reassembling data streams or analyzing HTTPS traffic.*

Wireshark Lab 38: Add/Sort an HTTP Response Time Column to Find HTTP Response Times

We will use the same steps that we used to create and sort the TCP Delta column to create
and sort an **http.time** column.

Step 1:   Open **tr-http-pcaprnet101.pcapng**.

Step 2:   The **http.time** field exists only in HTTP response packets. The first HTTP
response packet in this trace file is Packet 10 (HTTP 303 See Other). We will use
this packet to create our **http.time** column.

Right-click on the **Hypertext Transfer Protocol** section in the Packet Details pane
of Packet 10 and select **Expand Subtrees**.

Step 3:   Right-click on the **[Time since request: 0.026416000 seconds]** line and click
Apply as Column. The new `http.time` column appears with the label *Time since
request*. This is not a very descriptive column label. We will rename it in just a
moment.

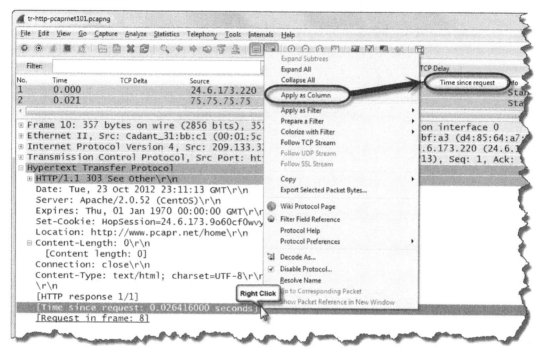

Step 4:   Your new column appears to the left of the Info column. Click and drag your
new column to the right of the existing **TCP Delta** column.

Step 5:   Rename your new column by right-clicking on the column heading and selecting
Edit Column Details. Consider changing the Title to **HTTP Delta**. Click **OK**.

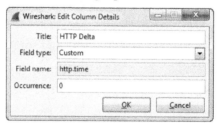

Step 6:   Click your new **HTTP Delta** column heading twice to sort from high to low. The
HTTP response packets with the largest delays preceding them appear at the top
of the list.

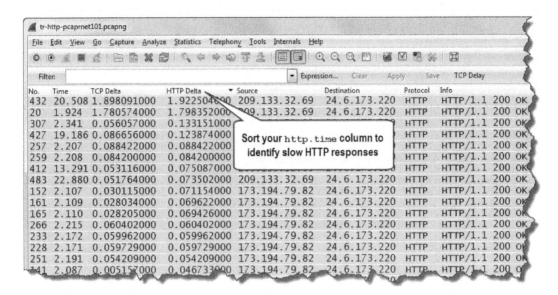

Packets 432 and 20 indicate that the HTTP response time from the HTTP server
(209.133.32.69) was over 1.7 seconds twice in this trace file.

Why is the server slow? We'd have to do more research on that server to find the answer
because Wireshark can always point to *where* the problem occurred, but it cannot always
tell us *why* the problem has occurred.

Wireshark Lab 39: Create a Button to Detect High HTTP Response Times

In this lab we will create a button to detect HTTP response times longer than 1 second.

Step 1:   Open **tr-http-pcaprnet101.pcapng**.

Step 2:   Type `http.time > 1` in the display filter area and click **Save**.

Step 3:   Name your button **HTTP Delay** and click **OK**.

Step 4:   Click your new **HTTP Delay** button. Two packets should be displayed—Packet 20 and Packet 432. It worked! Remember to clear your display filter when you are finished reviewing the results of this lab step.

Filter expression buttons can be used to detect delays and network errors fast. It is one of the most powerful features to improve your efficiency in locating network problems.

Wireshark Lab 40: Graph HTTP Response Times

These graphing steps should start feeling familiar now.

Step 1:   Open **tr-http-pcaprnet101.pcapng**.

Step 2:   Select **Statistics | IO Graph**.

Step 3:   In the **Y Axis Unit** area, select **Advanced...**

Step 4:   Select the **MAX(*)** Graph 1 Calc option and enter `http.time` in the Calc area.

Step 5:   Click the **Graph 1** button to graph your results. Remember to close this IO Graph when you finish examining the results.

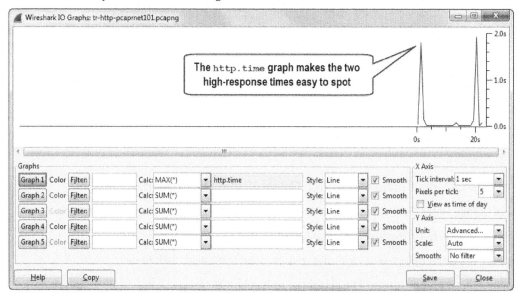

You may never need to build this graph—you already detected these problems by creating and sorting an `http.time` column. If you need to explain problems to others, however, these graphs are indispensable.

Identify High SMB Response Time

Display Filter Value

```
smb.time
smb2.time
```

Server Message Block (SMB) is the file sharing protocol used by Microsoft on Windows networks. There are two versions of SMB commonly seen on Windows-based networks — SMB and SMB version 2. Wireshark has separate dissectors for each version of SMB. We will need to consider this before we save a filter expression button that displays SMB delays.

SMB is request/response based with distinct, documented response codes available on Microsoft's Open Specification site (www.microsoft.com/openspecifications/).

Wireshark Lab 41: Add/Sort an SMB Response Time Column

We will use the same steps that we used to create and sort the TCP Delta column to create and sort an **smb.time** column.

Step 1:   Open **tr-smb-slow.pcapng**.

Step 2:   The **smb.time** field exists only in SMB response packets. The first SMB response packet is Packet 5 (Negotiate Protocol Response). We will use this packet to create a **smb.time** column.

Expand the **SMB (Server Message Block Protocol)** section and the **SMB Header** section in the Packet Details pane of Packet 5.

Step 3:   Right-click on the **[Time from request: 0.000766000 seconds] line** and click
Apply as Column.

The new `smb.time` column appears with the label *Time from request*. This label
does not indicate this column measures SMB time. This is why it is important to
rename new columns.

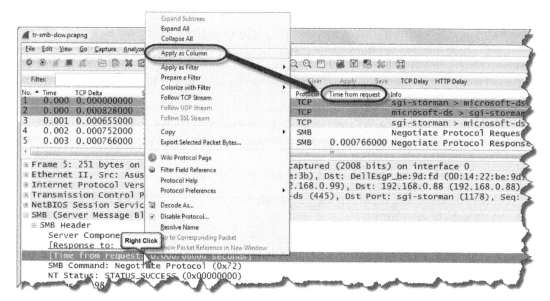

Step 4:   Your new column appears to the left of the Info column. Click and drag your
new column to the right of the existing **TCP Delta** column. (Since we do not need
HTTP time or DNS time information, we right-clicked on those column headings
and selected **Hide Column**.)

Step 5:   Rename your new column by right-clicking on the column heading and selecting
Edit Column Details. Change the title to **SMB Delta**. Click **OK**.

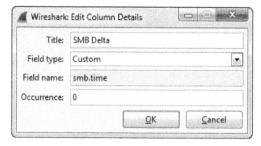

Step 6:   Click your new **SMB Delta** column heading twice to sort from high to low. The SMB response packets with the largest delays preceding them appear at the top of the list.

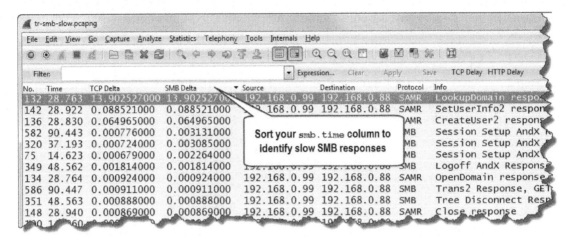

In this trace file, Packet 132 has a significant delay preceding it—almost 14 seconds.

Again, Wireshark can always point to *where* the problem occurred, but it cannot always tell us *why* the problem has occurred. We'd have to do more research on that server to find out why it is slow.

*If you are working with SMB version 2, the syntax for this column is **smb2.time**. To create an **smb2.time** column using this trace file, follow Step 3 and 4 to create another **smb.time** column. Right click your second **smb.time** column and select **Edit Column Details**. Change the Title to **SMB2 Delta** and the Field name to **smb2.time**. Click OK to save your new column.*

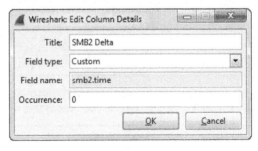

Wireshark Lab 42: Quickly Examine all SMB Statistics (Statistics | Service Response Times | SMB)

Wireshark creates and tracks a number of service response times, including SMB and SMB2 response times. Although we've added and sorted a column to find the biggest delay in the trace file, this SMB Service Response Time window will also point out high SMB response times.

Step 1:   Open **tr-smb-slow.pcapng**.

Step 2:   Select **Statistics | Service Response Time | SMB**. Click **Create Stat** when you are prompted for a filter since we are interested in all the SMB statistics in the trace file.

The SMB Service Response Time statistics window indicates the minimum, maximum and average Service Response Time (SRT) in the trace file.

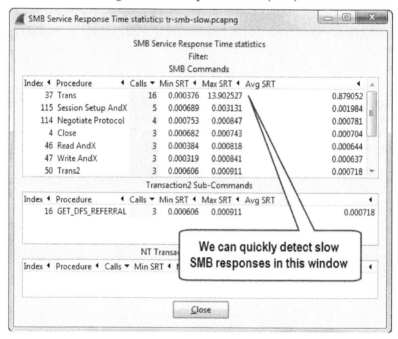

Although we've already detected the large response time delay in the trace file, this SMB Service Response Time statistics window provides a list of all the request procedures in the trace file.

Wireshark Lab 43: Create a Button to Detect High SMB and SMB2 Response Times

In this lab we will create a button to detect SMB and SMB2 response times larger than 1 second.

Step 1:   Open **tr-smb-slow.pcapng**.

Step 2:   Type `smb.time > 1 || smb2.time > 1` in the display filter area and click **Save**.

Step 3:   Name your button **SMB/SMB2 Delay** and click **OK**.

Step 4:   Click your new **SMB Delay** button. Packet 132 is the only packet that matched your filter. Remember to clear your display filter after you have examined the results.

Although I've been using one second in these delay buttons, you can adjust the time value as desired. To edit filter expression buttons, click the **Preferences** button on the Main Toolbar and select **Filter Expressions**.

Wireshark Lab 44: Graph SMB Response Times

Here's another graph using the same techniques we've used before in this book. This time we are graphing SMB response times.

Step 1:   Open **tr-smb-slow.pcapng**.

Step 2:   Select **Statistics | IO Graph**.

Step 3:   In the Y Axis **Unit** area, select **Advanced...**

Step 4:   Select the **MAX(*)** Graph 1 Calc option and enter `smb.time` in the Calc area.

Step 5:   Click the **Graph 1** button to graph your results. Remember to close your IO Graph after you have examined the results.

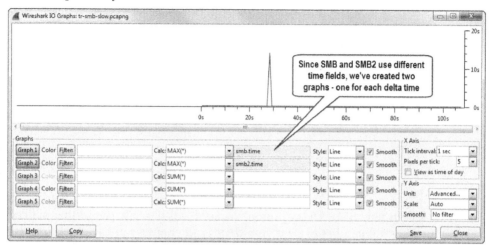

Again, this is a graph that you may never need to build—you can detect delays more quickly by sorting your `smb.time` and `smb2.time` columns.

If your application dissector does not have a time calculation function, you can always simply use the Time column (set to *Seconds Since Previous Displayed Packet*) and compare the time between the request and response.

CHAPTER 6: IDENTIFY PROBLEMS USING WIRESHARK'S EXPERT

The Expert system is one of Wireshark's greatest features for quickly spotting problems on a network.

Although primarily geared towards detecting TCP problems, the Expert contains numerous other error alerts embedded in various protocol and application dissectors.

In this section we will focus primarily on TCP problems.

Ruling out TCP problems will help you rule out various network and host issues—from congestion on the network to congestion at a receiver.

Chapter 6 Notes

I will always open the Expert Infos window to check for problems and navigate quickly to the problem points in a trace file.

- Watch for signs of packet loss (Previous Segment Not Captured, Duplicate ACKs, Retransmissions and Fast Retransmissions).

- Watch for signs of receiver congestion (Window Full and Zero Window).

- Watch for reused ports that occur near delays.

- Don't get distracted by checksum errors when capturing on a host that supports task offloading.

Overview of Wireshark's Expert Infos System

Wireshark consists of numerous Expert Infos notifications. The code for these notifications is contained in the application and protocol dissectors.

For example, below is a section of the *packet-tcp.c* file (the TCP dissector). This portion of *packet-tcp.c* defines the conditions for a lost packet indication.

```
900
901    /* LOST PACKET
902     * If this segment is beyond the last seen nextseq we must
903     * have missed some previous segment
904     *
905     * We only check for this if we have actually seen segments prior to this
906     * one.
907     * RST packets are not checked for this.
908     */
909    if( tcpd->fwd->nextseq
910    &&  GT_SEQ(seq, tcpd->fwd->nextseq)
911    &&  (flags&(TH_RST))==0 ) {
912        if(!tcpd->ta) {
913            tcp_analyze_get_acked_struct(pinfo->fd->num, seq, ack, TRUE, tcpd);
914        }
915        tcpd->ta->flags|=TCP_A_LOST_PACKET;
916
917        /* Disable BiF until an ACK is seen in the other direction */
918        tcpd->fwd->valid_bif = 0;
919
```

In the following pages, we will examine many TCP Expert Infos Errors, Warnings and Notes. We will also look inside *packet-tcp.c* code to determine why Wireshark marks a packet with a specific Expert indication.

Expert information covered in this section includes:

- Previous Segment Not Captured
- Duplicate ACKs
- Out-of-Order Segments
- Fast Retransmissions
- Retransmissions
- ACKed Unseen Segment
- Keep Alive and Keep Alive ACK
- Zero Window
- Window Full
- Zero Window Probe and Zero Window Probe ACK
- Window Update
- Reused Ports

Previous Segment Not Captured

Display Filter Value

`tcp.analysis.lost_segment`

Overview of Wireshark's Packet Loss Detection Process

Let's just get this over with quickly — 99.999999% of the time[25], packet loss occurs at an interconnecting device... a switch, a router, a firewall... anything that makes forwarding decisions.

Wireshark uses the TCP sequencing process to detect lost packets. This feature can be turned off by disabling the *Analyze TCP Sequence Numbers* TCP Preference setting.[26]

Wireshark adds together the Sequence Number field value of each packet to the number of data bytes in the packet to create a value called *nextseq* (displayed in the Next Sequence Number field). The *nextseq* value is the next expected sequence number from the sender.

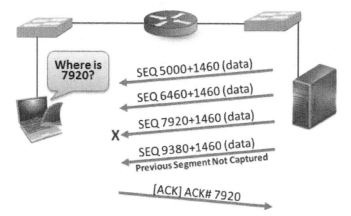

---

[25] Just my estimate, of course.

[26] I can't imagine why you would do that, however.

When Wireshark sees the sequence number jump beyond the *nextseq* value, it assumes that one or more packets have been lost[27]. For example, in the image on the previous page, Wireshark performed the following analysis:

- The server sends a packet with sequence number 5,000 and 1,460 bytes of data. The *nextseq* value is set to 6,460.
- When a packet with sequence number 6,460 is sent with 1,460 bytes of data, the *nextseq* value is set to 7,920.
- Instead of seeing sequence number 7,920 next however, Wireshark sees sequence number 9,380. Wireshark marks this packet with the `tcp.analysis.lost_segment` Expert tag.

What Causes Packet Loss?

There are many reasons why interconnecting devices might drop packets. A switch or router could be overloaded and unable to keep up with the required packet forwarding rate, or perhaps the device is simply faulty[28].

I've seen both cases. In one of the worst cases of packet loss on which I've worked, an enterprise switch was dropping one packet every 3 ms. The crucial switch was bringing an entire network to its knees. By moving around to capture traffic at different spots on the network we could definitively point to the offending switch.

---

[27] As of Wireshark version 1.10.x, the number of missing packets cannot automatically be determined by Wireshark. Even if 50 packets in a row were lost, Wireshark would generate a single Previous Segment Not Captured indication. To determine how many packets have been lost, examine Wireshark's Next Sequence Number field immediately prior to the lost packet indication and then look at the Sequence Number field in the lost packet indication. Subtract the first number from the second number and divide by the typical TCP segment size.

[28] When was the last time you looked at the statistics on your network switches, routers and other infrastructure devices? Hint, hint.

Packet Loss Recovery Method #1 – Fast Recovery

How TCP peers detect and recover from packet loss depends on if the receiver supports Fast Recovery.

If the receiver supports Fast Recovery and notices the jump in sequence number value, it will immediately begin sending Duplicate Acknowledgments requesting sequence number 7,920 (Acknowledgment Number field 7,920).

Upon receipt of four identical ACKs (the original and three Duplicate ACKs) requesting this packet, the server should retransmit the packet with sequence number 7,920 again.

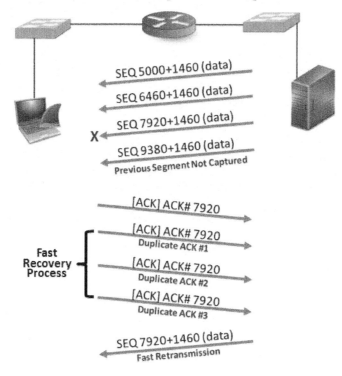

Packet Loss Recovery Method #2 – Sender Retransmission Timeout (RTO)

If the sender notices that a data packet has not been acknowledged within its Retransmission Timeout (RTO) timer value, it will retransmit the packet.

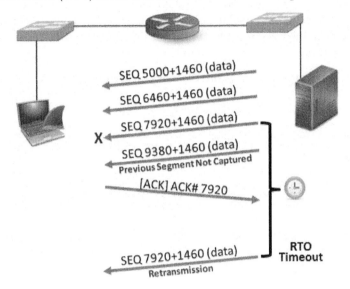

packet-tcp.c Code and Comments

You can clearly see the reference to *nextseq* in the *packet-tcp.c* code. You can also see that Wireshark only checks this if there is a preceding packet in the trace file. TCP RST (Reset) packets are not checked for this issue and can never be marked with *Previous Segment Not Captured* as indicated by *(flags&(TH_RST))==0*.

```
900
901    /* LOST PACKET
902     * If this segment is beyond the last seen nextseq we must
903     * have missed some previous segment
904     *
905     * We only check for this if we have actually seen segments prior to this
906     * one.
907     * RST packets are not checked for this.
908     */
909    if( tcpd->fwd->nextseq
910     && GT_SEQ(seq, tcpd->fwd->nextseq)
911     && (flags&(TH_RST))==0 ) {
912        if(!tcpd->ta) {
913            tcp_analyze_get_acked_struct(pinfo->fd->num, seq, ack, TRUE, tcpd);
914        }
915        tcpd->ta->flags|=TCP_A_LOST_PACKET;
916
917        /* Disable BiF until an ACK is seen in the other direction */
918        tcpd->fwd->valid_bif = 0;
919    }
```

Wireshark Lab 45: Use a Filter to Count Previous Segment Not Captured Indications

Step 1:   Open **tr-general101d.pcapng**.

Step 2:   In the display filter area, enter the filter **tcp.analysis.lost_segment**. Click
Apply. Notice the Status Bar indicates that Wireshark has detected packet loss
five times in the trace file. One of the packets displayed is Packet 10,417. We will
revisit that point in the trace file in the next lab.

Step 3:   Click **Clear** to remove your filter when you are done.

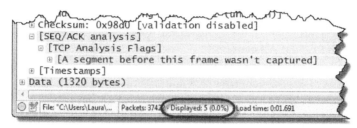

This is a very easy way to determine if packet loss is occurring in the trace file. In order to
determine how many packets were actually lost, however, we need to examine the TCP
sequence number information.

Wireshark Lab 46: Add TCP Sequencing Columns

In this lab exercise, you will create three columns to help you understand what is happening in the TCP sequencing in your trace file. You can use these columns to determine how many packets are actually lost when Wireshark indicates *Previous Segment Not Captured*.

Step 1:   Open **tr-general101d.pcapng**.

Step 2:   Expand the **TCP header** in Packet 1.

Step 3:   Right-click on the **Sequence Number** field and select **Apply as Column**. Right-click on your new **Sequence Number** column, select **Edit Column Details** and rename this column **SEQ#**.

Step 4:   Right-click on the **Next Sequence Number** field and select **Apply as Column**. Right-click on your new **Next Sequence Number** column, select **Edit Column Details** and rename this column **NEXTSEQ#**.

Step 5:   Right-click on the **Acknowledgment Number** field and select **Apply as Column**. Right-click on your new **Acknowledgment Number** column, select **Edit Column Details** and rename this column **ACK#**.

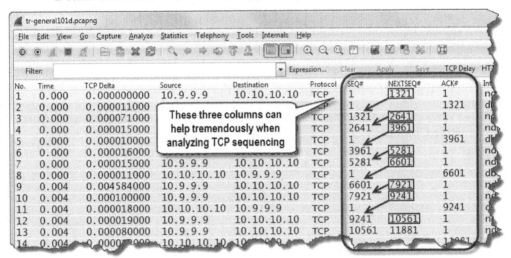

Step 6:   Click the **Go To Packet** button on the Main Toolbar. Enter **10417**[29] and click **Jump To**. This is one of the packets that is tagged with the *Previous Segment Not Captured* Expert indication.

The NEXTSEQ# column indicates that the next packet (after Packet 10,416) from 10.9.9.9 should use sequence number 9,164,761.

---

[29]   Do not use commas in the Go To Packet field. Wireshark does not understand commas and will generate an error if you try to use them here.

We see the next packet from 10.9.9.9 uses sequence number 9,175,321, however. This triggers Wireshark's Previous Segment Not Captured indication on Packet 10,417.

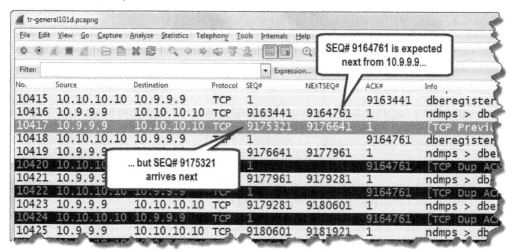

To determine how many bytes were dropped at this point, subtract 9,164,761 from 9,175,321. The result is 10,560. Examining the TCP header in Packet 10,417, we can see the packet contains 1,320 bytes of data.

If we assume that all the lost packets were 1,320 bytes long we can divide the number of missing bytes (10,417) by 1,320 to determine how many packets were lost. It appears 8 packets were lost prior to Packet 10,417.

Step 7:   When you are not using these columns, right-click on the columns and select **Hide Column**.

Wireshark Lab 47: Build a "Bad TCP" Filter Expression Button

This is a "must have" filter expression button. Click this button once to view many of the key TCP problems in the trace file. This button is based on the Bad TCP coloring rule string.

Step 1:   Open **tr-general101d.pcapng**.

Step 2:   If you'd rather not type the full filter, click the **Coloring Rules** button 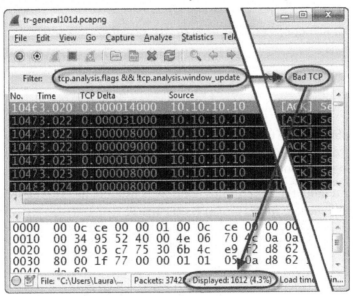. Double-click on the **Bad TCP coloring rule**, highlight and copy the **Bad TCP coloring rule string**. You will paste this into the display filter area in the next step. Close the **Coloring Rule** windows.

Step 3:   In the display filter area, paste your filter string. If you didn't use Step 2 to copy the Bad TCP coloring rule string, type the following:

```
tcp.analysis.flags && !tcp.analysis.window_update
```

Step 4:   Click **Save** on the display filter toolbar and name your new button **Bad TCP**.

Step 5:   Click your new **Bad TCP** button. There should be 1,612 packets that match your Bad TCP filter. Click **Clear** to remove your filter when you are finished.

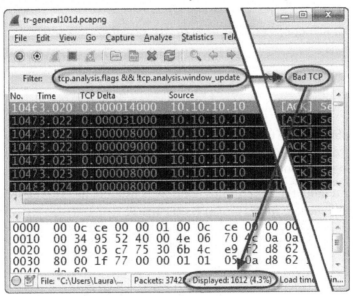

Although only 4.3% of the traffic matches our Bad TCP button, it is enough of a problem to affect the file transfer process to a noticeable extent.

Step 6:   Click **Clear** to remove your display filter.

We will graph these problems against throughput in *Correlate Drops in Throughput with TCP Problems (the "Golden Graph")* on page 280. First, let's open the Expert Infos window and see what other problems exist in this trace file.

Wireshark Lab 48: Find Packet Loss Counts with Expert Infos

Step 1:   Open **tr-general101d.pcapng**.

Step 2:   Click the **Expert Infos** button on the Status Bar.

Step 3:   Wireshark indicates there are 1,614 Expert Infos items in the title bar. We see
there are no entries under the Errors tab. Click the **Warnings** tab. The Warnings
tab indicates that Wireshark has seen packet loss 5 times in the trace file.
Remember, that does not mean that only 5 packets were lost. Wireshark just
indicates the sudden jump in sequence number, but does not take into account
the size of the increase.

Wireshark also indicates that there are 8 instances of Out-of-Order segments. We
will cover those issues in *Out-of-Order Packets* on page 174.

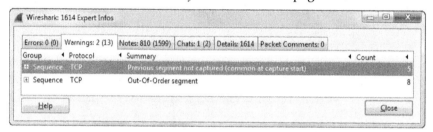

To jump to a problem in the trace file, simply expand one of the Expert Infos sections and
click on any packet listed. Remember to close the Expert Infos window when you are
finished analyzing the results.

Opening and examining the Expert Infos window is listed in the Troubleshooting Checklist
in *TCP-Based Application: Identify TCP Issues* on page 29.

Wireshark Lab 49: Find Out Where Packets are Being Dropped

Step 1:   Open **tr-general101d.pcapng**.

Step 2:   Click the **Expert Infos** button on the Status Bar if it is not still open.

Step 3:   Click the **Warnings** tab and expand the *Previous segment not captured (common at capture start)* section. Click on the listing for **Packet 10,417** and toggle back to the Wireshark window. Wireshark jumps to that packet.

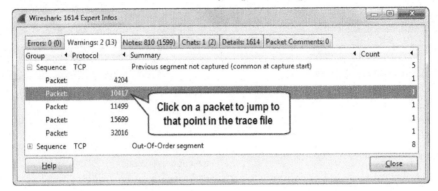

Step 4:   Look at what happens after the point of packet loss. Notice that you see numerous Duplicate ACKs after the missing packet indication.

The use of Duplicate ACKs indicates that 10.10.10.10 (the receiver) supports Fast Recovery. Each Duplicate ACK is a request for sequence number 9,164,761, as you can see in the Acknowledgment Number field in the Duplicate ACKs.

Remember to close the Expert Infos window when you are finished analyzing the results.

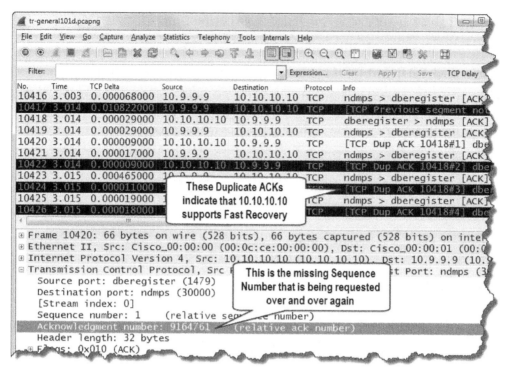

Step 5:   Now let's determine if we are upstream from the point of packet loss (closer to the data sender than the point of packet loss) or downstream from the point of packet loss (closer to the receiver than the point of packet loss).

If you are upstream from the point of packet loss you will see the original packet *and* the retransmission. In the image below we have set up a tap to listen to the traffic near 10.10.10.10 (the receiver of data).

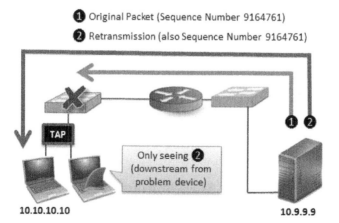

If you are downstream from the point of packet loss you will only see the retransmission. In the image below we have set up a tap on the other side of the switch that is closest to 10.10.10.10 (the receiver).

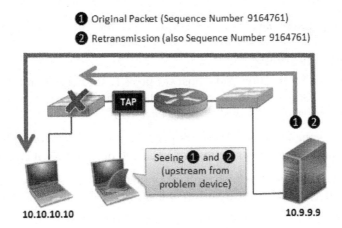

① Original Packet (Sequence Number 9164761)

② Retransmission (also Sequence Number 9164761)

Seeing **①** and **②** (upstream from problem device)

10.10.10.10   10.9.9.9

Step 6:   Since we know the sequence number of the packet that is missing, we can use that information to determine if we see the original and the Retransmission or just the Retransmission. That will tell us if we are upstream or downstream from packet loss.

In the display filter area, enter `tcp.seq==9164761`.

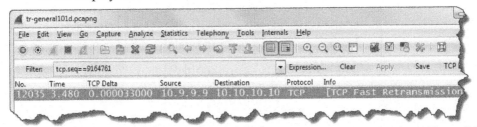

It appears we have captured traffic downstream from the point of packet loss. If possible, we should move Wireshark closer to the data sender. Remember to clear your display filter when you are finished reviewing the results of this lab.

Even though many functions have been added to TCP to improve recovery times after packet loss, packet loss always affects network performance.

When you see packet loss, get moving—you want to locate *where* packet loss is occurring and then figure out *why* it is happening.

Duplicate ACKs

Display Filter Value

`tcp.analysis.duplicate_ack`

Traffic Analysis Overview

Duplicate ACKs are an indication that a host supports Fast Recovery and noticed that a packet arrived with a sequence number beyond the calculated next sequence number. For details on Fast Recovery, see *RFC 5681, "TCP Congestion Control."*

Wireshark examines the Window Size, Sequence Number, and Acknowledgment Number fields as well as the number of data bytes in a packet to determine if it is a Duplicate ACK.

When two packets from a source have the same value in these fields and the packet contains no data, the second (and any future matching ACKs) are marked as duplicates of the first ACK.

The Acknowledgment Number field value in Duplicate ACKs indicates the requested sequence number. TCP hosts continue to send Duplicate ACKs until the missing packet arrives. For example, in the image below our client has sent a total of four identical ACKs so far—the original ACK requesting sequence number 7,920 and three Duplicate ACKs asking for the same sequence number.

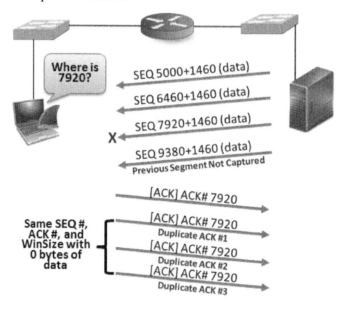

What Causes Duplicate ACKs?

Duplicate ACKs are usually a sign of packet loss, but Duplicate ACKs can also be an indication of out-of-order packets.

Duplicate ACKs are sent when a TCP receiver that supports Fast Recovery receives an out-of-order segment.

From the receiver's perspective at this point, it does not know if the packet is lost or if it is just out of order and will be arriving soon. It just knows that the incoming sequence number value jumped higher than expected.

Wireshark also doesn't know at this point if the packet has been lost along the path or this is simply an out-of-order packet that will be arriving soon. Wireshark will pay attention to what happens within the next 3 ms. to figure out which situation has occurred.

If the packet with the missing sequence number arrives within 3 ms, Wireshark marks that packet as Out-of-Order (`tcp.analysis.out_of_order`). If the packet with the missing sequence number arrives later than 3 ms. later, Wireshark will indicate that the packet is a either a Retransmission or a Fast Retransmission[30].

---

[30]   There are two retransmission types defined by Wireshark—a standard Retransmission and a Fast Retransmission. We will differentiate between these two types of retransmissions later in this Chapter.

packet-tcp.c Code and Comments

You can clearly see the reference to the *seglen* (amount of data in the packet), *lastack* (previous Acknowledgment Number field value), and *window* (Window Size value) in the TCP dissector.

In addition you will notice that Wireshark looks at the TCP SYN, FIN and RST flag settings. These flags must be set to 0 in packets defined as Duplicate ACK packets.

```
1013
1014      /* DUPLICATE ACK
1015       * It is a duplicate ack if window/seq/ack is the same as the previous
1016       * segment and if the segment length is 0
1017       */
1018      if( seglen==0
1019      && window
1020      && window==tcpd->fwd->window
1021      && seq==tcpd->fwd->nextseq
1022      && ack==tcpd->fwd->lastack
1023      && (flags&(TH_SYN|TH_FIN|TH_RST))==0 ) {
1024          tcpd->fwd->dupacknum++;
1025          if(!tcpd->ta) {
1026              tcp_analyze_get_acked_struct(pinfo->fd->num, seq, ack, TRUE, tcpd);
1027          }
1028          tcpd->ta->flags|=TCP_A_DUPLICATE_ACK;
1029          tcpd->ta->dupack_num=tcpd->fwd->dupacknum;
1030          tcpd->ta->dupack_frame=tcpd->fwd->lastnondupack;
1031      }
```

Wireshark Lab 50: Use a Filter to Count Duplicate ACKs

Step 1:   Open **tr-general101d.pcapng**.

Step 2:   In the display filter area, enter the filter **tcp.analysis.duplicate_ack**. Click
            Apply. Notice the Status Bar indicates that Wireshark has detected 1,019
            Duplicate ACKs in the trace file.

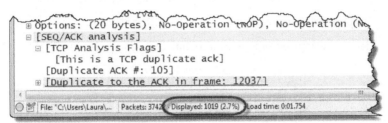

Step 3:   Right-click on any column header, select **Displayed Columns | ACK#**. This is a
            column that you created and renamed in *Wireshark Lab 46: Add TCP Sequencing
            Columns*. If you scroll through the trace, you will notice that many of these
            Duplicate ACKs are requests for a single missing packet with sequence number
            9,164,761.

            Only the original ACK and three duplicates are required to trigger the Fast
            Retransmission. You may see many more Duplicate ACKs as the host will not
            stop sending the Duplicate ACKs until the missing sequence number is resolved.

Step 4:   Since we aren't going to use this column again right now, right-click the **ACK#**
            column and select **Hide Column**. Click **Clear** to remove your display filter.

Wireshark Lab 51: Find Duplicate ACKs with Expert Infos

Wireshark counts Duplicate ACKs in an interesting fashion. Rather than count all Duplicate ACKs together, Wireshark groups Duplicate ACKs based on their number. For example, if packet loss occurs twice in a trace file and both times the original ACK and Duplicate ACK#1, Duplicate ACK#2, Duplicate ACK#3 and Duplicate ACK#4 were sent, Wireshark will list four Duplicate ACKs with an indication that each occurred twice.

Step 1:   Open **tr-general101d.pcapng**.

Step 2:   Click the **Expert Infos** button on the Status Bar.

Step 3:   Click the **Notes** tab to identify problems in this trace file. Notice how many Duplicate ACKs appear in this trace file.

There are 5 Duplicate ACK (#1) indications listed. This means the Fast Recovery process was launched 5 times. There are only 4 Duplicate ACK (#2) indications, however. This means that the receiver only had to send the first Duplicate ACK to recover from one of the skipped sequence number situations.

That is an indication that there is probably one out-of-order packet situation in the trace file near Packet 3,217.

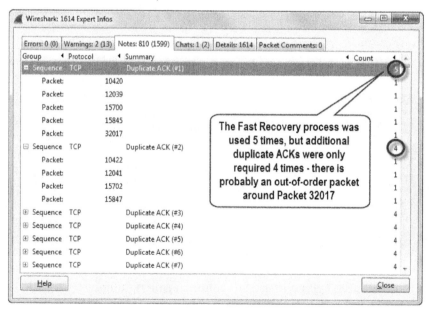

Step 4:   Scroll to the end of the **Notes** section[31]. The TCP receiver had to ask for a missing packet 809 times (do not forget to include the original ACK). That's not an out-of-order packet situation — we have a packet that was lost and the recovery took a significant amount of time. Remember to close the Expert Infos window when you are finished.

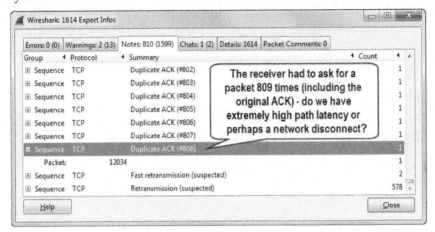

Refer back to *Previous Segment Not Captured* on page 154 to locate the point of packet loss.

These Duplicate ACKs complain about a missing sequence number. If SACK is in use we should see only the missing packets being retransmitted. The SACK Left Edge and SACK Right Edge fields in the TCP Options area acknowledge other data packets received while the Acknowledgment Number field still indicates the desired missing sequence number.

If SACK is not in use we may see many unnecessary retransmissions as the sender retransmits every data packet starting at the missing sequence number.

If you do not capture the TCP handshake, how do you know if SACK is in use? In the next lab we will examine Duplicate ACKs to determine if SACK is enabled on the connection.

---

[31]   Normally I tell students never to scroll—there is *almost* always a better way to work in Wireshark. In this case it would be great if you could sort the Summary column. Unfortunately, Wireshark does a text sort—this causes Duplicate ACK (#99) to appear above Duplicate ACK (#800) when you sort from high to low. Sigh.

Wireshark Lab 52: Determine if Selective ACK (SACK) is in Use

We can look inside Duplicate ACK packets to determine if SACK is in use.

Step 1:   Open **tr-general101d.pcapng**.

Step 2:   Click the **Expert Infos** button on the Status Bar.

Step 3:   Click on the **Notes** tab to locate Duplicate ACKs.

Step 4:   Expand the **Duplicate ACK (#1)** line and click on the first packet listed (Packet
           10,420). Toggle to Wireshark to examine that packet.[32]

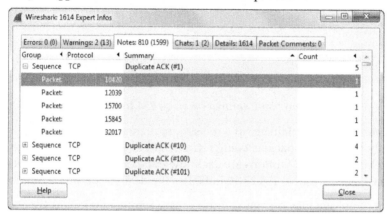

---

[32]   Note that if you have the Packet Bytes pane open, expand the SACK section in Packet 10,420 and click on
       the left edge field, there appears to be two bytes that do not match a field name (0x050a). These two bytes
       are the Kind field (0x05=SACK) and Length field (0x0a=10). As of Wireshark 1.10.5, these two fields were
       not dissected for some reason.

Step 5:   SACK Left Edge (SLE) and SACK Right Edge (SRE) information is listed in the
           Info column (you may need to scroll to the right). Alternately you can expand
           packet 10420 and look for the SLE and RLE values at the end of the TCP header
           (in the Options area).

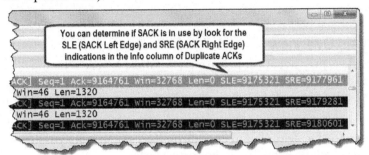

Duplicate ACKs are a sign of either out-of-order packets or packet loss. To differentiate
between the two conditions, we need to look at what happens after the Duplicate ACKs.

Let's begin by looking at the Out-of-Order Expert Infos indication.

Out-of-Order Packets

Display Filter Value

`tcp.analysis.out_of_order`

Traffic Analysis Overview

Out-of-order packets may not affect performance if there is very little time between their expected arrival and their actual arrival. For example, if two packets arrive in reverse order, but the packets both arrive within 1 ms, it is unlikely this will cause a problem.

If out-of-order packets arrive after quite a delay, or there are many out-of-order packets, there may be a noticeable degradation in performance. TCP cannot pass received data up to the application until all the bytes are in the correct order.

Wireshark marks a packet as out of order based on the fact that it (a) contains data, (b) does not advance the sequence number value, and (c) arrives within 3 ms of the highest sequence number seen. There may be one or more ACKs seen between the Previous Segment Not Captured point and the Out-of-Order packet.

What Causes Out-of-Order Packets?

Out-of-order packets can be caused by a stream using multiple different speed paths to reach the target (such as traffic traveling through the Internet), poorly configured queuing along a path or even asymmetric routing configurations.

In the case of queuing along a path, out-of-order packets can be caused when the queuing device does not forward packets in a first-in/first-out (FIFO) order.

In the image that follows, a queuing device has reordered the packets upon forwarding. Packets 1 and 2 would be marked as Out-of-Order if the packets arrive within 3 ms of each other. No network issue may be noticed if the total delay would be 6 ms in this case, however.

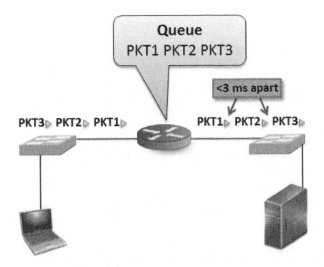

packet-tcp.c Code and Comments

This section of *packet-tcp.c* contains detailed notes on what makes a packet an out-of-order packet. It is defined inside the "Retransmission/Fast Retransmission/Out-of-Order" section.

The code begins with a general description of common characteristics shared by Retransmission, Fast Retransmission, and Out-of-Order packets:

- **Condition 1**: Segment contains data or has the SYN or FIN bits set to 1
- **Condition 2**: Segment does not advance the sequence number

Then the code begins differentiating between the three conditions. Each of the following items matches condition 1 and 2 above as well.

Fast Retransmission

- Conditions 1 and 2 are met
- At least 2 Duplicate ACKs in the reverse direction
- Sequence Number field matches Acknowledgment Number field value in those Duplicate ACKs
- Packet arrives within 20 ms of a Duplicate ACK

Out-of-Order

- Conditions 1 and 2 are met
- Packet arrives within 3 ms[33] of highest sequence number seen

Retransmission

- Matches Condition 1 and Condition 2 only

Confusing? It can be. The illustration that follows should help you differentiate these three types of Expert Infos indications.

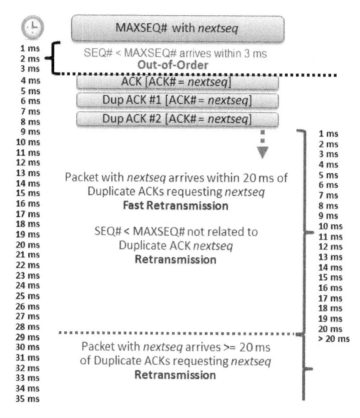

Determining if a packet is an Out-of-Order, Retransmission or Fast Retransmission is a matter of sequence number value, time and relationship to Duplicate ACKs (if Duplicate ACKs are present). In the *packet-tcp.c* code section that follows, the Out-of-Order designation mentions the sequence number not incrementing and 3 ms timing.

---

[33]   The 3 ms is an arbitrary time value selected by a developer.

```
1065
1066    /* RETRANSMISSION/FAST RETRANSMISSION/OUT-OF-ORDER
1067     * If the segments contains data (or is a SYN or a FIN) and
1068     * if it does not advance sequence number it must be either
1069     * of these three.
1070     * Only test for this if we know what the seq number should be
1071     * (tcpd->fwd->nextseq)
1072     *
1073     * Note that a simple KeepAlive is not a retransmission
1074     */
1075    if( (seglen>0 || flags&(TH_SYN|TH_FIN))
1076    && tcpd->fwd->nextseq
1077    && (LT_SEQ(seq, tcpd->fwd->nextseq)) ) {
1078        guint64 t;
1079
1080        if(tcpd->ta && (tcpd->ta->flags&TCP_A_KEEP_ALIVE) ) {
1081            goto finished_checking_retransmission_type;
1082        }
1083
1084        /* If there were >=2 duplicate ACKs in the reverse direction
1085         * (there might be duplicate acks missing from the trace)
1086         * and if this sequence number matches those ACKs
1087         * and if the packet occurs within 20ms of the last
1088         * duplicate ack
1089         * then this is a fast retransmission
1090         */
1091        t=(pinfo->fd->abs_ts.secs-tcpd->rev->lastacktime.secs)*1000000000;
1092        t=t+(pinfo->fd->abs_ts.nsecs)-tcpd->rev->lastacktime.nsecs;
1093        if( tcpd->rev->dupacknum>=2
1094        && tcpd->rev->lastack==seq
1095        && t<20000000 ) {
1096            if(!tcpd->ta) {
1097                tcp_analyze_get_acked_struct(pinfo->fd->num, seq, ack, TRUE, tcpd);
1098            }
1099            tcpd->ta->flags|=TCP_A_FAST_RETRANSMISSION;
1100            goto finished_checking_retransmission_type;
1101        }
1102
1103        /* If the segment came <3ms since the segment with the highest
1104         * seen sequence number and it doesn't look like a retransmission
1105         * then it is an OUT-OF-ORDER segment.
1106         *   (3ms is an arbitrary number)
1107         */
1108        t=(pinfo->fd->abs_ts.secs-tcpd->fwd->nextseqtime.secs)*1000000000;
1109        t=t+(pinfo->fd->abs_ts.nsecs)-tcpd->fwd->nextseqtime.nsecs;
1110        if( t<3000000
1111        && tcpd->fwd->nextseq != seq + seglen ) {
1112            if(!tcpd->ta) {
1113                tcp_analyze_get_acked_struct(pinfo->fd->num, seq, ack, TRUE, tcpd);
1114            }
1115            tcpd->ta->flags|=TCP_A_OUT_OF_ORDER;
1116            goto finished_checking_retransmission_type;
1117        }
1118
1119        /* Then it has to be a generic retransmission */
1120        if(!tcpd->ta) {
1121            tcp_analyze_get_acked_struct(pinfo->fd->num, seq, ack, TRUE, tcpd);
1122        }
1123        tcpd->ta->flags|=TCP_A_RETRANSMISSION;
1124        nstime_delta(&tcpd->ta->rto_ts, &pinfo->fd->abs_ts, &tcpd->fwd->nextseqtime);
1125        tcpd->ta->rto_frame=tcpd->fwd->nextseqframe;
1126    }
```

Wireshark Lab 53: Use a Filter to Count Out-of-Order Packets

Step 1:   Open **tr-general101d.pcapng**.

Step 2:   In the display filter area, enter the filter `tcp.analysis.out_of_order`. Click **Apply**. The Status Bar indicates that Wireshark has detected eight Out-of-Order packets.

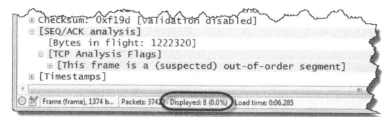

It appears we have a single out-of-order packet, then a group of out-of-order packets in close proximity, then another single out-of-order packet.

When you see multiple Out-of-Order indications in close proximity, it is likely that a set of packets have been lost and these Out-of-Order packets are actually Retransmissions that arrived within 3 ms of the higher sequence number value.

We will examine these different points in the trace file further in this section.

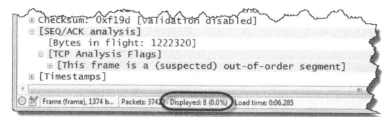

Step 3:   Click the **Clear** button to remove your filter when you are done.

Wireshark Lab 54: Find Out-of-Order Packets with Expert Infos

Step 1:   Open **tr-general101d.pcapng**.

Step 2:   Click the **Expert Infos** button on the Status Bar.

Step 3:   Click the **Warnings** tab. Expand the **Out-of-Order segment** section. Click on the
first entry, **Packet 4,206**. Click the **Close** button and toggle back to the main
Wireshark window.

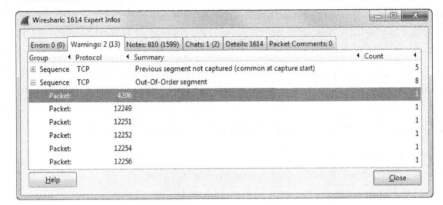

Step 4:   Right-click on any column heading and display your **SEQ#**, **NEXTSEQ#** and
ACK# columns (created in an earlier lab). In the image below we have hidden
several other columns to fit the interesting columns in the screenshot.

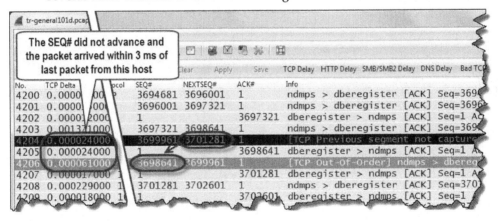

The sequence number value of Packet 4,206 is lower than the sequence number in
Packet 4,204. In addition, the out-of-order packet arrived .000085 (85 microseconds) after
the previous packet from 10.9.9.9. That is within the 3 ms time value set in the Out-of-Order
definition in the TCP dissector.

Next we will look at Wireshark's Retransmissions and Fast Retransmissions detection
processes. You will once again find that an arbitrary number in the Wireshark *packet-tcp.c*
code is used to differentiate these Expert Infos Notes.

Fast Retransmissions

Display Filter Value

`tcp.analysis.fast_retransmission`

Traffic Analysis Overview

Fast Retransmissions are part of the Fast Recovery process and another sign that packet loss has occurred. Fast Retransmissions are triggered by receipt of three identical ACKs (the original ACK and two Duplicate ACKs).

In *Out-of-Order Packets* on page 174, you learned that Wireshark's detection of Fast Retransmissions, Retransmissions and Out-of-Order packets are interrelated in the *packet-tcp.c* code.

The characteristics of Fast Retransmissions are the following:

- The segment contains data or has the SYN or FIN bits set to 1.
- The segment does not advance the sequence number.
- At least 2 Duplicate ACKs were coming from the reverse direction.
- The Sequence Number field value matches Acknowledgment Number field value in the preceding Duplicate ACKs.
- The packet arrived within 20 ms of the last Duplicate ACK.

There may be times when Fast Retransmissions are listed as simply "Retransmissions". This happens when a Fast Retransmission arrives 20 ms or longer after a Duplicate ACK. The 20 ms value is an arbitrary value defined by the developers.

What Causes Fast Retransmissions?

Fast Retransmissions indicate that a host that supports Fast Recovery believes there is packet loss and has sent at least four identical ACKs (the original ACK and at least three Duplicate ACKs) requesting the missing segment.

Ultimately, this is a packet loss problem and packet loss typically occurs at infrastructure devices. Refer to *Previous Segment Not Captured* on page 154 to determine the location of packet loss.

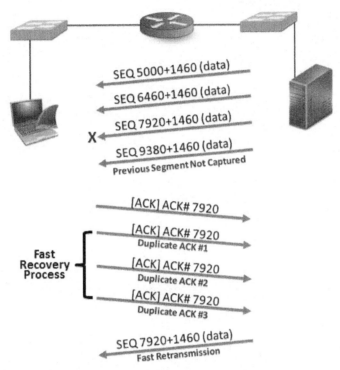

packet-tcp.c Code and Comments

You can clearly see the reference to at least two Duplicate ACKs (*dupacknum>=2*) in the *packet-tcp.c* code. In addition, you can see the reference to the 20 ms limit (*t<20000000*).

```
1065
1066      /* RETRANSMISSION/FAST RETRANSMISSION/OUT-OF-ORDER
1067       * If the segments contains data (or is a SYN or a FIN) and
1068       * if it does not advance sequence number it must be either
1069       * of these three.
1070       * Only test for this if we know what the seq number should be
1071       * (tcpd->fwd->nextseq)
1072       *
1073       * Note that a simple KeepAlive is not a retransmission
1074       */
1075      if( (seglen>0 || flags&(TH_SYN|TH_FIN))
1076      &&  tcpd->fwd->nextseq
1077      &&  (LT_SEQ(seq, tcpd->fwd->nextseq)) ) {
1078          guint64 t;
1079
1080          if(tcpd->ta && (tcpd->ta->flags&TCP_A_KEEP_ALIVE) ) {
1081              goto finished_checking_retransmission_type;
1082          }
1083
1084          /* If there were >=2 duplicate ACKs in the reverse direction
1085           * (there might be duplicate acks missing from the trace)
1086           * and if this sequence number matches those ACKs
1087           * and if the packet occurs within 20ms of the last
1088           * duplicate ack
1089           * then this is a fast retransmission
1090           */
1091          t=(pinfo->fd->abs_ts.secs-tcpd->rev->lastacktime.secs)*1000000000;
1092          t=t+(pinfo->fd->abs_ts.nsecs)-tcpd->rev->lastacktime.nsecs;
1093          if( tcpd->rev->dupacknum>=2
1094          &&  tcpd->rev->lastack==seq
1095          &&  t<20000000 ) {
1096              if(!tcpd->ta) {
1097                  tcp_analyze_get_acked_struct(pinfo->fd->num, seq, ack, TRUE, tcpd);
1098              }
1099              tcpd->ta->flags|=TCP_A_FAST_RETRANSMISSION;
1100              goto finished_checking_retransmission_type;
1101          }
1102
1103          /* If the segment came <3ms since the segment with the highest
1104           * seen sequence number and it doesn't look like a retransmission
1105           * then it is an OUT-OF-ORDER segment.
1106           *   (3ms is an arbitrary number)
1107           */
1108          t=(pinfo->fd->abs_ts.secs-tcpd->fwd->nextseqtime.secs)*1000000000;
1109          t=t+(pinfo->fd->abs_ts.nsecs)-tcpd->fwd->nextseqtime.nsecs;
1110          if( t<3000000
1111          &&  tcpd->fwd->nextseq != seq + seglen ) {
1112              if(!tcpd->ta) {
1113                  tcp_analyze_get_acked_struct(pinfo->fd->num, seq, ack, TRUE, tcpd);
1114              }
1115              tcpd->ta->flags|=TCP_A_OUT_OF_ORDER;
1116              goto finished_checking_retransmission_type;
1117          }
1118
1119          /* Then it has to be a generic retransmission */
1120          if(!tcpd->ta) {
1121              tcp_analyze_get_acked_struct(pinfo->fd->num, seq, ack, TRUE, tcpd);
1122          }
1123          tcpd->ta->flags|=TCP_A_RETRANSMISSION;
1124          nstime_delta(&tcpd->ta->rto_ts, &pinfo->fd->abs_ts, &tcpd->fwd->nextseqtime);
1125          tcpd->ta->rto_frame=tcpd->fwd->nextseqframe;
1126      }
```

Wireshark Lab 55: Use a Filter to Count Fast Retransmission Packets

Step 1:   Open **tr-general101d.pcapng**.

Step 2:   In the display filter area, enter the filter `tcp.analysis.fast_retransmission`.
           Click **Apply**.

           The Status Bar indicates that Wireshark has detected two Fast Retransmissions in
           the trace file.

Step 3:   Expand the **[SEQ/ACK analysis]** section on one of the Fast Retransmissions. This
           area is colored cyan by Wireshark. Cyan is the color associated with Expert Infos
           Notes.

           You may also notice that Wireshark has two Expert Infos indications on this one
           packet. It indicates that the frame is a Fast Retransmission and a Retransmission.
           After all, a Fast Retransmission is actually just a flavor of Retransmission.

Step 4:   Click the **Clear** button to remove your filter when you are done.

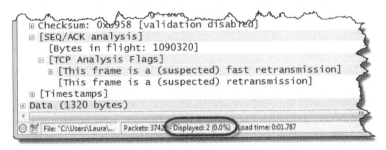

Wireshark Lab 56: Find Fast Retransmission Packets with Expert Infos

Step 1:   Open **tr-general101d.pcapng**.

Step 2:   Click the **Expert Infos** button on the Status Bar.

Step 3:   Click the **Notes** tab. Expand the Fast Retransmissions section and click on the first entry, **Packet 12,035**. Click the **Close** button to return to the main Wireshark window.

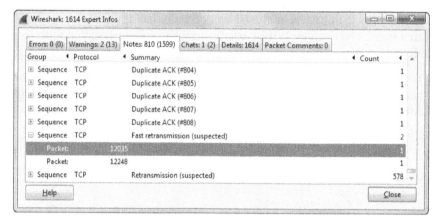

Step 4:   Display your **SEQ#**, **NEXTSEQ#** and **ACK#** columns if they are hidden. Notice that we have 808 Duplicate ACKs before the Fast Retransmission — the term Fast Retransmission indicates the packet is part of the Fast Recovery process only.

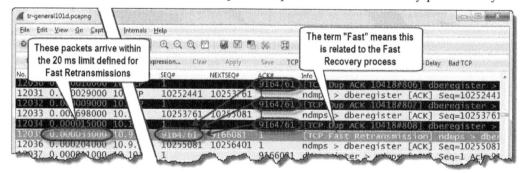

The Fast Retransmission occurred within 20 ms of the last Duplicate ACK, as we can see in the TCP Delta column.

Remember to ALWAYS consider time when troubleshooting. It is easy to look at the 808 Duplicate ACKs and think 'wow-that receiver had to buffer up all the data and not hand it off to the application until the Fast Retransmission- I bet that had a huge impact on performance." If you look at the time when sequence number 9,164,761 went missing and measure to the Fast Retransmission, only about 465 ms have passed. The user may not even notice this ½-second delay. If this problem occurs repeatedly, however, the user may start to notice and complain.

Next we will look at Wireshark's detection process for Retransmissions. Keep in mind that both Fast Retransmissions and Retransmissions are indications of packet loss. Refer back to *Previous Segment Not Captured* for instructions for finding the location of packet loss.

Retransmissions

Display Filter Value

`tcp.analysis.retransmission`

Traffic Analysis Overview

Wireshark defines a packet as a Retransmission if the following conditions are met:

- The segment contains data or has the SYN or FIN bits set to 1.
- The segment does not advance the sequence number.
  The Retransmission is not triggered by Duplicate ACKs.
- The segment arrives > 3 ms later than the previous packet with a higher sequence number.

Standard Retransmissions are not triggered by Duplicate ACKs. Standard Retransmissions are triggered by a Retransmission Time Out (RTO) at the sender. The RTO timer is used to ensure data delivery continues even if the TCP peer stops communicating (with ACKs).

Each TCP host calculates and maintains a RTO timer. This timer value is based on the round trip time learned through previous data transmissions and related acknowledgments. The RTO value consistently changes through the conversation.

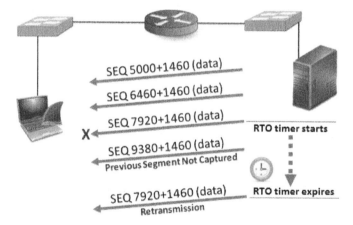

What Causes Retransmissions?

When a TCP host sends a data packet, it begins counting down the RTO. When the RTO timer expires without receiving an ACK for the data packet, the sender retransmits the unacknowledged data packet. The sender does not know if the original packet was lost or the acknowledgment was lost. The sender just knows it did not receive an ACK within the RTO.

packet-tcp.c Code and Comments

The reference to standard Retransmissions is short since Condition 1 and Condition 2 were defined early in the file.

```
1065
1066    /* RETRANSMISSION/FAST RETRANSMISSION/OUT-OF-ORDER
1067     * If the segments contains data (or is a SYN or a FIN) and
1068     * if it does not advance sequence number it must be either
1069     * of these three.
1070     * Only test for this if we know what the seq number should be
1071     * (tcpd->fwd->nextseq)
1072     *
1073     * Note that a simple KeepAlive is not a retransmission
1074     */
1075    if( (seglen>0 || flags&(TH_SYN|TH_FIN))
1076    && tcpd->fwd->nextseq
1077    && (LT_SEQ(seq, tcpd->fwd->nextseq)) ) {
1078        guint64 t;
1079
1080        if(tcpd->ta && (tcpd->ta->flags&TCP_A_KEEP_ALIVE) ) {
1081            goto finished_checking_retransmission_type;
1082        }
1083
1084        /* If there were >=2 duplicate ACKs in the reverse direction
1085         * (there might be duplicate acks missing from the trace)
1086         * and if this sequence number matches those ACKs
1087         * and if the packet occurs within 20ms of the last
1088         * duplicate ack
1089         * then this is a fast retransmission
1097
1098                        ecs-tcpd->rev->lastacktime.secs)*1000000000;
1099            tcpd->ta->fla          d->rev->lastacktime.nsecs;
1100            goto finished_checking_r
1101        }
1102
1103        /* If the segment came <3ms since the segment with the highe
1104         * seen sequence number and it doesn't look like a retransmission
1105         * then it is an OUT-OF-ORDER segment.
1106         *   (3ms is an arbitrary number)
1107         */
1108        t=(pinfo->fd->abs_ts.secs-tcpd->fwd->nextseqtime.secs)*1000000000;
1109        t=t+(pinfo->fd->abs_ts.nsecs)-tcpd->fwd->nextseqtime.nsecs;
1110        if( t<3000000
1111        && tcpd->fwd->nextseq != seq + seglen ) {
1112            if(!tcpd->ta) {
1113                tcp_analyze_get_acked_struct(pinfo->fd->num, seq, ack, TRUE, tcpd);
1114            }
1115            tcpd->ta->flags|=TCP_A_OUT_OF_ORDER;
1116            goto finished_checking_retransmission_type;
1117        }
1118
1119        /* Then it has to be a generic retransmission */
1120        if(!tcpd->ta) {
1121            tcp_analyze_get_acked_struct(pinfo->fd->num, seq, ack, TRUE, tcpd);
1122        }
1123        tcpd->ta->flags|=TCP_A_RETRANSMISSION;
1124        nstime_delta(&tcpd->ta->rto_ts, &pinfo->fd->abs_ts, &tcpd->fwd->nextseqtime);
1125        tcpd->ta->rto_frame=tcpd->fwd->nextseqframe;
1126    }
```

Wireshark Lab 57: Use a Filter to Count Retransmission Packets

Interestingly, a Wireshark filter for Retransmissions (`tcp.analysis.retransmission`) will also display Fast Retransmissions. In order to see packets that are only flagged as standard Retransmissions you must exclude Fast Retransmissions in your filter. We will try both filtering methods in this lab.

Step 1:   Open **tr-general101d.pcapng**.

Step 2:   In the display filter area, enter the filter `tcp.analysis.retransmission`. Click **Apply**. The Status Bar indicates that Wireshark has detected 580 Retransmissions in the trace file. This includes the two Fast Retransmissions that we found in the previous section.

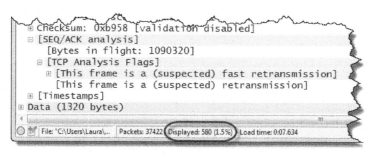

Step 3:   Expand your filter to the following:

`tcp.analysis.retransmission && !tcp.analysis.fast_retransmission`

Click **Apply**. You now only see 578 packets that match your filter — you have removed the Fast Retransmissions from view.

Step 4:   Click the **Clear** button to remove your filter before continuing.

Wireshark Lab 58: Find Retransmission Packets with Expert Infos and Use a Time Reference to Compare Expert Infos Designations

In this lab we will examine how Wireshark differentiates between Out-of-Order, Retransmission and Fast Retransmission Expert Infos designations.

Step 1:   Open **tr-general101d.pcapng**.

Step 2:   Click the **Expert Infos** button on the Status Bar.

Step 3:   Click the **Notes** tab. Expand the **Retransmissions** section and click on **Packet 12,259**. Click the **Close** button to return to the main Wireshark window.[34]

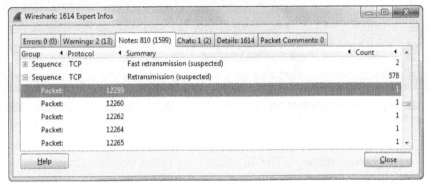

Step 4:   This point in the trace file is very interesting. It contains Duplicate ACKs, Out-of-Order, Fast Retransmission and Retransmission indications. We will set and use a Time Reference to analyze why Wireshark used each of these designations.

Display your **SEQ#**, **NEXTSEQ#** and **ACK#** columns if they are hidden. Also make certain your Time column is displayed. The Time column is the only column affected by Wireshark's Time Reference feature.

Notice that Packet 12,246 is a data packet from 10.9.9.9. It appears to have the highest Sequence Number field value at this point.

Right-click on **Packet 12,246** in the Packet List pane, and select **Set Time Reference (toggle)**.

Now review the Expert Infos indications in the trace file. Take the time values into consideration when determining why Wireshark indicates a packet is an Out-of-Order, Retransmission or Fast Retransmission.

---

[34]   In Wireshark 1.10.x, Fast Retransmissions and Retransmissions are listed separately. In later versions of Wireshark Fast Retransmissions are considered a subset of Retransmissions.

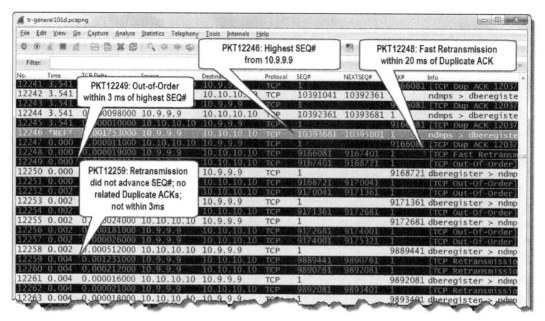

The image indicates why each packet is marked as Out-of-Order, Retransmission, or Fast Retransmission. The differentiating factor involves time.

Step 5:   To remove the Time Reference, right-click on **Packet 12,246**, and select **Set Time Reference (toggle)** or select **Edit | Unset All Time References**.

It is important to understand why Wireshark defines a packet as Out-of-Order, Retransmission, or Fast Retransmission.

You do not want to spend time troubleshooting Retransmissions or Fast Retransmissions when these packets are actually Out-of-Order packets that did not arrive within 3 ms of the higher Sequence Number field value.

Remember, Duplicate ACKs lead to Fast Retransmissions. An expired RTO at the sender leads to Retransmissions. Each of these is an indication of packet loss which typically occurs at interconnecting devices. Capturing at different points on the network can help you find the point of packet loss.

Applications cannot pick up data from the buffer until all sequential bytes have been received. Out-of-Order problems typically aren't felt by network users unless there is a large gap in time between the expected arrival time and actual arrival time.

ACKed Unseen Segment

Display Filter Value

`tcp.analysis.ack_lost_segment`

Traffic Analysis Overview

This Expert Infos warning indicates that Wireshark sees an ACK, but it did not see the data packet that is being acknowledged.

Just as Wireshark tracks sequence number, next sequence number, and acknowledgment number values for each host, it also tracks a "Maximum Sequence Number to be ACKed" (*maxseqtobeacked*) value. This value changes as data is received.

If an ACK is sent to acknowledge a data packet that has a higher Sequence Number field value than *maxseqtobeacked*, Wireshark indicates that is has missed the data packet that is being ACKed.

For example, in the image below we have captured an ACK being sent to acknowledge all sequence numbers up to 9,380, but we did not see sequence number 7,920 which should have arrived after sequence number 6460. We know the data packet must have reached the target because it is being ACKed, but Wireshark did not see that data packet.

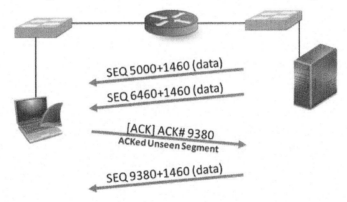

What Causes ACKed Unseen Segment?

ACKed Unseen Segments can be caused by problems during the capture process. If you are using switch port spanning, perhaps the switch is oversubscribed and dropping packets that should be forwarded to Wireshark. It is more likely the switch will drop data packets as they are larger than the ACK packets.

ACKed Unseen Segments can also be a sign of asymmetric routing. Perhaps data is flowing along one path on the network while ACKs flow along another path. If Wireshark was capturing on the second path, we would not see the data—we would only see the ACK packets. This is not a good place to capture traffic because we are only seeing a portion of the data streams.

I avoid performing analysis on trace files that contain ACKed Unseen Segments indications. There will be too many false positives—a new trace that contains the complete picture must be taken.

packet-tcp.c Code and Comments

You can see the reference to *maxseqtobeacked* in the *packet-tcp.c* code. You can also see that Wireshark can only apply this to packets that have the ACK bit set to 1 — *(flags&(TH_ACK))!=0.*

```
1042
1043    /* ACKED LOST PACKET
1044     * If this segment acks beyond the 'max seq to be acked' in the other direction
1045     * then that means we have missed packets going in the
1046     * other direction
1047     *
1048     * We only check this if we have actually seen some seq numbers
1049     * in the other direction.
1050     */
1051    if( tcpd->rev->maxseqtobeacked
1052    && GT_SEQ(ack, tcpd->rev->maxseqtobeacked )
1053    && (flags&(TH_ACK))!=0 ) {
1054  /*QQQ tested*/
1055        if(!tcpd->ta) {
1056            tcp_analyze_get_acked_struct(pinfo->fd->num, seq, ack, TRUE, tcpd);
1057        }
1058        tcpd->ta->flags|=TCP_A_ACK_LOST_PACKET;
1059        /* update 'max seq to be acked' in the other direction so we don't get
1060         * this indication again.
1061         */
1062        tcpd->rev->maxseqtobeacked=tcpd->rev->nextseq;
1063    }
```

Wireshark Lab 59: Use a Filter to Count ACKed Unseen Segment Warnings

Just as we have done in the previous labs, we will create a quick filter to view the ACKed Unseen Segment warnings.

Step 1:   Open **tr-badcapture.pcapng**.

Step 2:   In the display filter area, enter the filter `tcp.analysis.ack_lost_segment`. Click **Apply**.

The Status Bar indicates that Wireshark detected ACKed Unseen Segment a total of 24 times.

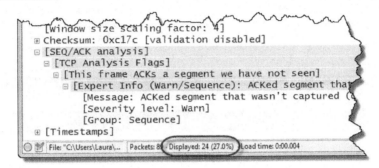

Step 3:   Click the **Clear** button to remove your filter when you are done.

Wireshark Lab 60: Find ACKed Unseen Segment Indications Using Expert Infos

Again, this is another way to count the ACKed Unseen Segment indications in a trace file.

Step 1:   Open **tr-badcapture.pcapng**.

Step 2:   Click the **Expert Infos** button on the Status Bar.

Step 3:   Click the **Warnings** tab and expand the **ACKed segment that wasn't captured (common at capture start)** section.

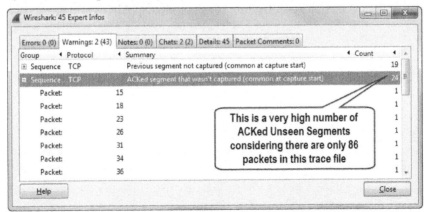

Step 4:   Click on the first entry, **Packet 15** and then click the **Close** button to return to the main Wireshark window.

Display your **SEQ#**, **NEXTSEQ#** and **ACK#** columns if you have hidden them. As you look at the SEQ# column, you will see the value jump although we see no Retransmissions, Duplicate ACKs, or Fast Retransmissions. No packets have been lost as far as the TCP peers are concerned.

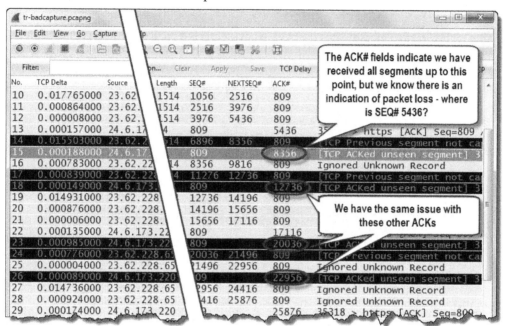

This trace file is almost unusable. The spanned switch is not sending all the traffic down the port to which Wireshark is connected. We aren't seeing a complete picture, so we can't make a solid diagnosis of the situation.

Next we will look at Wireshark's detection process for Keep Alives and Keep Alive ACKs.

Keep Alive and Keep Alive ACK

Display Filter Values

```
tcp.analysis.keep_alive
tcp.analysis.keep_alive_ack
```

Traffic Analysis Overview

Keep Alives are used to detect dead connections, detect dead TCP peers, and prevent a connection from terminating when idle.

Keep Alives (also referred to as TCP Keep Alive Probe packets) are strange packets in the TCP world. Keep Alives are ACK packets that are either empty or contain 1 byte of data. The interesting thing is that the sequence number value is 1 less than the next expected sequence number. TCP SYN, FIN and RST packets cannot be marked as Keep Alives.

Since Wireshark tracks the Sequence Number field values in all TCP streams, it can easily detect Keep Alives.

What Causes Keep Alives?

This process is invoked by applications written to use Keep Alives on sockets they establish. There are three parameters that are usually defined for Keep Alives:

- **Keep Alive Time**: The amount of time between the last data packet and the first Keep Alive probe
- **Keep Alive Interval**: Interval between Keep Alive Probes
- **Keep Alive Probes**: Number of unacknowledged Keep Alive Probes that should be sent before considering the connection dead

Standard Keep Alives are not a concern. The *lack of response to Keep Alives* is a concern. Keep Alives/Keep Alive ACKs are listed under the Notes column heading in the Expert Infos window.

packet-tcp.c Code and Comments

You can see the reference to 0 or 1 data byte in the packet (*seglen==0* or *seglen==1*) and the reference to the Sequence Number field decrementing by 1 (*nextseq-1*). You'll also notice TCP SYN, FIN and RST flags must be set to 0 (off) on Keep Alive packets.

```
921
922    /* KEEP ALIVE
923     * a keepalive contains 0 or 1 bytes of data and starts one byte prior
924     * to what should be the next sequence number.
925     * SYN/FIN/RST segments are never keepalives
926     */
927  /*QQQ tested */
928    if( (seglen==0||seglen==1)
929    && seq==(tcpd->fwd->nextseq-1)
930    && (flags&(TH_SYN|TH_FIN|TH_RST))==0 ) {
931       if(!tcpd->ta) {
932          tcp_analyze_get_acked_struct(pinfo->fd->num, seq, ack, TRUE, tcpd);
933       }
934       tcpd->ta->flags|=TCP_A_KEEP_ALIVE;
935    }
```

Designation as a Keep Alive ACK is based on seeing a Keep Alive arriving from the TCP peer.

```
972
973    /* KEEP ALIVE ACK
974     * It is a keepalive ack if it repeats the previous ACK and if
975     * the last segment in the reverse direction was a keepalive
976     */
977  /*QQQ tested*/
978    if( seglen==0
979    && window
980    && window==tcpd->fwd->window
981    && seq==tcpd->fwd->nextseq
982    && ack==tcpd->fwd->lastack
983    && (tcpd->rev->lastsegmentflags&TCP_A_KEEP_ALIVE)
984    && (flags&(TH_SYN|TH_FIN|TH_RST))==0 ) {
985       if(!tcpd->ta) {
986          tcp_analyze_get_acked_struct(pinfo->fd->num, seq, ack, TRUE, tcpd);
987       }
988       tcpd->ta->flags|=TCP_A_KEEP_ALIVE_ACK;
989       goto finished_fwd;
990    }
991
```

Wireshark Lab 61: Use a Filter to Count Keep Alive/Keep Alive ACK Packets

Step 1:   Open **tr-keepalives.pcapng**.

Step 2:   In the display filter area, enter the filter `tcp.analysis.keep_alive ||`
            `tcp.analysis.keep_alive_ack`. Click **Apply**.

Only two packets matched your filter.

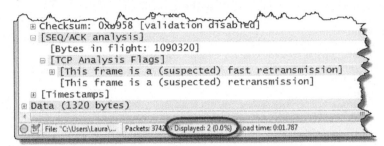

Step 3:   Make sure your **TCP Delta** column is visible. Notice the TCP Delta before
            Packet 61. It appears 10.2.122.80 has a 300 second Keep Alive Time value.
            Packet 62 is the Keep Alive ACK packet.

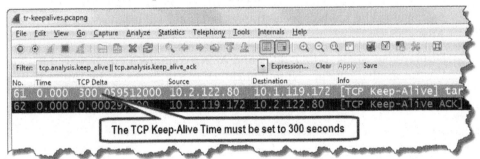

Step 4:   Click the **Clear** button to remove your filter when you are done.

Wireshark Lab 62: Find Keep Alive/Keep Alive ACK Packets with Expert Infos

Step 1:   Open **tr-keepalives.pcapng**.

Step 2:   Click the **Expert Infos** button on the Status Bar.

Step 3:   Click the **Notes** tab to identify Keep Alives and Keep Alive ACKs. Expand the **Keep Alive** and **Keep Alive ACK** lines and you should see Packets 61 and 62 listed. This is a quick way to locate these packets.

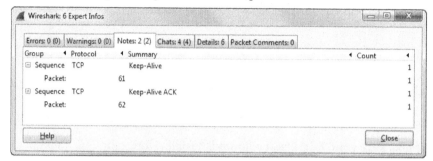

Step 4:   Click on the **Keep Alive** entry (Packet 61) and click the **Close** button to return to the main Wireshark window. In Packet 61, the Sequence Number field value has decremented by 1, which feels strange, but is normal behavior for TCP Keep Alives.

Display your **SEQ#**, **NEXTSEQ#** and **ACK#** columns if you have hidden them. We can see the Sequence Number field value has decreased by 1 from 10,943 to 10,942 in Packet 61.

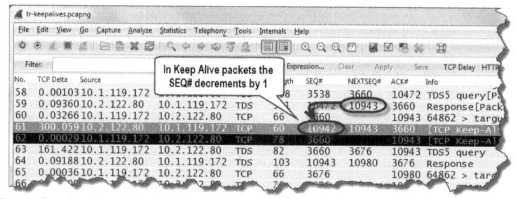

Remember that Keep Alives and Keep Alive ACKs are usually not indications of problems—they are typically used to check for dead TCP peers and avoid time out of idle connections.

Sometimes you will see hosts send TCP Keep Alives in place of Window Zero Probes. In the next lab you will analyze a trace file that depicts this usage.

Wireshark Lab 63: Identify Keep Alive Packets used in Zero Window Conditions

It is not unusual to see a TCP host send a Keep Alive to a peer that is advertising a Zero Window condition. In that case you will not see Keep Alive ACK responses. We will look at this traffic pattern in this lab.

Step 1:   Open **tr-youtubebad.pcapng**.

Step 2:   Click the **Expert Infos** button on the Status Bar and then click the **Notes** tab.

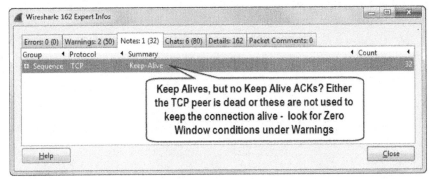

In this case we see Keep Alives, but no Keep Alive ACKs. That doesn't sound like a successful keep alive process. Either the peer is dead (and not sending Keep Alive ACKs) or this is not a standard keep alive process.

Step 3:   Expand the **Keep-Alive** section and click on the first Keep Alive listed — **Packet 2,721**. Click the Close button to return to the main Wireshark window.

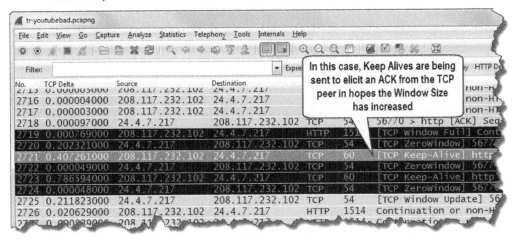

These Keep Alives are not used to check for a dead peer — we can see the first Keep Alive occurs just over 400 ms after a packet from the peer. This set of Keep Alives are being used to elicit an ACK from the peer to determine if the Window Size value has increased (Window Update) and data can flow again over the connection.

Next we will look at Wireshark's detection process for receiver congestion. During a receiver congestion process we may see Window Full, Zero Window, Zero Window Probe, Zero Window Probe ACK and Window Update indications. We may also see Keep Alive indications as we did in this section.

Zero Window

Display Filter Value

`tcp.analysis.zero_window`

Traffic Analysis Overview

Each side of a TCP conversation advertises its receive buffer space in the Window Size Value field (`tcp.window_size_value`). This is a 2-byte field that can advertise a maximum value of 65,535 bytes. That is certainly not a sufficient buffer space for today's high-speed links and large file sizes, however.

When a receiving application cannot pull data out of the receive buffer fast enough, this advertised Window Size value can drop to zero (or to a size too low to fit a full-sized data segment).

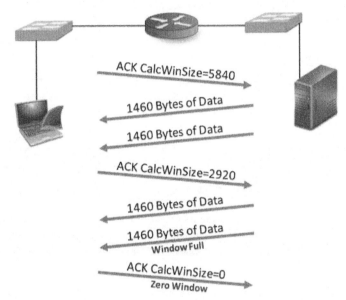

When Wireshark detects an advertised Window Size of zero, it marks the packet "Zero Window" and lists it in the Expert Infos Warnings area. TCP packets with the SYN, FIN or RST bits set to 1 are never marked as Window Zero.

What Causes a Zero Window Condition?

The cause of a Zero Window condition is a full receive buffer. This is caused by an application that is not picking up data from the receive buffer fast enough to keep up with the data receipt rate.

Why wouldn't an application be able to keep up with the data transfer rate? It could be that the application does not have the processing time necessary, the host machine is lacking in memory, or perhaps the application is just poorly written or intentionally written to generate these Zero Window packets[35].

Window Size Value Field vs. Calculated Window Size Field

The Window Size Value field indicates the actual Window Size being advertised. When Window Scaling is in use, Wireshark multiplies the Scaling Factor by the advertised Window Size Value field to provide the scaled Window Size (Calculated window size field). You are always safe focusing on the Calculated window size field whether Window Scaling is in use or not.

```
⊞ Frame 9: 1514 bytes on wire (12112 bits), 1514 bytes captured (12112 bits)
⊞ Ethernet II, Src: PaceAmer_11:e2:b9 (ac:5d:10:11:e2:b9), Dst: Hewlett-_a7:b
⊞ Internet Protocol Version 4, Src: 101.234.75.20 (101.234.75.20), Dst: 192.1
⊟ Transmission Control Protocol, Src Port: http (80), Dst Port: 9872 (9872),
    Source port: http (80)
    Destination port: 9872 (9872)
    [Stream index: 0]
    Sequence number: 2921     (relative sequence number)
    [Next sequence number: 4381     (relative sequence number)]
    Acknowledgment number: 530     (relative ack number)
    Header length: 20 bytes
  ⊞ Flags: 0x010 (ACK)
    Window size value: 1047
    [Calculated window size: 8376]
    [Window size scaling factor: 8]
  ⊟ Checksum: 0x4229 [validation disabled]
    [Good Checksum: False]
    [Bad Checksum: False]
  ⊟ [SEQ/ACK analysis]
    [Bytes in flight: 4380]
  ⊟ [Timestamps]
    [Time since first frame in this TCP stream: 0.394532000 seconds]
```

When Wireshark sees Window Scaling successfully established during the TCP handshake, it includes the scaling factor and the Calculated Window Size value in the packets

Window Scaling (*RFC 1323, "TCP Extensions for High Performance"*) is one improvement to TCP. During the TCP handshake, TCP peers can advertise support for Window Scaling and provide a Shift Count. This Shift Count is used to determine what the Window Size value should be multiplied by.

Both sides of a TCP connection must support Window Scaling in order for it to be used.[36] Once Wireshark sees this successful Window Scaling setup in the TCP handshake, it will multiply the Window Size Value field in all successive packets by the scaling factor.

---

[35] We will examine a printer that stops picking up data from the receive buffer and eventually sends Zero Window packets during the "ink drying time" when performing double-sided printing.

[36] Window Sizes (with or without Window Scaling) are not negotiated. Each side of a TCP connection defines its own Window Size value (and Shift Count if Window Scaling is enabled).

packet-tcp.c Code and Comments

You can see the reference to *window=0* in the *packet-tcp.c* code. You can also see that Wireshark will not mark TCP SYN, FIN, and RST packets as Zero Window even if these packets have a Window Size Value of zero.

```
887
888    /* ZERO WINDOW
889     * a zero window packet has window == 0   but none of the SYN/FIN/RST set
890     */
891  /*QQQ tested*/
892    if( window==0
893    && (flags&(TH_RST|TH_FIN|TH_SYN))==0 ) {
894        if(!tcpd->ta) {
895            tcp_analyze_get_acked_struct(pinfo->fd->num, seq, ack, TRUE, tcpd);
896        }
897        tcpd->ta->flags|=TCP_A_ZERO_WINDOW;
898    }
899
```

Wireshark Lab 64: Use a Filter and Column to Count and Analyze Zero Window Packets

Step 1:   Open **tr-youtubebad.pcapng**.

Step 2:   In the display filter area, enter the filter **tcp.analysis.zero_window**. Click **Apply**. The Status Bar indicates that Wireshark has detected 41 Zero Window packets in this trace file.

Step 3:   Click on the first packet listed — **Packet 2,720**.

Step 4:   Expand the **TCP header**. Right-click on the **[Calculated window size: 0]** line and select **Apply as Column**. This is another great column to display when you are working with TCP-based applications.

Step 5:   Right-click on this new **Calculated Window Size** column and select **Align Center**.

Step 6:   Right-click again on your new Calculated Window Size column and select **Edit Column Details**. Enter **WinSize** in the Title area and click **OK**.

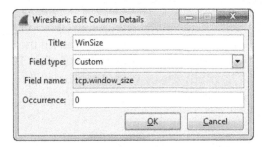

Let's see how we can use this new column to identify Window Zero conditions in a trace file.

Step 7:   Click **Clear** to remove your filter.

Step 8:   Click once on the **WinSize** column heading to sort from low to high.

Step 9:   Click the **Go to First Packet** button 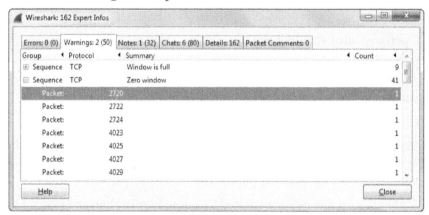 on the Main Toolbar. All the Zero Window packets are on the top of the Packet List pane.

If the trace file contained TCP FIN or RST packets with a calculated window size of 0 they would also appear at the top of the sorted packet list. The TCP FIN or RST packets would not be colored by the Bad TCP or have the [TCP ZeroWindow] designation in the Info column because those packets are explicitly excluded from the Zero Window expert designation in the TCP dissector.

Wireshark Lab 65: Find Zero Window Packets with Expert Infos

Step 1:   Open **tr-youtubebad.pcapng**.

Step 2:   Click the **Expert Infos** button on the Status Bar.

Step 3:   Click the **Warnings** tab. Expand the **Zero window** section.

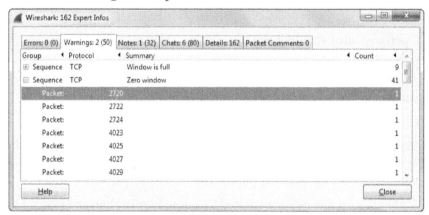

Step 4:   Click on **Packet 2,720** and then click the **Close** button to return to the main Wireshark window.

Let's examine this Zero Window condition:

- In Packet 2,718, the client is advertising only 1,460 bytes of receive buffer space.
- Packet 2,719 contains 1,460 bytes of data[37]. This will fill the target's receive buffer completely. Wireshark detects that and marks the packet TCP Window Full.
- In Packet 2,720, 24.4.7.217 advertises a Window Size of zero. Wireshark marks this as a TCP Zero Window packet.

---

[37] Add a 20-byte TCP header, 20-byte IP header and 14-byte Ethernet header (the Ethernet trailer has been stripped off by the capturing network interface card) and you have 54 bytes of overhead. Add this to the 1,460 bytes of data and the frame is 1,514 bytes—the value shown in the Length column.

- The sender, 208.117.232.102, sends TCP Keep Alives to elicit ACKs from the peer in the hope that the Window Size has increased.
- In Packet 2,725, 24.4.7.217 does advertise a larger Window Size value—243,820 bytes. Wireshark sees the increase in the Window Size value on this packet and marks it as a TCP Window Update.

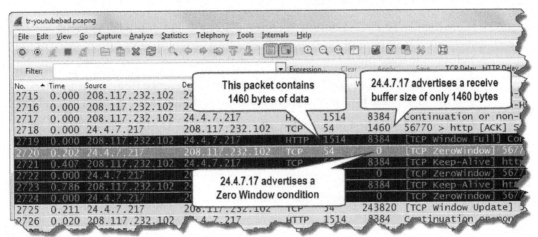

Remember to watch the time. Note how much time passes during a Zero Window condition. If the condition is cleared up quickly, it is probably not the cause of the performance issue bothering the user. If it took 30+ seconds to clear up, you probably have discovered at least one of the reasons the user is complaining. See *Wireshark Lab 66: Measure the Delay Caused by a Window Full Condition* on page 206.

Interestingly, a Zero Window condition is *not* the network's fault.

Window Full Precedes the Problem

Many people mistakenly believe the Window Full packet indicates a problem on the host that sent the packet. Actually, Window Full packets are heading towards the host who's buffer is about to be full.

Window Full packets precede the Zero Window condition and travel towards the host that is having buffer size problems.

Wireshark Lab 66: Measure the Delay Caused by a Window Full Condition

Once you've identified the host that is experiencing a Zero Window condition, consider measuring the delay caused by this problem. You can estimate the time delay by looking at the Time column or use a Time Reference to measure the delay more precisely.

Step 1:   Open **tr-youtubebad.pcapng**.

Step 2:   Click the **Go To Packet** button ![button]. Enter **4022** and click **Jump to**. We will measure the amount of delay time caused by a lack of receive buffer space at this point in the trace file.

Step 3:   Right-click on **Packet 4,022** and select **Set Time Reference (toggle)**. Wireshark sets the time value for this packet to 0.000000 and puts *REF* in the Time column.

Look down to the first data packet after the Window Update. This is the point at which data begins flowing again in this connection. The Time column indicates the total delay time is 25.658 seconds. Yes, this would be noticeable.

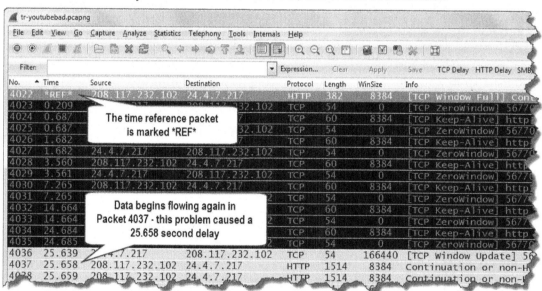

Step 4:   To remove the Time Reference, right-click on **Packet 4,022** and select **Set Time Reference (toggle)** again.

Step 5:   Wireshark returns the Time column to the Seconds Since Beginning of Capture setting.

If your Time column had been set to Seconds Since Previous Displayed Packet before using a time reference, it may not properly restore this setting.

To restore the Time setting to Seconds Since Previous Displayed Packet, you must select **View | Time Display Format** and choose some other setting (such as **Time of Day**) and then select **View | Time Display Format | Seconds Since Previous Displayed Packet**.

This is a bug as of Wireshark 1.10.x that may be fixed in later versions.

Next we will more closely at Wireshark's Window Full detection process.

Window Full

Display Filter Value

`tcp.analysis.window_full`

Traffic Analysis Overview

Wireshark constantly monitors the advertised Window Size values as well as the amount of data flowing in each direction.

When Wireshark notices a packet of data that contains exactly the number of data bytes required to fill the target's available buffer space, Wireshark marks that packet *Window Full*.

What Causes Window Full?

Window Full is an indication that the target will be out of receive buffer space when the data packet arrives. The condition may be cleared up immediately if the target sends a Window Update. Otherwise, the target will send a Zero Window packet.

Remember that the cause of a Zero Window condition is a full receive buffer. This is caused by a receiving application that is not picking up data from the receive buffer fast enough to keep up with the data receipt rate.

Again, we do not know why the application is not keeping up with the data transfer rate. We know this process can cause significant delays and we know that we need to look further at the host that is advertising the Zero Window condition. Perhaps there are too many applications running on the host. Perhaps the application is just a lame application. A Zero Window condition can occur for many reasons.

packet-tcp.c Code and Comments

You can see the reference to a data packet (*seglen>0*) and a reference to the advertised window (*window*). You can also see that Wireshark will not mark TCP SYN, FIN, and RST packets as Window Full.

```
953
954      /* WINDOW FULL
955       * If we know the window scaling
956       * and if this segment contains data and goes all the way to the
957       * edge of the advertised window
958       * then we mark it as WINDOW FULL
959       * SYN/RST/FIN packets are never WINDOW FULL
960       */
961   /*QQQ tested*/
962      if( seglen>0
963      && tcpd->rev->win_scale!=-1
964      && (seq+seglen)==(tcpd->rev->lastack+(tcpd->rev->window<<
965          (tcpd->rev->win_scale==-2?0:tcpd->rev->win_scale)))
966      && (flags&(TH_SYN|TH_FIN|TH_RST))==0 ) {
967          if(!tcpd->ta) {
968              tcp_analyze_get_acked_struct(pinfo->fd->num, seq, ack, TRUE, tcpd);
969          }
970          tcpd->ta->flags|=TCP_A_WINDOW_FULL;
971      }
```

Wireshark Lab 67: Use a Filter to Count Window Full Packets

In these Window Full labs, you will analyze traffic sent to a network printer. This printer is a network printer/fax/copier product (an HP OfficeJet 6500A Plus).

Step 1:   Open **tr-winzero-print.pcapng**.

Step 2:   In the display filter area, enter the filter `tcp.analysis.window_full`. Click **Apply**. The Status Bar indicates that Wireshark has detected 12 Window Full conditions in the trace file.

Step 3:   Expand the **[SEQ/ACK analysis]** section in one of the Window Full packets. Notice that this area is colored yellow by Wireshark. Yellow is the color associated with Expert Infos Warnings.

```
⊕ Flags: 0x010 (ACK)
   Window size value: 1536
   [Calculated window size: 6144]
   [Window size scaling factor: 4]
⊕ Checksum: 0x0f33 [validation disabled]
⊟ [SEQ/ACK analysis]
     [Bytes in flight: 17520]
   ⊟ [TCP Analysis Flags]
      ⊟ [The transmission window is now completely full]
         ⊟ [Expert Info (Warn/Sequence): Window is full]
            [Message: Window is full]
            [Severity level: Warn]
            [Group: Sequence]
⊟ [Timestamps]
     [Time since first frame in this TCP stream: 8.463796000 seconds]
     [Time since previous frame in this TCP stream: 0.000083000 seconds]
⊕ Data (1460 bytes)
```
```
File: "C:\Users\Laura\...  Packets: 85 · Displayed: 12 (14%) · Load time: 0:00.037
```

Step 4:   Click the **Clear** button to remove your filter when you are done.

Wireshark Lab 68: Find Window Full Packets with Expert Infos

Step 1:   Open **tr-winzero-print.pcapng**.

Step 2:   Click the **Expert Infos** button on the Status Bar.

Step 3:   Click the **Warnings** tab. Expand the **Window is Full** section and click on the first entry, **Packet 36**. Click the **Close** button to return to the main Wireshark window.

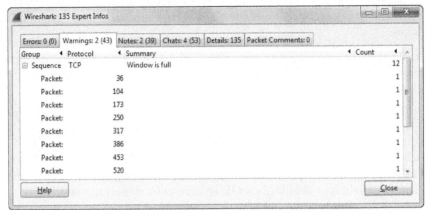

Packet 36 contains just enough data to completely fill the buffer space of the target (192.168.1.101). Data does not begin flowing again until Packet 41.

Step 4:   Use the **Time Reference process** to measure the delay caused by this Zero Window condition (see *Wireshark Lab 66: Measure the Delay Caused by a Window Full Condition* on page 206 for step-by-step instructions on using the Time Reference feature). You should find the delay was only 542 ms (about ½ second).

If your Time column had previously been set to Seconds Since Previous Displayed Packet, you will need to select another setting and then return it to Seconds Since Previous Displayed Packet after using the Time Reference feature. This 1.10.x bug was mentioned in Wireshark Lab 66.

Wireshark Lab 69: Use Bytes in Flight to Watch a "Stuck" Application

This network printer is located at IP address 192.168.1.101. The network client, 192.168.1.111 is sending a document to the printer using the double-sided print setting. In this trace file you will be able to see when the network printer stops pulling data out of its TCP buffer.

This printer (an HP OfficeJet 6500A Plus) stops pulling data from the buffer each time it "waits" for the ink to dry on one side of the page. This eventually leads to the Window Zero condition.

You will create and use a new column, Bytes in Flight, and watch this column increase as data is sent to the printer and no ACKs are sent back. "Bytes in Flight" are unacknowledged data bytes.

Step 1:   To add a column to track unacknowledged bytes, the *Track Number of Bytes in Flight* TCP preference setting must be enabled.

Click the **Preferences** button 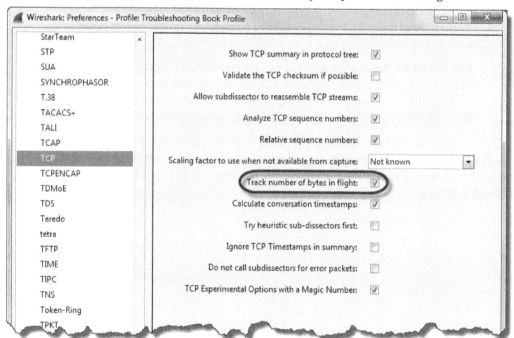 on the Main Toolbar and expand **Protocols**. Type **TCP** to jump to that preference area and check to make sure *Track Number of Bytes in Flight* is enabled. Click **OK** to save your preference settings.

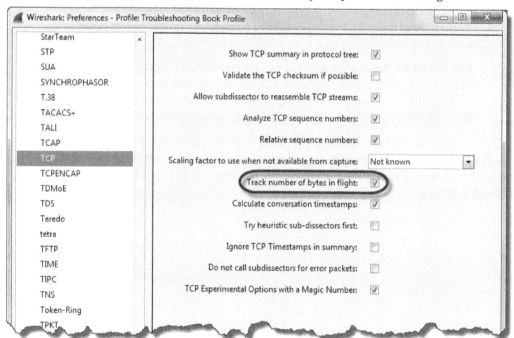

Step 2:   Open **tr-winzero-print.pcapng**.

Step 3:   Jump to **Packet 173**. This is the first Window Full packet in the trace file.

Step 4:   Expand the **TCP header** to view the contents of the **[SEQ/ACK analysis]** section.

If *Track Number of Bytes in Flight* is enabled, you will see a Bytes in Flight section in square brackets. Remember that fields surrounded by square brackets are interpretations by Wireshark—they are not actual fields in the packet.

Step 5:   Right-click the **[Bytes in flight: 17520]** line and select **Apply as Column**.

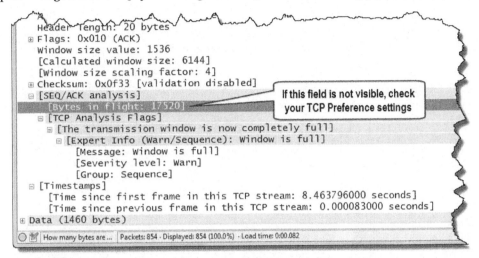

Step 6:   Display your WinSize (Calculated Window Size) column if it is hidden. If you must recreate the column, right-click on the **Calculated window size** field in any TCP header and select **Apply as Column**.

Step 7:   Look up in the Packet List pane to the last ACK packet sent from the printer— **Packet 161**. In this ACK packet, the printer advertises 17,520 bytes of available buffer space in the Calculated window size field. Then the printer stops sending ACKs for the incoming data.

The client continues to send data until it reaches 17,520 bytes of data in flight. Wireshark knows we are at a Window Full condition and marks the packet as such.

This printer takes 25 seconds to "dry the ink" when printing in double-sided mode. During this "drying time," the printer seems to completely lock up. The page with one side printed is hanging halfway out of the paper tray. The printer does not acknowledge receipt of data during this time.

Why? Good question. Remember that Wireshark can always show you where the problem is located, but not why the problem is occurring. Doesn't this printer have enough memory to keep up with the incoming data?

This printer boasts 64-MB memory standard yet this printer only allocates 17,520 bytes of memory for this TCP connection receive buffer. The printer advertises a Window Scaling Factor of 1. Maybe it reserves most of its memory for incoming fax retention in case the paper runs out. We can't tell the reason for this problem by looking at the packets — we can only detect that the problem exists.

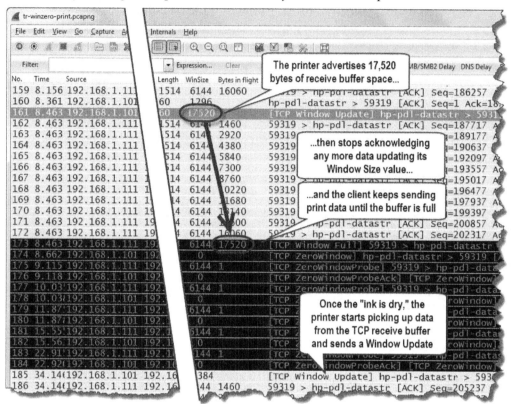

Next we will look at Wireshark's identification process for Zero Window Probe and Zero Window Probe ACK packets.

Zero Window Probe and Zero Window Probe ACK

Display Filter Value

```
tcp.analysis.zero_window_probe
tcp.analysis.zero_window_probe_ack
```

Zero Window Probe packets may be sent by a host to a TCP peer that is advertising a Zero Window condition in the hope of eliciting a Window Update response. Keep in mind that a host may send a TCP Keep Alive (decrementing the sequence number by 1) instead of a Zero Window Probe packet.

Wireshark looks for Zero Window Probe packets after Zero Window packets. A Zero Window probe packet advances the sequence number by 1.

Although Zero Window Probes and Zero Window Probe ACKs are not a problem, they are a symptom of an issue — a Zero Window issue.

What Causes Zero Window Probes?

These packets follow a Zero Window condition. Essentially you are troubleshooting an application issue on the host that advertises the Zero Window.

The ultimate cause of a Zero Window issue is a lack of buffer space on a host. When an application does not keep up with the receipt rate, the receive buffer will become full.

packet-tcp.c Code and Comments

In *packet-tcp.c*, you can clearly see the reference to 1-byte length (*seglen==1*), and the Window Size in the reverse direction (*rev*) is set at zero (*window==0*). In addition, there is a reference to the sequence number being the next expected one (*fwd->nextseq*).

```
870        /* ZERO WINDOW PROBE
871         * it is a zero window probe if
872         *  the sequence number is the next expected one
873         *  the window in the other direction is 0
874         *  the segment is exactly 1 byte
875         */
876    /*QQQ tested*/
877        if( seglen==1
878        && seq==tcpd->fwd->nextseq
879        && tcpd->rev->window==0 ) {
880            if(!tcpd->ta) {
881                tcp_analyze_get_acked_struct(pinfo->fd->num, seq, ack, TRUE, tcpd);
882            }
883            tcpd->ta->flags|=TCP_A_ZERO_WINDOW_PROBE;
884            goto finished_fwd;
885        }
886
```

Wireshark Lab 70: Use a Filter to Count Zero Window Probe and Zero Window Probe ACK Packets

Step 1:   Open **tr-winzero-print.pcapng**.

Step 2:   In the display filter area, enter the filter **tcp.analysis.zero_window_probe ||
            tcp.analysis.zero_window_probe_ack**. Click **Apply**.

            The Status Bar indicates that Wireshark has detected 39 Zero Window Probes
            and Zero Window Probe ACKs in the trace file.

```
 Window size value: 1536
 [Calculated window size: 6144]
 [Window size scaling factor: 4]
⊞ Checksum: 0xe865 [validation disabled]
⊟ [SEQ/ACK analysis]
    [Bytes in flight: 1]
  ⊟ [TCP Analysis Flags]
    ⊟ [This is a TCP zero-window-probe]
      ⊟ [Expert Info (Note/Sequence): Zero window probe]
          [Message: Zero window probe]
          [Severity level: Note]
          [Group: Sequence]
⊟ [Timestamps]
    [Time since first frame in this TCP stream: 0.899945000 seconds]
    [Time since previous frame in this TCP stream: 0.322519000 seconds]
⊞ Data (1 byte)
```

```
○ 🗒 File: "C:\Users\Laura\...  Packets: 854  Displayed: 39 (4.6%)  Load time: 0:00.089
```

Step 3:   Click the **Clear** button to remove your filter when you are done.

Wireshark Lab 71: Find Zero Window Probe and Zero Window Probe ACK Packets with Expert Infos

Step 1:   Open **tr-winzero-print.pcapng**.

Step 2:   Click the **Expert Infos** button on the Status Bar.

Step 3:   Click the **Notes** tab. Expand the **Zero Window Probe ACK** section. A longer Zero Window problem will generate a higher number of Zero Window Probe/Zero Window Probe ACKs in close proximity.

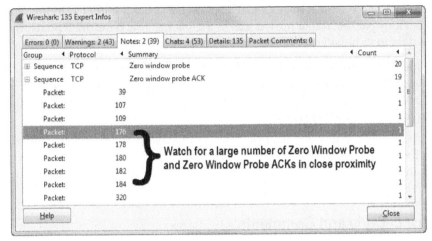

Step 4:   Click on the link to **Packet 176** and click the **Close** button.

If you keep your Bytes in Flight column visible, you can see the 1-byte value of the Zero Window Probe packets in this column.

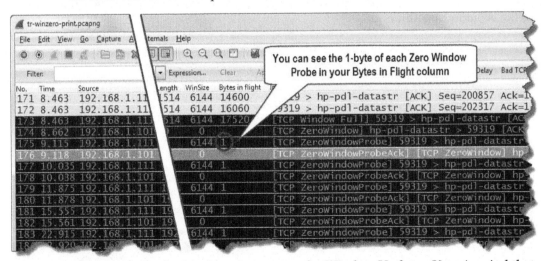

Next we will look at Wireshark's detection process for Window Updates. Keep in mind that Window Updates are the only solution to a Window Zero condition.

Window Update

Display Filter Value

`tcp.analysis.window_update`

Traffic Analysis Overview

Window Updates indicate that an application at a host has picked data up out of the receive buffer. When Wireshark sees an ACK packet that has a higher Window Size value than the previous packet from a host, it marks the packet as a Window Update. If the packet has data in it, however, Wireshark does not mark that packet as a Window Update.

Window Updates are good! Window Updates are explicitly excluded from Wireshark's Bad TCP coloring rule (`tcp.analysis.flags && !tcp.analysis.window_update`).

What Causes Window Updates?

Window Updates are sent when an application takes data out of the receive buffer. As you will see in the labs in this section, Window Updates may occur at many points in a TCP communication. When a Window Zero condition occurs, a Window Update is the only remedy.

packet-tcp.c Code and Comments

You can clearly see the reference to a zero-byte packet (*seglen=0*) and a new Window Size value (*window!=tcpd->fwd->window*). Window Updates do not advance the sequence number (*seq==tcpd->fwd->nextseq*) or acknowledgment number (*ack==tcpd->fwd->lastack*).

Wireshark will never mark TCP SYN, FIN or RST packets as Window Updates, regardless of the Window Size value.

```
937     /* WINDOW UPDATE
938      * A window update is a 0 byte segment with the same SEQ/ACK numbers as
939      * the previous seen segment and with a new window value
940      */
941     if( seglen==0
942     &&  window
943     &&  window!=tcpd->fwd->window
944     &&  seq==tcpd->fwd->nextseq
945     &&  ack==tcpd->fwd->lastack
946     &&  (flags&(TH_SYN|TH_FIN|TH_RST))==0 ) {
947         if(!tcpd->ta) {
948             tcp_analyze_get_acked_struct(pinfo->fd->num, seq, ack, TRUE, tcpd);
949         }
950         tcpd->ta->flags|=TCP_A_WINDOW_UPDATE;
951     }
952
```

Wireshark Lab 72: Use a Filter to Count Window Update Packets

Step 1:   Open **tr-winzero-print.pcapng**.

Step 2:   In the display filter area, enter the filter **tcp.analysis.window_update**. Click **Apply**. The Status Bar indicates that Wireshark detected 49 Window Updates.

```
Header length: 20 bytes
⊞ Flags: 0x010 (ACK)
  Window size value: 17520
  [Calculated window size: 17520]
  [Window size scaling factor: 1]
⊞ Checksum: 0x3ba5 [validation disabled]
⊟ [SEQ/ACK analysis]
  ⊟ [TCP Analysis Flags]
    ⊟ [This is a tcp window update]
      ⊟ [Expert Info (Chat/Sequence): Window update]
        [Message: Window update]
        [Severity level: Chat]
        [Group: Sequence]
⊟ [Timestamps]
    [Time since first frame in this TCP stream: 8.463224000 seconds]
    [Time since previous frame in this TCP stream: 0.101763000 seconds]

File: "C:\Users\Laura\...   Packets: 854   Displayed: 49 (5.7%)   Load time: 0:00.054
```

Step 3:   Select **Packet 40** and expand the **[SEQ/ACK analysis]** section of the TCP header. This area is colored blue by Wireshark because blue is the color associated with Expert Infos Chats (the Expert Infos section under which Window Updates are listed).

Step 4:   Click the **Clear** button to remove your filter you are done.

Wireshark Lab 73: Find Window Update Packets with Expert Infos

Step 1:   Open **tr-winzero-print.pcapng**.

Step 2:   Click the **Expert Infos** button on the Status Bar.

Step 3:   Click the **Chats** tab to locate Window Updates. Expand the **Window updates** section and click on the first entry, **Packet 40**. Click the **Close** button to return to the main Wireshark window.

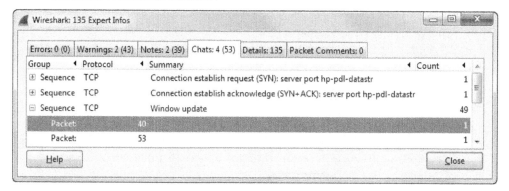

Packet 40 resolves the Zero Window condition by indicating the printer now has 16,384 bytes of available buffer space. Based on the Time column value, this Zero Window condition resolved relatively quickly.

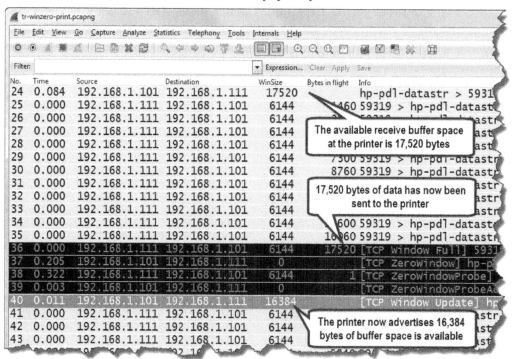

*You can also locate Expert Infos packets using Wireshark's Find feature. Select **Edit | Find Packet**. Enter `tcp.analysis.window_update`. Click **Find**.*

Step 4:   Scroll down to **Packet 53**. This is another Window Update. Prior to this Window Update, the printer advertised only 324 bytes of available receive buffer space. That is not enough buffer space to accept the 1,460 bytes of data the client has queued up. We notice a delay at this time in the trace file as we wait for a Window Update from the printer.

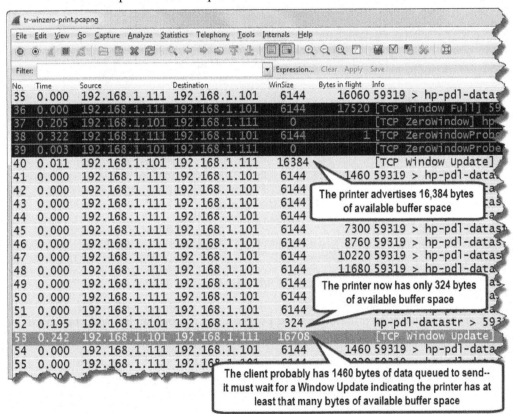

Keep a close watch on low window conditions as well as Zero Window conditions. Wireshark does not have an Expert warning or note to call your attention to low window conditions, so you need to catch them yourself.

Next we will look at Wireshark's detection process for Reused Ports. Sometimes Reused Ports are not a problem. Other times Reused Ports can cause significant delays in communications.

Reused Ports

Display Filter Value

`tcp.analysis.reused_ports`

Traffic Analysis Overview

Wireshark marks SYN packets with the Reused Ports Expert Analysis definition when it detects a previous SYN packet using the same IP address/port combination in the trace file.

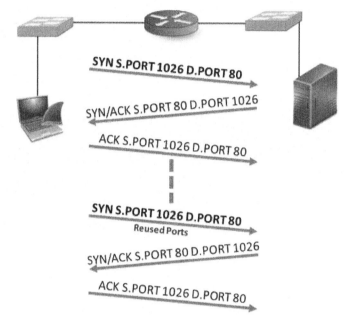

If the first connection is terminated, reused ports are not a problem. Reused ports become a problem when the previous connection has not terminated (either through TCP FINs or TCP RSTs).

For example, if a print server uses the same source port number in each connection to a printer, but does not terminate the previous connection, then reused ports can be a problem.

Be careful of splitting trace files that might have a Reused Port indication. Wireshark does not look across file sets to see if a port has been reused.

What Causes Reused Ports?

Reused ports may be seen if an application defines a static source port number or a very small range of source port numbers.

Reused ports may also be seen if a host is going through a lot of source port numbers very quickly.

packet-tcp.c Code and Comments

The note in *packet-tcp.c* indicates how Wireshark evaluates the TCP SYN packets. Wireshark looks at the source port number, source IP address and the Sequence Number field. If the three match a previous SYN packet, it is a retransmission. If the sequence number is different, then it is a different connection request and marked as a Reused Port.

In this case Wireshark is evaluating the true Sequence Number field value, not a relative sequence number value.

```
4206    /* If this is a SYN packet, then check if its seq-nr is different
4207     * from the base_seq of the retrieved conversation. If this is the
4208     * case, create a new conversation with the same addresses and ports
4209     * and set the TA_PORTS_REUSED flag. If the seq-nr is the same as
4210     * the base_seq, then do nothing so it will be marked as a retrans-
4211     * mission later.
4212     */
4213    if(tcpd && ((tcph->th_flags&(TH_SYN|TH_ACK))==TH_SYN) &&
4214        (tcpd->fwd->base_seq!=0) &&
4215        (tcph->th_seq!=tcpd->fwd->base_seq) ) {
4216        if (!(pinfo->fd->flags.visited)) {
4217            conv=conversation_new(pinfo->fd->num, &pinfo->src, &pinfo->dst,
4218                pinfo->ptype, pinfo->srcport, pinfo->destport, 0);
4219            tcpd=get_tcp_conversation_data(conv,pinfo);
4220        }
4221        if(!tcpd->ta)
4222            tcp_analyze_get_acked_struct(pinfo->fd->num, tcph->th_seq, tcph->th_ack, TRUE, tcpd);
4223        tcpd->ta->flags|=TCP_A_REUSED_PORTS;
4224    }
```

Wireshark Lab 74: Use a Filter to Count Reused Port Packets

Step 1:   Open **tr-reusedports.pcapng**.

Step 2:   In the display filter area, enter the filter `tcp.analysis.reused_ports`. Click **Apply**. The Status Bar indicates that Wireshark has detected one Reused Port in the trace file.

Step 3:   Expand the **[SEQ/ACK analysis]** section on the Reused Port packet. Notice that this area is colored cyan by Wireshark. Cyan is the color associated with Expert Infos Notes.

```
 ⊞ Maximum segment size: 1460 bytes
 ⊞ No-Operation (NOP)
 ⊞ Window scale: 2 (multiply by 4)
 ⊞ No-Operation (NOP)
 ⊞ No-Operation (NOP)
 ⊞ TCP SACK Permitted Option: True
 ⊟ [SEQ/ACK analysis]
   ⊟ [TCP Analysis Flags]
     ⊟ [A new tcp session is started with the same ports as an earlier ses
       ⊟ [Expert Info (Note/Sequence): TCP Port numbers reused for new sess
           [Message: TCP Port numbers reused for new session]
           [Severity level: Note]
           [Group: Sequence]
 ⊟ [Timestamps]
     [Time since first frame in this TCP stream: 0.000000000 seconds]
     [Time since previous frame in this TCP stream: 0.000000000 seconds]
 ○ 📝 File: "C:\Users\Laura\...   Packets: 316   Displayed: 1 (0.3%)   Load time: 0:00.017
```

Step 4:   Click the **Clear** button to remove your filter when you are done.

Wireshark Lab 75: Find Reused Ports with Expert Infos

Step 1:   Open **tr-reusedports.pcapng**.

Step 2:   Click the **Expert Infos** button on the Status Bar.

Step 3:   Click the **Notes** tab to identify Reused Port packets. Expand the **TCP Port numbers reused for new session** section and click on the first entry, **Packet 317**. Click the **Close** button to return to the main Wireshark window.

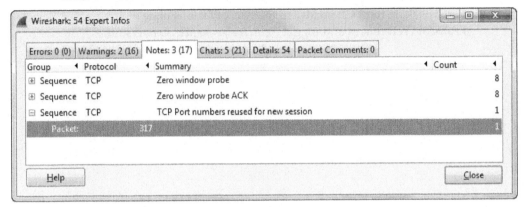

Step 4:   Hide any irrelevant columns (such as WinSize and Bytes in Flight) by clicking on the column headings and selecting **Hide Column**.

The Reused Ports packet shown is a SYN packet (which is expected). This packet uses IP address 192.168.1.44 and port 59319.

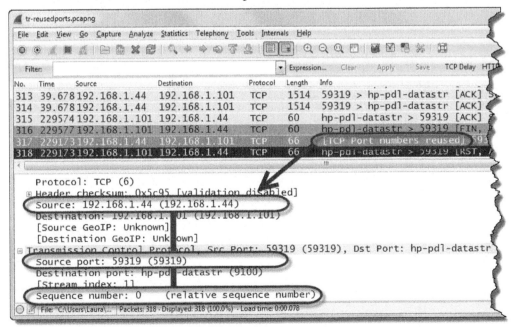

Step 5:   The TCP dissector (*packet-tcp.c*) indicated that the sequence number field is examined to determine whether the SYN is a unique connection request, a retransmission or a reused port.

We want to compare the sequence number in this SYN packet to the sequence number in the previous SYN packet, but Wireshark applies a relative sequence number to TCP conversations. Wireshark displays 0 for the sequence numbers of both SYNs.

Right-click on the **TCP header** in the Packet Details pane of any packet. Select **Protocol Preferences** and toggle *Relative sequence numbers* off.

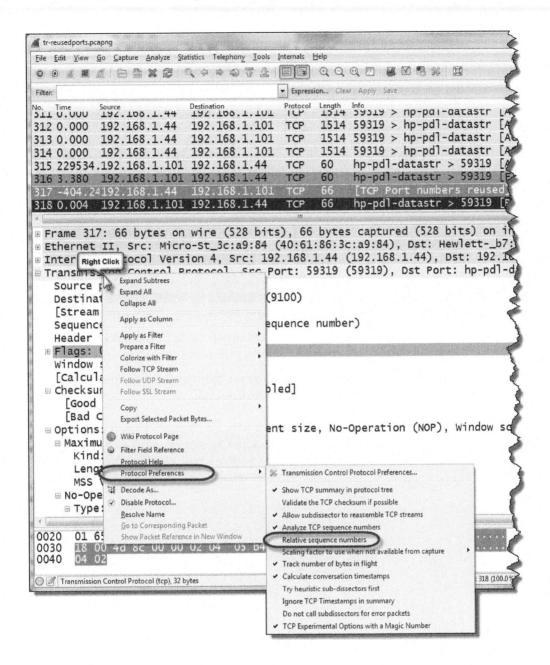

Step 6:   Let's look at the sequence number value of SYN packets in this trace file. Enter
           `tcp.flags==0x0002`[38] in the display filter area and click **Apply**.

           Only 2 packets match this filter.

Step 7:   If you want to quickly compare the sequence number values, display your
           sequence number column again.

           We can see the sequence numbers are different in each of the SYN packets. If the
           sequence numbers were the same, Packet 317 would be marked as a
           Retransmission.

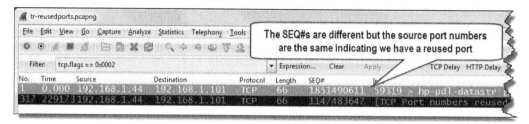

Step 8:   Click on a **TCP header** in the Packet Details pane, select **Protocol Preferences,**
           and toggle the *Relative sequence numbers* preference setting on.

Step 9:   If you want to hide your sequence number column, right-click on the **Sequence
           number** column heading and select **Hide Column**.

Next we will look at Wireshark's detection process for Checksum errors — an error
indication that has caused a lot of folks to analyze network problems incorrectly over the
past years.

---

[38]   This filter looks for the SYN bit on, but all other TCP flags off. You could also use `tcp.flags.syn==1`
       `&& tcp.flags.ack==0`.

Checksum Errors

Display Filter Value

`ip.checksum_bad==1 || tcp.checksum_bad==1 || or udp.checksum_bad==1`

Traffic Analysis Overview

By default, Wireshark does not perform TCP or UDP checksum validation. If you have updated Wireshark from an earlier version that did perform these Checksum validations, you may have retained these settings.

You can easily disable Wireshark's Checksum validation processes using the Preference settings.

What Causes Checksum Errors?

Checksum errors can be caused by faulty Network Interface Cards (NICs) or any device that alters the content of the packets along the path. Most likely, however, incorrect checksums are due to task offloading on the capturing device.

If you have loaded Wireshark on a machine and you are capturing your own traffic to and from that machine, you would see Checksum Errors on all outbound traffic if (a) task offloading is enabled on that host and (b) Wireshark checksum validation processes are enabled.

When task offloading is in use, some protocol functions, such as checksum validation may be passed to the NIC.

When capturing on a task offloading host, Wireshark may display a packet that looks quite different from the one that is actually sent on the network.

For example, when you capture on a Windows host that is using task offloading, WinPcap (the Windows packet capture driver) uses the Netgroup Packet Filter to capture traffic. If this host supports task offloading, Netgroup is saving a copy of the packets before the checksums have been calculated.

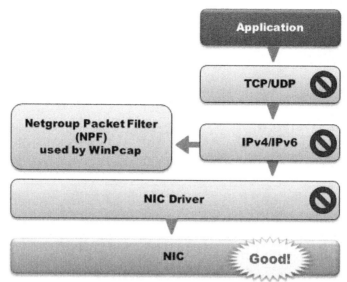

If you really were experiencing checksum errors on the network, you'd know it. Packets with checksum errors do not receive responses because they would be discarded at the layer on which the checksum error occurred.

packet-tcp.c Code and Comments

The checksum error area in *packet-tcp.c* refers to the fields upon which to perform checksum validation, and will only run if checksum validation is enabled.

```
4512    if (tcp_check_checksum) {
4513        /* We haven't turned checksum checking off; checksum it. */
4514
4515        /* Set up the fields of the pseudo-header. */
4516        cksum_vec[0].ptr = (guint8 *)pinfo->src.data;
4517        cksum_vec[0].len = pinfo->src.len;
4518        cksum_vec[1].ptr = (guint8 *)pinfo->dst.data;
4519        cksum_vec[1].len = pinfo->dst.len;
4520        cksum_vec[2].ptr = (const guint8 *)phdr;
4521        switch (pinfo->src.type) {
4522
4523        case AT_IPv4:
4524            phdr[0] = g_htonl((IP_PROTO_TCP<<16) + reported_len);
4525            cksum_vec[2].len = 4;
4526            break;
4527
4528        case AT_IPv6:
4529            phdr[0] = g_htonl(reported_len);
4530            phdr[1] = g_htonl(IP_PROTO_TCP);
4531            cksum_vec[2].len = 8;
4532            break;
```

Wireshark Lab 76: Detect Checksum Errors with Expert Infos

Keep in mind that you can only detect checksum errors if checksum validation is enabled. In this lab we will enable checksum validation to examine traffic from a host that supports task offload.

Step 1:   Open **tr-checksums.pcapng**.

Step 2:   First we need to enable checksum validation for IPv4, TCP and UDP. Select the **Preferences** button 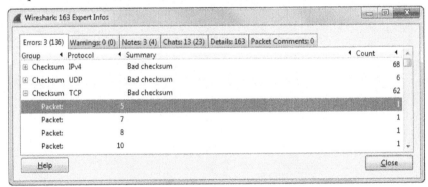 on the Main Toolbar.

Step 3:   Expand the Protocols section and select **IPv4**. Toggle on the *Validate the IPv4 checksum if possible* preference setting.

Step 4:   Select **TCP** off the protocol list. Toggle on the *Validate the TCP checksum if possible* preference setting.

Step 5:   Select **UDP** off the protocol list. Toggle on the *Validate the UDP checksum if possible* preference setting.

Click **OK** to save these preference settings. The coloring in your Packet List pane will change dramatically. Every packet from 192.168.1.72 will have a black background and red foreground.

Step 6:   Click the **Expert Infos** button on the Status Bar.

Step 7:   The Errors tab is open by default. You can see 68 bad IPv4 checksums, 6 bad UDP checksums and 62 bad TCP checksums.

Expand the **TCP Bad Checksum** section.

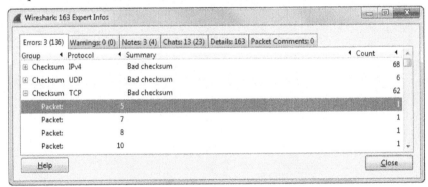

Step 8:   Click on the first TCP Bad Checksum entry—**Packet 5**. Toggle back to the main Wireshark window.

Notice that the Packet List pane now colors each packet from 192.168.1.72 with a black background and red foreground. Each of those packets has a bad IP and UDP checksum or bad IP and TCP checksum.

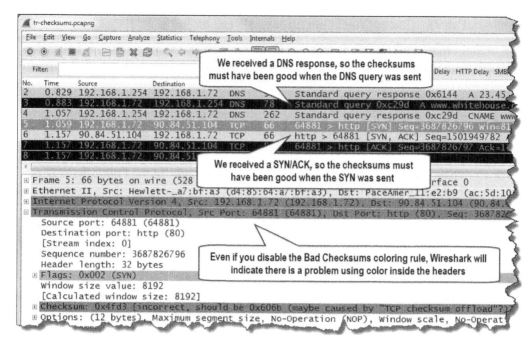

Looking closely at the trace file, you can see that the packets from 192.168.1.72 must have been good when the packets arrived at the target because the target acknowledged receipt of the packets, processed the packets, and replied to the requests in those packets.

That host, 192.168.1.72, is configured to use task offloading, as shown in the image below.

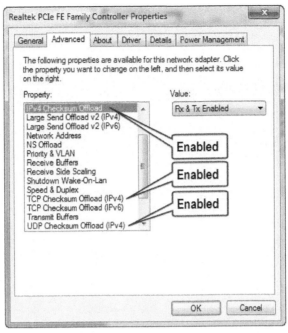

Step 9:   We will use the right-click method to disable Ethernet, IP, UDP and TCP checksum validation before closing this trace file.

In the Packet Details area of Packet 3, right-click on the **Ethernet II header**, select **Protocol Preferences** and toggle off *Validate the Ethernet checksum if possible*.

In the Packet Details area of Packet 3, right-click on the **IP header**, select **Protocol Preferences** and toggle off *Validate the IPv4 checksum if possible*.

In that same packet (Packet 3), right-click on the **UDP header**, select **Protocol Preferences** and toggle off *Validate the UDP checksum if possible*.

In the Packet Details area of Packet 7, right-click on the **TCP header**, select **Protocol Preferences** and toggle off *Validate the TCP checksum if possible*.

In this chapter we have covered a LOT of material. Knowing how to efficiently use and analyze Expert Infos is essential in troubleshooting.

This page intentionally left blank.

CHAPTER 7: IDENTIFY APPLICATION ERRORS

Application errors are easy to catch as long as Wireshark has a dissector for the application.

Application dissectors know the structure of the application traffic as well as the commands and responses used by the application.

In this chapter, you will quickly detect DNS, HTTP, SMB and SIP error responses. Expand your error detection capabilities to other applications using these same techniques.

Chapter 7 Notes

You can quickly detect application error responses when you know the error response syntax and field name.

- Create a set of filter expression buttons that you can quickly click on to find application response errors (such as HTTP, DNS, SMB/SMB2 and SIP errors).

- Keep adding to this basic set of application error buttons as you determine how your applications indicate an error has occurred.

Detect DNS Errors

Display Filter Value

`dns.flags.rcode > 0`

Traffic Analysis Overview

DNS is a request/response-based application. A host sends a request for name resolution, and we want to see a successful response arrive within a reasonable amount of time. Unlike most other applications that run on the network, DNS can run over UDP (common for basic name resolution queries) or TCP (used for zone transfers).

Although Wireshark does not have a coloring rule or Expert Infos item to highlight DNS errors, Wireshark's DNS dissector (*packet-dns.c*) recognizes most DNS errors, as shown in the following list.

Reply Code	Name	Description
0	NoError	No Error
1	FormErr	Format Error
2	ServFail	Server Failure
3	NXDomain	Non-Existent Domain
4	NotImp	Not Implemented
5	Refused	Query Refused
6	YXDomain	Name Exists when it should not
7	YXRRSet	RR Set Exists when it should not
8	NXRRSet	RR Set that should exist does not
9	NotAuth	Server Not Authoritative for zone (RFC 2136)
9	NotAuth	Not Authorized (RFC 2845)
10	NotZone	Name not contained in zone
16	BADVERS	Bad OPT Version (RFC 6891)
16	BADSIG	TSIG Signature Failure (RFC 2845)
17	BADKEY	Key not recognized
18	BADTIME	Signature out of time window
19	BADMODE	Bad TKEY Mode
20	BADNAME	Duplicate key name
21	BADALG	Algorithm not supported

In this section we will focus on the most common DNS errors seen: a server failure (Reply Code 2) and a name error, listed as Non-Existent Domain, (Reply Code 3).

Server failures indicate that the responding DNS server could not obtain information from another DNS server. There is a problem upstream from the responding server. Name errors indicate the name could not be resolved. The name resolution process itself worked properly, but no DNS servers could provide the information requested.

Wireshark Lab 77: Create and Use a "DNS Errors" Filter Expression Button

After this lab you will be able to click this one button to quickly identify DNS errors in your trace files. Although you could type the display filter value to create your filter expression button, in this lab we will use the right-click method to create the filter expression button.

Step 1:   Open **tr-dnserrors.pcapng**.

Step 2:   Click on **Packet 5**. This is the first DNS response in this trace file. The Info column indicates this is a Server Failure reply.

Step 3:   In the Packet Details pane, right-click on the **Domain Name System (response)** line and select **Expand Subtrees**. The DNS Reply Code field is inside the Flags section in this DNS response.

```
⊞ Frame 5: 72 bytes on wire (576 bits), 72 bytes captured (576 bits) on interface
⊞ Ethernet II, Src: D-Link_cc:a3:ea (00:13:46:cc:a3:ea), Dst: Elitegro_40:74:d2 (0
⊞ Internet Protocol Version 4, Src: 192.168.0.1 (192.168.0.1), Dst: 192.168.0.113
⊞ User Datagram Protocol, Src Port: domain (53), Dst Port: 52502 (52502)
⊟ Domain Name System (response)
    [Request In: 4]
    [Time: 1.095858000 seconds]
    Transaction ID: 0xa570
  ⊟ Flags: 0x8182 Standard query response, Server failure
    1... .... .... .... = Response: Message is a response
    .000 0... .... .... = Opcode: Standard query (0)
    .... .0.. .... .... = Authoritative: Server is not an authority for domain
    .... ..0. .... .... = Truncated: Message is not truncated
    .... ...1 .... .... = Recursion desired: Do query recursively
    .... .... 1... .... = Recursion available: Server can do recursive queries
    .... .... .0.. .... = Z: reserved (0)
    .... .... ..0. .... = Answer authenticated: Answer/authority portion was not
    .... .... ...0 .... = Non-authenticated data: Unacceptable
    .... .... .... 0010 = Reply code: Server failure (2)
    Questions: 1
    Answer RRs: 0
    Authority RRs: 0
    Additional RRs: 0
  ⊟ Queries
```

Step 4:   Right-click on the **Reply code** field and select **Prepare a Filter | Selected**.

This filter would detect only Server Failures. We want our button to display any DNS errors. These DNS error packets have values larger than 0 in the **dns.flags.rcode** field.

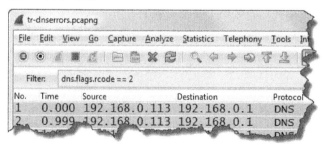

Step 5:   Edit the display filter to read **dns.flags.rcode > 0**[39] and click the **Save** button. Enter **DNS Errors** as your button label and click **OK**.

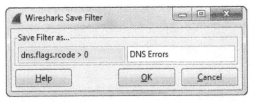

Step 6:   Click your new **DNS Errors** button to locate the eight DNS error responses in this trace file.

Step 7:   To quickly determine what name(s) generated these responses, expand the Queries section in the Packet Details pane of any of these responses. Right-click on the **Name** field and choose **Apply as Column**.

```
⊞ Frame 5: 72 bytes on wire (576 bits), 72 bytes captured (576 bits
⊞ Ethernet II, Src: D-Link_cc:a3:ea (00:13:46:cc:a3:ea), Dst: Eli
⊞ Internet Protocol Version 4, Src: 192.168.0.1 (192.168.0.1), Dst
⊞ User Datagram Protocol, Src Port: domain (53), Dst Port: 52502
⊟ Domain Name System (response)
    [Request In: 4]
    [Time: 1.095858000 seconds]
    Transaction ID: 0xa570
  ⊞ Flags: 0x8182 Standard query response, Server failure
    Questions: 1
    Answer RRs: 0
    Authority RRs: 0
    Additional RRs: 0
  ⊟ Queries
    ⊟ www.nmap.org: type A, class IN
        Name: www.nmap.org
        Type: A (Host address)
        Class: IN (0x0001)
```

Add the query name field as a column
for faster DNS troubleshooting

---

[39]   You could also use **dns.flags.rcode != 0**, but Wireshark will color the display filter area background yellow because you are using the **!=** operator. Oftentimes, using this operator does not yield the expected results. For example, **ip.addr != 10.10.10.10** does not remove traffic to or from 10.10.10.10 from view. The proper syntax would be **!ip.addr==10.10.10.10**.

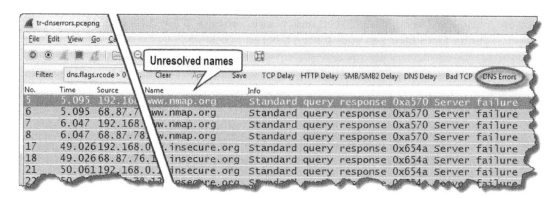

In this case, it appears as if a server upstream from our local server is not responding to recursive DNS queries. The client can't get to www.nmap.org or www.insecure.org because of upstream DNS server problems.

Step 8:   Click the **Clear** button to remove your filter. Right-click on the **Name** column and select **Hide Column**.

Detect HTTP Errors

Display Filter Value

```
http.response.code >= 400 or
http.response.code > 399
```

Traffic Analysis Overview

HTTP is a request/response-based application. An HTTP client sends a request for something and, since HTTP runs over TCP, we hope to see an ACK to our request packet within a reasonable amount of time and then a successful response (also within a reasonable amount of time).

Alternatively we may see the HTTP response piggybacked onto the ACK packet.

HTTP Response Codes[40] are separated into five groups. Each group of HTTP Response Codes begins with a different number.

- 1xx: Informational - Request received, continuing process
- 2xx: Success - The action was successfully received, understood, and accepted
- 3xx: Redirection - Further action must be taken in order to complete the request
- 4xx: Client Error - The request contains bad syntax or cannot be fulfilled
- 5xx: Server Error - The server failed to fulfill an apparently valid request

In this section we are interested in any HTTP Response Codes that begin with 4xx (Client Errors) or 5xx (Server Errors).

Although Wireshark does not have a coloring rule or Expert Infos entry for HTTP errors, Wireshark's HTTP dissector (*packet-http.c*) recognizes the current list of HTTP 4xx and 5xx errors. Open and examine *packet-http.c* to view the list of detected HTTP Response Codes.

---

[40]   Referred to as "Status Codes" in the HTTP specification.

```
300
301     /* --- HTTP Status Codes */
302     /* Note: The reference for uncommented entries is RFC 2616 */
303   ☐static const value_string vals_status_code[] = {
304         { 100, "Continue" },
305         { 101, "Switching Protocols" },
306         { 102, "Processing" },                    /* RFC 2518 */
307         { 199, "Informational - Others" },
308
309         { 200, "OK"},
310         { 201, "Created"},
311         { 202, "Accepted"},
312         { 203, "Non-authoritative Information"},
313         { 204, "No Content"},
314         { 205, "Reset Content"},
315         { 206, "Partial Content"},
316         { 207, "Multi-Status"},                    /* RFC 4918 */
317            { 226, "IM Used"},                       /* RFC 3229 */
318         { 299, "Success - Others"},
319
320         { 300, "Multiple Choices"},
321         { 301, "Moved Permanently"},
322         { 302, "Found"},
323         { 303, "See Other"},
324         { 304, "Not Modified"},
325         { 305, "Use Proxy"},
326         { 307, "Temporary Redirect"},
327         { 399, "Redirection - Others"},
328
329         { 400, "Bad Request"},
330         { 401, "Unauthorized"},
331         { 402, "Payment Required"},
```

Wireshark Lab 78: Create and Use an "HTTP Errors" Filter Expression Button

After this lab you will be able to click this one button to quickly identify HTTP errors in your trace files. In this lab you will simply type the display filter value to create your filter expression button.

Step 1:   Open **tr-chappellu.pcapng**.

Step 2:   Type **http.response.code >= 400** in the display filter area and click the **Save** button. Name your button **HTTP Errors** and click **OK**.

Step 3:   Click your new **HTTP Errors** button to locate the two HTTP error responses in this trace file. Both errors are 404 Not Found errors.

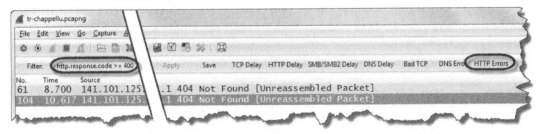

*If different packet numbers appear after applying your filter, check to ensure your TCP Allow subdissector to reassemble TCP streams preference setting is **disabled** (see Wireshark Lab 11: Change the TCP Dissector Reassembly Setting to Properly Measure HTTP Response Times on page 59).*

Step 4:   If you want to know what item could not be found, right-click on **Packet 61** and select **Follow TCP Stream**. Wireshark applies a filter based on the Stream Index number and opens a window that depicts the conversation without headers.

The Follow Stream capability offers a quick way to view what hosts send to each other without having to move from one packet to the next or scroll through a trace file.

It looks like the file *reader_2_728x90.png* can't be found on the server.

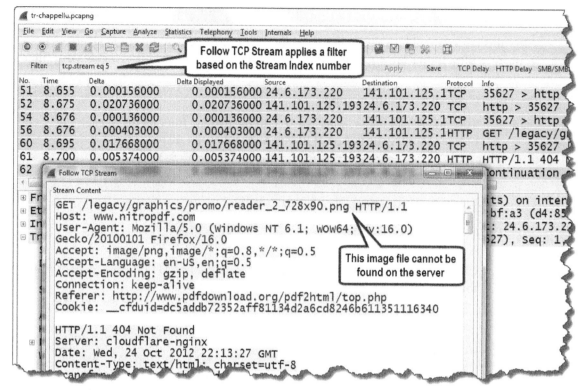

Step 5: Click **Clear** to remove your filter before continuing.

If you ever want to know the syntax to use in a display filter, expand the Packet Details pane and click on the field of interest. The first column in the Status Bar shows the name and description of the field.

Using the filter `http.response.code >= 400` (or `http.response.code > 399`, which is equivalent) makes catching HTTP errors easy. Next we look at the simple process of detecting SMB and SMB2 errors. We will make a filter expression button for these errors as well.

Detect SMB/SMB2 Errors

Display Filter Value

`smb.nt_status > 0 || smb2.nt_status > 0`

Traffic Analysis Overview

Server Message Block (SMB) and Server Message Block Version 2 (SMB2) are request/response applications. The client sends a request for a file or service and since SMB and SMB2 run over TCP, we hope to see an ACK to our request packet within a reasonable amount of time and then a successful response (also within a reasonable amount of time).

Although Wireshark does not have a coloring rule or Expert Infos entry for SMB/SMB2 errors, Wireshark's SMB and SMB2 dissectors (*packet-smb.c* and *packet-smb2.c*) recognize the current list of SMB and SMB2 errors.

A response code (NT Status code) of 0 indicates the request was successful. Anything else and you have a problem. Only a partial list of SMB errors follows as there are too many SMB/SMB2 errors to list them all. The full list can be obtained from Microsoft's Open Specification document entitled "[MS-CIFS] Common Internet File System (CIFS) Protocol" (Section 2.2.2.4 SMB Error Classes and Codes).

Error Code	NT Status Values	Description
ERRbadfunc 0x0001	STATUS_NOT_IMPLEMENTED 0xC0000002 STATUS_INVALID_DEVICE_REQUEST 0xC0000010 STATUS_ILLEGAL_FUNCTION 0xC00000AF	Invalid Function.
ERRbadfile 0x0002	STATUS_NO_SUCH_FILE 0xC000000F STATUS_NO_SUCH_DEVICE 0xC000000E STATUS_OBJECT_NAME_NOT_FOUND 0xC0000034	File not found.

ERRbadpath 0x0003	STATUS_OBJECT_PATH_INVALID 0xC0000039 STATUS_OBJECT_PATH_NOT_FOUND 0xC000003A STATUS_OBJECT_PATH_SYNTAX_BAD 0xC000003B STATUS_DFS_EXIT_PATH_FOUND 0xC000009B STATUS_REDIRECTOR_NOT_STARTED 0xC00000FB	A component in the path prefix is not a directory.
ERRnofids 0x0004	STATUS_TOO_MANY_OPENED_FILES 0xC000011F	Too many open files. No FIDs are available.
ERRnoaccess 0x0005	STATUS_ACCESS_DENIED 0xC0000022 STATUS_INVALID_LOCK_SEQUENCE 0xC000001E STATUS_INVALID_VIEW_SIZE 0xC000001F STATUS_ALREADY_COMMITTED 0xC0000021 STATUS_PORT_CONNECTION_REFUSED 0xC0000041 STATUS_THREAD_IS_TERMINATING 0xC000004B STATUS_DELETE_PENDING 0xC0000056 STATUS_PRIVILEGE_NOT_HELD 0xC0000061 STATUS_LOGON_FAILURE 0xC000006D STATUS_FILE_IS_A_DIRECTORY 0xC00000BA STATUS_FILE_RENAMED 0xC00000D5 STATUS_PROCESS_IS_TERMINATING 0xC000010A STATUS_DIRECTORY_NOT_EMPTY 0xC0000101 STATUS_CANNOT_DELETE 0xC0000121 STATUS_FILE_DELETED 0xC0000123	Access denied.

ERRbadfid	STATUS_SMB_BAD_FID	Invalid FID.
0x0006	0x00060001	
	STATUS_INVALID_HANDLE	
	0xC0000008	
	STATUS_OBJECT_TYPE_MISMATCH	
	0xC0000024	
	STATUS_PORT_DISCONNECTED	
	0xC0000037	
	STATUS_INVALID_PORT_HANDLE	
	0xC0000042	
	STATUS_FILE_CLOSED	
	0xC0000128	
	STATUS_HANDLE_NOT_CLOSABLE	
	0xC0000235	

In this section, we begin by creating a simple SMB/SMB2 Errors filter expression button so we can find these errors more quickly.

Wireshark Lab 79: Create and Use an "SMB/SMB2 Errors" Filter Expression Button

After this lab you will be able to click this one button to quickly identify SMB and SMB2 errors in your trace files.

Step 1:   Open **tr-smbjoindomain.pcapng**.

Step 2:   Click on **Packet 15**. This is the first SMB response in this trace file. The Info column indicates this is a Negotiate Protocol response.

Step 3:   Right-click on the **SMB (Server Message Block Protocol)** line in the Packet Details pane and select **Expand Subtrees**. The response code (NT Status) field is directly after the SMB Command field.

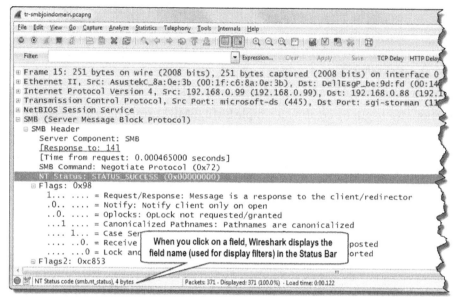

Step 4:   Enter **smb.nt_status > 0 || smb2.nt_status > 0** in the display filter area and click **Save**. Name your new filter expression button **SMB/SMB2 Errors**.

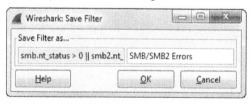

Step 5:   Click your new **SMB/SMB2 Errors** button to locate the two SMB error responses in this trace file.

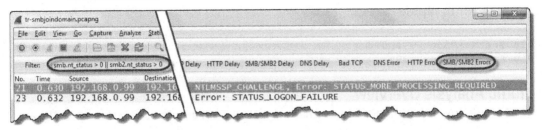

One error is an NTLMSSP_Challenge error indicating that more processing is required. The other is a Logon Failure.

At this point, we need to do some research into the configuration of the client and server and those two NT Status responses.

Step 6:   Click the **Clear** button to remove your filter when you are done.

We create filter expression buttons to quickly locate problems in a trace file that may contain thousands if not hundreds of thousands of packets. In larger trace files (over 100 MB), the process of applying display filters may take a long time to complete.

You could split the trace file and apply the filter to each file in a file set. Alternately you could use Tshark and the –Y parameter to apply this display filter to the trace file. The syntax in this case would be:

```
tshark -r "<filename>" -Y "<displayfilter> " -w <newfilename>
```

```
Command Prompt

C:\traces-general>tshark -r "tr-smbjoindomain.pcapng" -Y "smb.nt_status > 0
|| smb2.nt_status > 0" -w smberrors.pcapng

C:\traces-general>
```

Using the commands shown above, our file (*smberrors.pcapng*) contains only two packets — Packet 21 and Packet 23 (now listed as Packet 1 and Packet 2 in the new trace file).

Next we will look at SIP error detection using the same techniques we've used on DNS, HTTP, and SMB error detection.

Detect SIP Errors

Display Filter Value

```
sip.Status-Code >= 400 or
sip.Status-Code > 399
```

Traffic Analysis Overview

Session Initiation Protocol (SIP) is a signaling protocol commonly used to set up VoIP calls.

Although Wireshark does not have a coloring rule or Expert Infos entry for SIP errors, Wireshark's SIP dissector (*packet-sip.c*) recognizes the current list of SIP errors.

SIP is a request/response-based application. A SIP client sends a request for something and we hope to see a successful SIP response. SIP can run over UDP or TCP. When SIP is configured to run over TCP, we hope to see an ACK to our SIP request in a reasonable amount of time and then a successful response (also within a reasonable amount of time).

SIP Status Codes (response codes) are separated into six groups. Each group of SIP Status Codes begins with a different number.

- 1xx: Provisional — request received, continuing to process the request.
- 2xx: Success — the action was successfully received, understood, and accepted.
- 3xx: Redirection — further action needs to be taken in order to complete the request.
- 4xx: Client Error — the request contains bad syntax or cannot be fulfilled at this server.
- 5xx: Server Error — the server failed to fulfill an apparently valid request.
- 6xx: Global Failure — the request cannot be fulfilled at any server.

The SIP error grouping is very similar to the HTTP error code grouping.

In this section, we are interested in any SIP Status Codes that begin with 4xx (Client Errors), 5xx (Server Errors) and 6xx (Global Failure).

4xx Request Failure

400	Bad Request
401	Unauthorized
402	Payment Required
403	Forbidden
404	Not Found
405	Method Not Allowed
406	Not Acceptable
407	Proxy Authentication Required
408	Request Timeout
409	Conflict
410	Gone

412	Conditional Request Failed [RFC 3903]
413	Request Entity Too Large
414	Request-URI Too Long
415	Unsupported Media Type
416	Unsupported URI Scheme
417	Unknown Resource-Priority [RFC4412]
420	Bad Extension
421	Extension Required
422	Session Interval Too Small [RFC4028]
423	Interval Too Brief
424	Bad Location Information [RFC 6442]
428	Use Identity Header [RFC 4474]
429	Provide Referrer Identity [RFC 3892]
430	Flow Failed [RFC 5626]
433	Anonymity Disallowed [RFC 5079]
436	Bad Identity-Info [RFC 4474]
437	Unsupported Certificate [RFC 4474]
438	Invalid Identity Header [RFC 4474]
439	First Hop Lacks Outbound Support [RFC 5626]
440	Max-Breadth Exceeded [RFC 5393]
469	Bad Info Package [RFC 6086]
470	Consent Needed [RFC 5360]
480	Temporarily Unavailable
481	Call/Transaction Does Not Exist
482	Loop Detected
483	Too Many Hops
484	Address Incomplete
485	Ambiguous
486	Busy Here
487	Request Terminated
488	Not Acceptable Here
489	Bad Event [RFC 6665]
491	Request Pending
493	Undecipherable
494	Security Agreement Required [RFC 3329]

5xx Server Failure

500	Server Internal Error
501	Not Implemented
502	Bad Gateway
503	Service Unavailable
504	Server Time-out
505	Version Not Supported
513	Message Too Large
580	Precondition Failure [RFC 3312]

6xx Global Failures

600	Busy Everywhere
603	Decline
604	Does Not Exist Anywhere
606	Not Acceptable

Wireshark Lab 80: Create and Use a "SIP Errors" Filter Expression Button

After this lab you will be able to click this one button to quickly identify SIP errors in your trace files.

Step 1:   Open **tr-voip-extension.pcapng**.

Step 2:   Click on **Packet 2**. This is the first SIP response in this trace file. The Info column indicates this is a 100 Trying response.

Step 3:   Right-click on the **Session Initiation Protocol (100)** line and select **Expand Subtrees**.

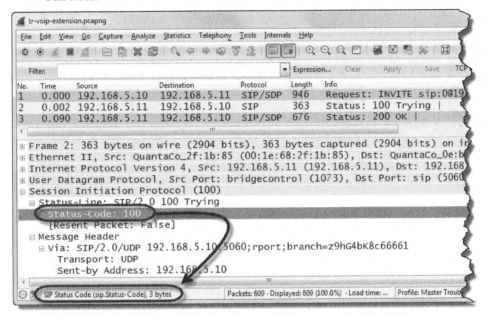

Step 4:   Enter `sip.Status-Code >= 400` in the display filter area and click **Save**. Name your new filter expression button **SIP Errors**.

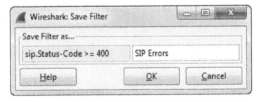

Step 5:   Click your new **SIP Errors** button to locate the two SIP error responses in this trace file. Two 488 Not Acceptable Here messages were sent from 192.168.5.11. This is where we would focus our troubleshooting efforts.

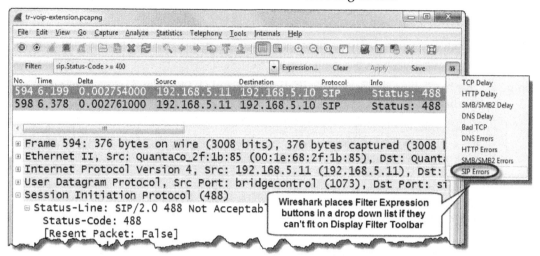

Step 6:   Click the **Clear** button to remove your filter.

What if you are interested in other application error codes? In the next section, we will look at how to create display filters to detect error responses from other applications.

Detect Error Responses of Other Applications

If Wireshark has a dissector for your application, building a filter expression button to detect the errors sent by your application is as simple as locating the response code field and determining what values indicate failures.

For example, let's use the Expression… button to locate and create a filter expression button for FTP errors.

Wireshark Lab 81: Build Other Application Error Filters and Filter Expression Buttons

In this lab we will use Wireshark's Expression function to determine the value of error responses and build our filter expression button.

Step 1:   Open **tr-ftpfail.pcapng**.

Step 2:   Click the **Expression** button on the Filter Display toolbar.

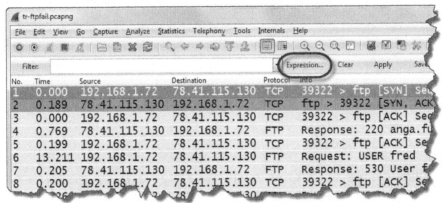

Step 3:   Type **ftp** to jump to the first match in the Field name area. We are not interested in the FTP DATA line. Expand the **FTP – File Transfer Protocol (FTP)** selection.

Step 4:   Scroll down and select **ftp.response.code – Response Code**. Notice the Predefined Values column is populated with response codes.[41]

---

[41]   The developers often do not populate the field values. For example, under HTTP, the **http.response.code** field does not contain any predefined values.

Step 5:   In the Relation area, click **==** to activate the Predefined Values column. If you
want to create a filter for a specific response code, you can select it from the list or
type the response code number in the Value area.

For example, if you want to create a display filter (and then a filter expression
button) for response code **Service Not Available; Closing Control
Connection (421)**, select that line and click **OK**.

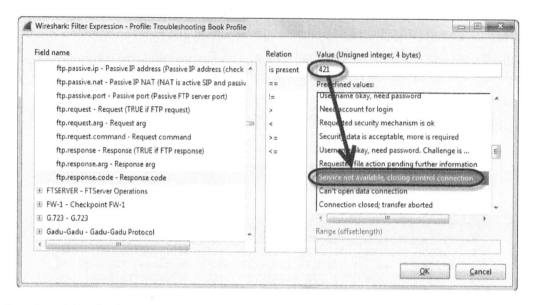

Step 6:   Wireshark creates a display filter for this FTP error (`ftp.response.code==421`).
If you want to save this as a filter expression button, simply click the **Save** button
in the display filter area and provide a button label. We will edit this filter before
saving it.

Step 7:   A quick Google for "ftp error response codes" reveals that any FTP response
code number over 399 indicates an error.

Change your filter to `ftp.response.code > 399` and click **Save**.[42] Name your
button **FTP Errors** and click **OK**.

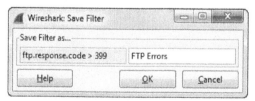

---

[42]   The filter `ftp.response.code >= 400` is functionally the same as `ftp.response.code > 399`.

Step 8:   Click your new **FTP Errors** button to apply it to this trace file. Two packets in this
trace file match your FTP errors filter. (Clear your filter when you are finished
reviewing the results of this lab.)

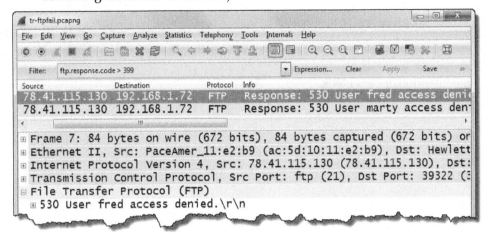

Use this same process to build other error buttons. If Wireshark does not have predefined
values for error responses, you can research the application or protocol to obtain those
response codes.

This page intentionally left blank.

Part 3: Use Graphs to Detect Problems

If you followed along with the *Troubleshooting Checklist* that began on page 27, you probably already know where the problems lie in your network communications.

Some graphs can help you prioritize your troubleshooting efforts. For example, if you open the IO Graph and notice three spots where the throughput drops suddenly, you can identify the most severe drop in throughput and start troubleshooting that problem first.

Graphs are also useful when you need to explain the issue to others in a visual manner.

"A picture is worth a thousand packets" to people who do not understand network analysis terminology or enjoy looking inside the TCP handshake options or headers. A graph depicting the throughput alongside indications of packet loss and recovery (the "Golden Graph") may help these folks understand the correlation between the two.

This page intentionally left blank.

CHAPTER 8: MASTER BASIC AND ADVANCED IO GRAPH FUNCTIONS

Since Wireshark's graphs are linked to the packets in the trace file, you can bring up a graph, spot an issue and click on the location of the problem. Wireshark jumps to that point in the trace file so you can analyze the situation further.

In *Chapter 5: Troubleshoot with Time*, we created a few graphs. In this chapter we will cover some basic and advanced IO graph functions before applying them to specific network problems.

A picture is worth a thousand packets.

Chapter 8 Notes

Although I often already know the cause of network problems before building graphs, these graphs can "paint a picture" of network problems and help explain what is causing performance issues.

- Use an IO Graph to compare the throughput of separate conversations.

- Use an IO Graph to compare application throughput based on port numbers in use.

- Consider using Advanced IO Graphs when you need the Calc functions (such as MIN, AVG, MAX).

Graph Individual Conversations

Many times your trace files will have intertwined conversations to/from multiple hosts. You may have lots of irrelevant traffic depending on where you capture (such as Spanning Tree traffic, OS update traffic, and virus detection signature update traffic).

The first skill you should master is the ability to graph a single conversation or a set of conversations. For example, you may want to graph the throughput level of a file download process captured in a trace file that contains numerous web browsing sessions and other background traffic.

There are several ways you can do this. You could apply a display filter for a conversation, save just that traffic in a separate trace file, and then graph the contents of the new file. Alternately you can use the original file and apply a display filter for the conversation of interest to your IO graph. This is the function we will practice in the next Wireshark Lab.

Wireshark Lab 82: Graph and Compare Throughput of Two Conversations

In this lab you will open a trace file that contains the traffic to and from two hosts. One host complains of slow download speeds from a site while the other host does not.

Step 1:   Open **tr-twohosts.pcapng**.

Step 2:   Select **Statistics | Conversations**. Notice that there are two IP conversations. We will graph and compare these two conversations based on the client IP addresses 192.168.1.72 and 192.168.1.119.

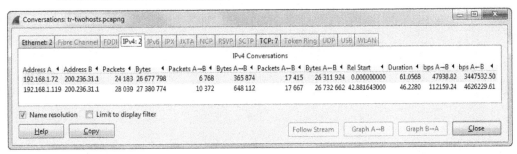

Step 3:   Click the **Close** button to close the **Conversations** window.

Select **Statistics | IO Graph**. The graph appears with a single graph line active—Graph 1. The black line represents the throughput of all traffic in the trace file.

By default, Wireshark graphs the throughput rate of all traffic based on packets per tick with each tick being one second. To change that, in the Y Axis Unit area, click the drop down arrow and select **Bits/Tick**. Notice the Y Axis automatically adjusts based on the maximum bits per second rate in the trace file.

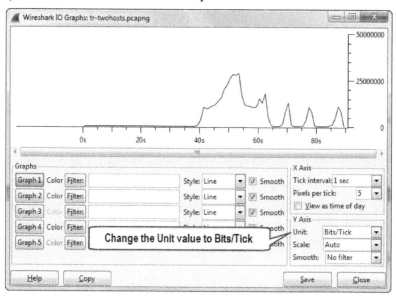

Step 4:   Click the **Graph 1** button to disable the black graph line.

In the Graph 2 Filter area, enter `ip.addr==192.168.1.72` and click the **Graph 2** button. Set the Style to **Dot**.

In the Graph 4 Filter area, enter `ip.addr==192.168.1.119` and click the **Graph 4** button. Leave the Style as **Line**.

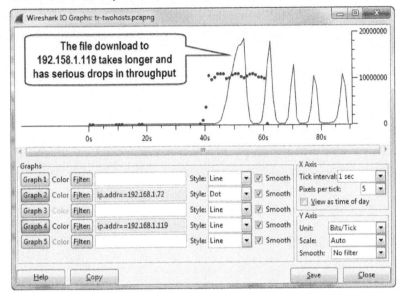

We can definitely see the difference in throughput between the two download processes. The download by 192.168.1.72 completes much more quickly than the download to 192.168.1.119.

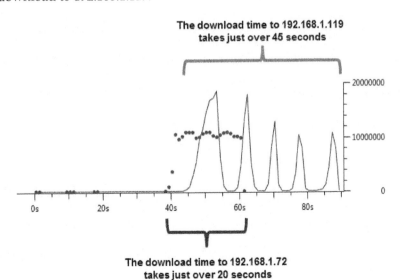

When we look at the Graph 4 line, we see large increases in throughput followed by drops to almost no throughput. The drops occur four times in the graph.

Those are the points we would examine more closely in the trace. Clicking around the near-zero throughput areas and toggling back to the main Wireshark window, you will see packet loss occurring at these points in the trace file.

The graph helped us see the effects of packet loss, but we would already know this was the issue by following the *Troubleshooting Checklist* that started on page 27. This issue would have been apparent when we opened the Expert Infos window.

Step 5:   Click the Close button when you are finished examining the graph.

Graph all Traffic for a Single Application

You can extract and graph a single application's traffic to perform throughput analysis for that one application.

When the application runs over TCP and you have the option of using an application name filter (such as **http**), it is recommend you use a port-based filter (such as **tcp.port==80**) instead in order to include the TCP overhead (such as TCP handshake packets, ACKs, FINs, and RSTs) in your graph.

UDP-based applications can be graphed using port numbers or application names.

Wireshark Lab 83: Graph and Compare Traffic for Two Applications

In this lab exercise you will open a trace file that contains FTP and HTTP traffic. You will graph the FTP traffic (including both FTP commands and data transfer) and the HTTP traffic based on the TCP port numbers in use.

Step 1:   Open **tr-ftphttp.pcapng**.

You'll notice the HTTP traffic runs over TCP port 80. We will use that port number for the HTTP graph line.

FTP data can run over any port so we will look at the conversations window to determine which port is used for the FTP file transfer.

Step 2:   Select **Statistics | Conversations | TCP**. Uncheck **Name resolution** to view the port numbers in use in these TCP conversations. This provides a list of all HTTP and FTP port numbers in use.

Port 80 is used for the HTTP traffic. Port 21 is used for the FTP command traffic. Port 22487 is used for the FTP data channel.

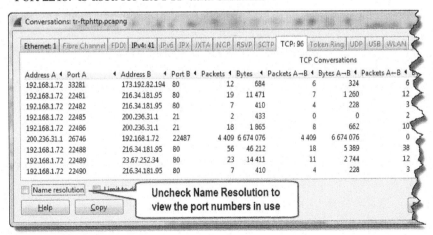

Step 3:   The Graph buttons on this window would open the TCP Time-Sequence graphs. We will use the IO graph, however. For more information on the TCP Time-Sequence graphs, see *Graph Packet Loss and Recovery* on page 295.

Click the **Close** button and return to the main Wireshark window.

Step 4:   Select **Statistics | IO Graph**. We will make numerous changes to this graph in order to compare the throughput of the HTTP traffic with the FTP traffic and be able to see the FTP command traffic.

Step 5:   First let's set up the graph area. Select **Bits/Tick** in the Y Axis Unit area. Click the **Graph 1** button to disable this graph line.

Step 6:   Enter the following filters in Graph 2 and Graph 4 Filter areas:

Graph 2 filter: `tcp.port==80` (line style)
Graph 4 filter: `tcp.port==21 or tcp.port==22487` (Impulse style)

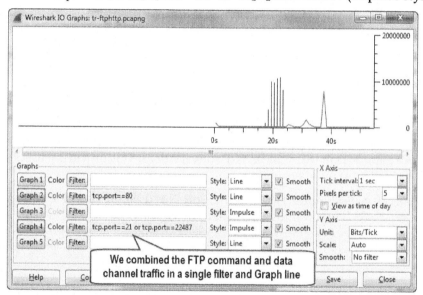

The graph indicates that the HTTP traffic is almost non-existent until approximately 39 seconds into the trace file. The FTP command/data channel traffic peaks at 20 seconds into the trace file.

The peak rates of traffic make it difficult to see if there is a lower rate of traffic at points in this trace file. Applying a logarithmic scale helps visualize the lower traffic rates.

Step 7:   In the Y Axis Scale area, click the dropdown menu to select **Logarithmic**. This changes the graph significantly.

Now we can see that the HTTP traffic rate is active, but not running at a high bits-per-second rate.

Remember to close the IO Graph when you are finished.

When graphing two disparate numbers, set the Y Axis Scale to logarithmic to view the smaller numbers alongside the larger numbers.

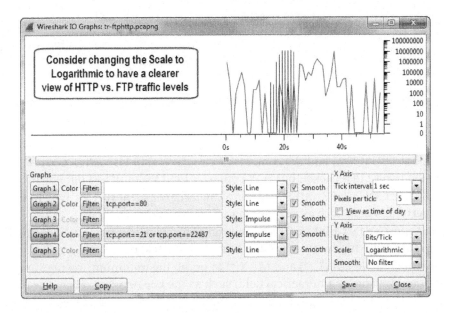

In *Correlate Drops in Throughput with TCP Problems (the "Golden Graph")* on page 280 you will use this logarithmic graphing technique to detect and correlate TCP-based problems with drops in throughput.

Use CALC Functions on the Advanced IO Graph

The Advanced IO Graph is accessible under the Y Axis Unit menu in the IO Graph (**Statistics | IO Graph**).

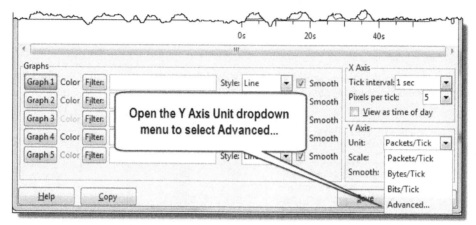

The Advanced IO Graph offers Calc functions for summing the contents of a field, counting the occurrences of a field and more.

- Use Calc: SUM(*) to add the contents of a numerical field, such as `tcp.len`, which does not exist in a packet, but is Wireshark's field to count just data bytes in packets.
- Use Calc: COUNT FRAMES(*) to count the occurrence of specific type of frame or Expert Infos item such as `tcp.analysis.retransmission`.
- Use Calc: COUNT FIELDS(*) to count the occurrence of a field, such as the IP ID (`ip.id`) field which occurs twice in some ICMP packets.
- Use Calc: MIN(*), AVG(*) and MAX(*) to graph the minimum, average and maximum value of a numerical field, such as the `tcp.window_size field`.
- Use Calc: LOAD(*) to graph response time fields, such as `smb.time`.

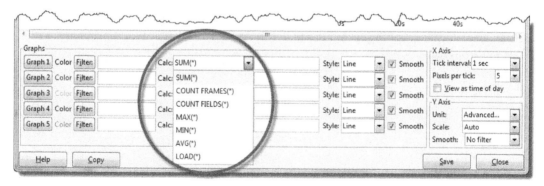

Let's run through a lab using some of these Calc functions.

Wireshark Lab 84: Graphing the TCP Payload Throughput with an Advanced IO Graph

There is no field in a packet called **tcp.len**, but Wireshark uses this value to define the number of data bytes in each TCP segment. We will use **tcp.len** to graph the throughput level of the payload only (no header values will be counted in our calculation).

Step 1:   Open **tr-twohosts.pcapng**.

This trace file depicts two hosts downloading files, 192.168.1.72 and 192.168.1.119.

Step 2:   Select **Statistics | IO Graph** and choose **Advanced...** in the Y Axis Unit dropdown menu.

Step 3:   In the Graph 2 area, enter **ip.dst==192.168.1.72** in the filter area. Leave the Calc value at **SUM(*)** and enter **tcp.len** to the right of the Calc area.

Click the **Graph 2** button.

Step 4:   In the Graph 3 area, enter **ip.dst==192.168.1.119** in the filter area. Leave the Calc value at **SUM(*)** and enter **tcp.len** to the right of the Calc area. Set the Style to **Impulse**.

Click the **Graph 3** button.

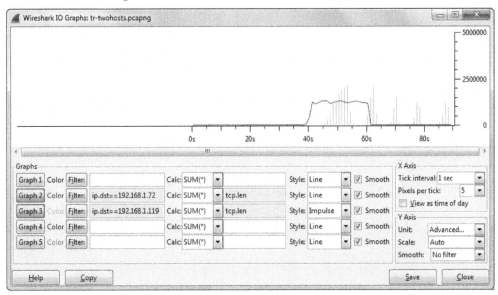

Unlike in Wireshark Lab 82, this graph depicts each file download throughput value without counting headers (Ethernet, IP or TCP).

We can easily see the download process to 192.168.1.72 is more efficient than the file download process to 192.168.1.119. The Graph 3 depiction of the download process indicates there are several points when the data transfer to 192.168.1.119 stops.

CHAPTER 9: GRAPH THROUGHPUT PROBLEMS

Now we will take a look at graphing throughput issues, including throttled traffic, traffic held in queues, and the "Golden Graph."

The Golden Graph plots TCP problems along side general throughput to look for a correlation between drops in throughput and increases in TCP problems. A lack of correlation indicates that the problem is not due to TCP issues such as packet loss or Zero Window conditions.

You will likely already know the cause of performance problems before moving to the graphing stage. The graphs are a good way to explain what is creating performance issues.

Chapter 9 Notes

The "Golden Graph" (based on an IO Graph) is one of my favorite graphs. I use this graph to correlate TCP problems with drops in through-put. Queuing along a path can also be detected using an IO Graph.

- Pull the Bad TCP coloring rule string into your IO graph to create the "Golden Graph."

- If your trace file only covers a short period of time, adjust the Tick interval.

- If you are comparing very different numerical values, use a logarithmic scale.

- Click on a point of concern in a graph to jump to that point in the trace file.

Detect Consistently Low Throughput due to Low Packet Sizes

Transferring files using small packet sizes is like going to the store to buy a dozen eggs and bringing them home one egg at a time. It will take too long.

Low packet sizes may be caused by an application that intentionally wants to transfer smaller amounts of data. Low packet sizes can also be an indication of a low Maximum Segment Size (MSS) setting.

A low MSS may be due to a misconfiguration at the client or even additional functionality (such as a VLAN driver loaded).

Wireshark Lab 85: Graph Low Throughput Due to Itty Bitty Stinkin' Packets

This trace file consists of an HTTPS connection between hosts. Since we do not have the key to decrypt the traffic, we can only analyze up to the point of the TCP layer.

Step 1:   Open **tr-throughput.pcapng**. Scroll through the trace file and look at your Length column value. There are a lot of small data packets in this trace file. First let's rule out low MSS settings as a reason for small packet sizes.

Step 2:   Examine the **TCP Option** section in Packet 1 and Packet 2. Notice the MSS values advertised by each host – Packet 1 and Packet 2 both advertise an MSS of 1,460 bytes. We know the MSS configuration isn't the reason for small packet sizes.

Step 3:   Select **Statistics | IO Graph**. Set the Y Axis Unit value to **Bits/Tick**. Change the Y Axis Scale to **2000**. Wow, that is a low throughput rate.

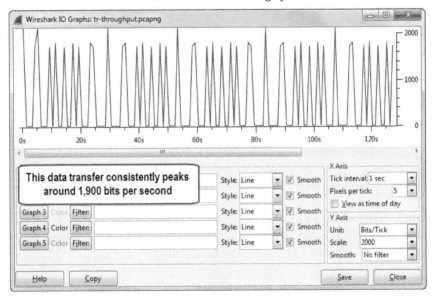

Step 4:   Now click **Close**. Select **Statistics | Summary**. This will give us the average packet size in the trace file.

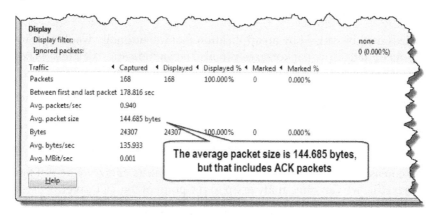

This average packet size includes ACK packets. Let's apply a filter to the traffic to determine the average data packet size.

Step 5:   Click **OK** to close the Summary window. Enter `tcp.len > 0` in the display filter area and click **Apply**. Now you are only seeing packets that contain data.

Step 6:   Select **Statistics | Summary**. Now look at the **Displayed** column. This column indicates the average data packet size is 213.011 bytes.

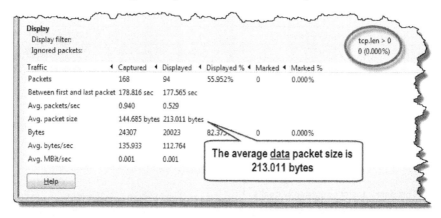

Why are smaller packets being used? We identified that it isn't a limitation defined by the TCP connection. This is likely an application setting. We must look at the application to determine if this is intentional or a configuration problem.

Identify Queuing Delays along a Path

Interconnecting devices can inject delays by queuing (holding the packets temporarily before forwarding them) along a path.

Consider using a traffic generator to detect queuing along a path. A tool such as iPerf/jPerf can be used to transmit traffic at a steady rate. We need that steady rate of transmission to identify distinct queuing patterns when you capture traffic on the other side of a queuing device.

In the next lab, we will look at the IO Graph indication of traffic that has been queued along the path.

Wireshark Lab 86: Identify the Queued Traffic Pattern in an IO Graph

This trace file contains a video multicast that transmits packets to the multicast address 239.255.0.1.

Step 1:   Open **tr-queuing.pcapng**.

Step 2:   Select **Statistics | IO Graph**. You will see a very boring graph. There are only 2,016 packets in the trace file and the packet transmit rate is over 1,100 packets per second.

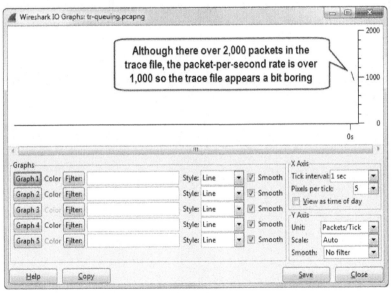

Step 3:   We must change the Tick interval to look more closely at the traffic. In the X Axis Tick Interval area, change the value from 1 sec to **0.01 sec**.

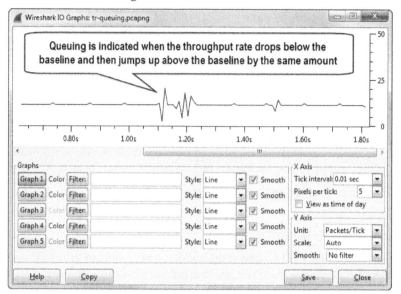

Now the queuing is easier to detect. Since the traffic is sent at a steady rate, we can establish a baseline for the traffic rate. When the traffic drops below the baseline and then pops up above the baseline by the same amount, we can deduce that the traffic has been queued along the path.

How do we know this is not a packet loss condition? Let's look into that in Step 4.

Step 4:   Leave the IO Graph open and toggle back to the main Wireshark window. Open
tr-notqueuing.pcapng.

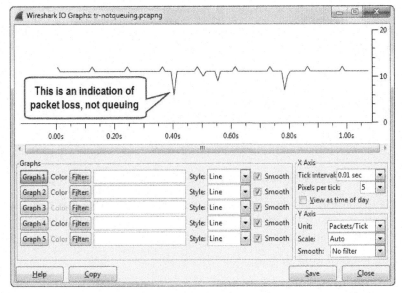

This time we see the graph line drops below the baseline and does *not* pop up above the
baseline. This is an indication of packet loss. There is no retransmission capability built into
the transport mechanism (UDP) and the application we used does not detect or retransmit
lost packets.

Next we will create the "Golden Graph" to correlate TCP problems with drops in
throughput. Remember to close the IO Graph when you are done with this lab.

Correlate Drops in Throughput with TCP Problems (the "Golden Graph")

This graph can determine if throughput issues are related to network problems such as lost packets or zero window sizes.

This is one of my favorite graphs (hence the name "Golden Graph"). Honestly though, when troubleshooting problems you want to find the problem quickly. This is a great graph, but a quick look at the Expert Infos warnings and notes would have indicated TCP problems already.

Wireshark Lab 87: Identify Network Problems with the "Golden Graph"

This trace file was captured as a client was connecting to a site and downloading a file using FTP. The download was very slow. We will create and use a Golden Graph to correlate performance issues with network problems.

Step 1:   Open **tr-goldengraph.pcapng**.

Step 2:   Select **Statistics | IO Graph**. In the Y Axis Unit area, change the value to **Bits/Tick**. (If you kept the IO Graph open from the previous lab, change the Tick interval to **1 sec**.)

Step 3:   Enter `tcp.analysis.flags && !tcp.analysis.window_update` in the Graph 2 filter area. This is the filter string used by the Bad TCP coloring rule. Click the **Graph 2** button.

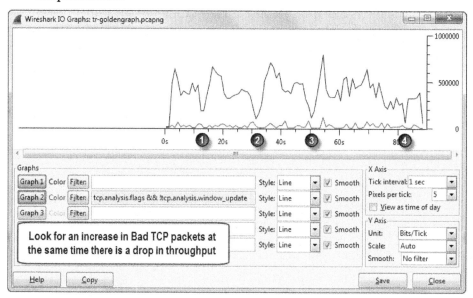

Examine the graph. There are four distinct points where throughput drops to almost zero. Although there are Bad TCP issues throughout this trace file, there is a slight increase in Bad TCP at the points where the throughput level drops.

Step 4:   Click on any of the **major throughput drops** on the graph. Toggle back to the main Wireshark window. You will notice a lot of packets colored with the Bad TCP coloring rule at those points in the trace file.

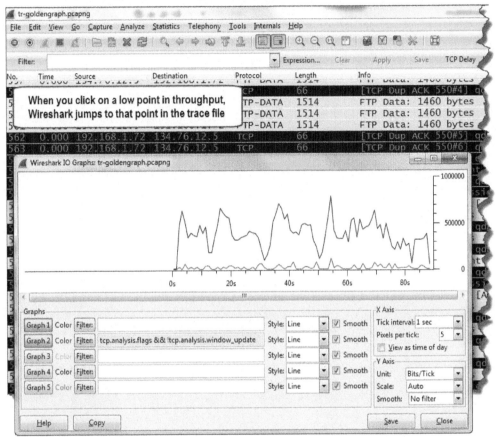

Consider changing the Y Axis Scale to logarithmic if the throughput rate is too high and the Bad TCP line is difficult to see. Don't forget to close the IO Graph when you are done with this lab.

This is a great graph to build whenever anyone complains about slow performance of a TCP-based application.

This page intentionally left blank.

CHAPTER 10: GRAPH TIME DELAYS

In this short chapter, you will graph slow DHCP server responses and then graph high TCP delta times.

Again, you likely know these problems exist by simply sorting the various time columns that you create. These graphs may help you explain the delays to management or non-technical people.

Chapter 10 Notes

You can graph Wireshark's response time fields to identify delays in the trace files. This is one of the best uses of Wireshark's Advanced IO Graph.

- Use the MAX Calc function to find the points when response times suddenly increased.

- You can graph Wireshark's primary time values (such as frame.time_delta), TCP time (tcp.time_delta), as well as application response times (http.time).

- These time values must be graphed in the Advanced IO Graph, not in the basic IO Graph.

Graph High Delta Times (UDP-Based Application)

In *Identify High DNS Response Time* on page 135, we added a **dns.time** column to detect DNS delays. Now we will graph the delta time for an application that does not have a delta time function — DHCP.

Wireshark Lab 88: Graph a Slow DHCP Server Response

This trace file contains only DHCP traffic. We are going to graph the response time of the DHCP Offer packets.

Step 1:   Open **tr-bootp.pcapng**.

Step 2:   Select **Statistics | IO Graph**.

Step 3:   In the Y Axis Unit area, select **Advanced...**

Step 4:   In the Filter area of Graph 1, enter **bootp.option.dhcp == 2**. This is the option used by DHCP Offer packets. In the Calc area, select **MAX(*)** and type **frame.time_delta**.

Click the **Graph 1** button.

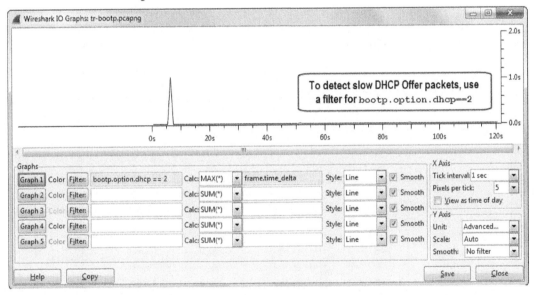

You can see there is one point in the trace file where the DHCP Offer arrived over 1 second after the previous frame. This is a great way to identify slow responses for an application that does not have a delta time function. Don't forget to close the IO Graph when you are done with this lab.

Graph High TCP Delta Time (TCP-Based Application)

Some TCP-based applications (such as HTTP and SMB) have a delta time tracking function in Wireshark. If the application does not have the delta time tracking function built into the dissector, you can still graph high delta times using `tcp.time_delta`.

We will practice graphing high TCP delta times in this lab.

Wireshark Lab 89: Graph and Analyze High TCP Delta Times

This trace file contains a single encrypted TCP conversation. We will need to use Wireshark's `tcp.time_delta` function because we do not have an application delta time function available to us.

Step 1:   Open **tr-tcpdeltatime.pcapng**.

Step 2:   Select **Statistics | IO Graph**. In the Y Axis Unit area, select **Advanced...**

Step 3:   In the Graph 2 Calc area, select **MIN(*)** and enter `tcp.time_delta`. Click the **Graph 2** button to enable this graph.

Step 4:   In the Graph 3 Calc area, select **AVG(*)** and enter `tcp.time_delta`. Set the Style to **Impulse** and click the **Graph 3** button to enable this graph.

Step 5:   In the Graph 4 Calc area, select **MAX(*)** and enter `tcp.time_delta`. Set the Style to **Dot** and click the **Graph 4** button to enable this graph.

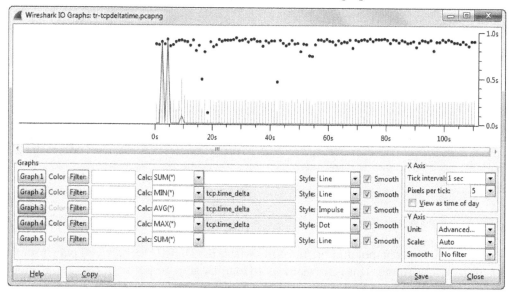

The graph clearly shows that the average response time in the trace file is slightly less than 300 ms and there are higher TCP response times in the beginning of the trace file.

When you use more than one graph in this window, keep in mind that Graph 1 is in the foreground and Graph 5 is in the background. If you use the Fbar style on Graph 1 and that graph plots the highest points in the IO Graph, the Fbar graph may block Graphs 2-5 from view.

You can use this `tcp.time_delta` graph to detect high response times for any TCP-based application.

This page intentionally left blank.

CHAPTER 11: GRAPH OTHER NETWORK PROBLEMS

Once again, you probably already detected these problems by checking the Expert Infos window or adding and sorting custom columns, but you can use these additional graphs to create a picture of various network problems.

Chapter 11 Notes

Consider building pictures of other network problems, such as receiver congestion and packet loss/recovery processes.

- You can graph window size issues based on the TCP analysis flag (tcp.analysis.zero_window) or the actual Calculated Window Size field value.

- You can graph packet loss and recovery processes using the TCP analysis flags for each part of the process.

- Although the TCP Time-Sequence graph can be very busy, it can depict not only packet loss, duplicate ACKs and retransmissions, but it can also depict Selective ACKs.

Graph Window Size Problems

Wireshark can identify Zero Window problems through the Expert Infos function, but there is no "Low Window" detection capability. Window size problems can be detected by adding and sorting a Window Size column (`tcp.window_size`), or by creating a graph of the Window Size field value.

In this section, we will first graph Window Size issues using `tcp.analysis` filters. Then we will graph Window Size issues using the Advanced IO Graph and the TCP Stream Graph/Window Size Graph.

Wireshark Lab 90: Graph Window Size Issues Using TCP Analysis Filters

In this trace file, a client is trying to watch a video on YouTube. The video download appears to stall at several points. We will use an IO Graph to watch the decreasing TCP Window Size value of the client.

Step 1:   Open **tr-youtubebad.pcapng**.

Step 2:   Select **Statistics | IO Graph**. In the Y Axis Unit area, select **Advanced...**

Step 3:   In the Graph 2 Calc area, select **COUNT FRAMES(*)** and enter `tcp.analysis.window_full`. Set the Style to **Dot**. Click the **Graph 2** button to enable this graph.

Step 4:   In the Graph 3 Calc area, select **COUNT FRAMES(*)** and enter `tcp.analysis.zero_window`. Set the Style to **FBar**. Click the **Graph 3** button to enable this graph.

Step 5:   In the Graph 4 Calc area, select **COUNT FRAMES(*)** and enter `tcp.analysis.window_update`. Set the Style to **FBar**. Click the **Graph 4** button to enable this graph.

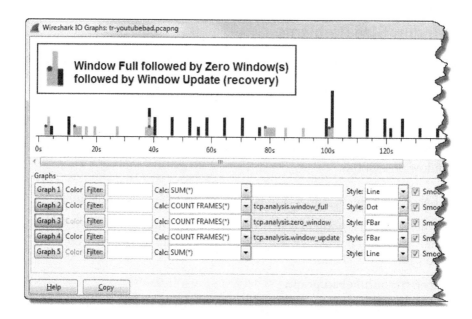

This graph clearly depicts the Zero Window problem from the point that the Window Full Expert Infos warning is seen through the recovery process (Window Updates). You can also see the periodic Window Updates throughout the trace file.

Don't forget to close the IO Graph when you are done with this lab.

Wireshark Lab 91: Graph Window Size Issues Using the Calculated Window Size Field and Window Size Graph

Now we will use an Advanced IO Graph and Wireshark's TCP Stream Graph/Window Size Graph to watch the decreasing TCP Window Size value advertised by the client.

Step 1:   Open **tr-youtubebad.pcapng**.

Step 2:   Select **Statistics | IO Graph**. In the Y Axis Unit area, select **Advanced...**

Step 3:   In the Graph 2 filter area, enter **ip.src==24.4.7.217**. In the Calc area, select **AVG(*)** and enter **tcp.window_size**. Click the **Graph 2** button to enable this graph.

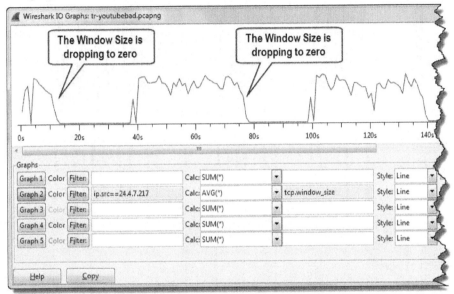

We can see there are several points in this trace file where the client's application is not picking up data from the buffer. The client's advertised window size decreases until it reaches zero.

If you click on this graph at the points where the line reaches zero, Wireshark jumps to that point in the trace file. You will see Window Full, Zero Window and TCP Keep-Alive packets at this point in the trace file.

Unfortunately, the Window Size graph line does not disappear when there are no packets in the trace file—such as when the data transfer stops completely. If you click on those flat-line points, Wireshark will not jump to the packets because there are none at that location. Click just before or just after the flat-line spots to see what happened immediately before or immediately after the points where we see no throughput.

Step 4:   Wireshark also offers a Window Scaling Graph.

Toggle back to the main Wireshark window.

Click on a packet sent from **24.4.7.217** in the Packet List pane. Select **Statistics | TCP Stream Graph | Window Scaling Graph**.

Every dot in the graph represents a Window Size field value in a packet. When a spot in the graph does not have a dot there are no packets to plot. This is another way to graph a low or zero window size issue.

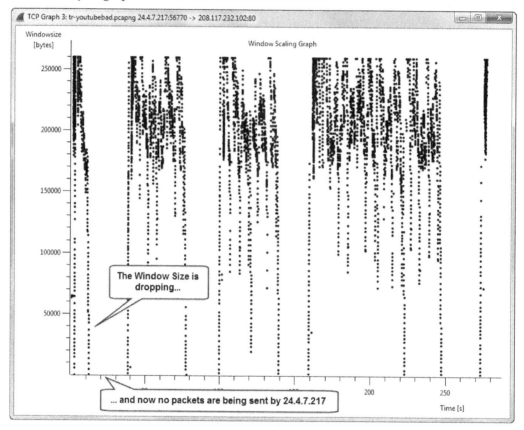

The Window Scaling Graph can be a bit difficult to understand because it will fit the entire trace file within one window—there is no scroll bar across the bottom.

Fortunately you can click and drag over an area to zoom in to investigate a point in the graph further.

Don't forget to close the IO Graph and Window Scaling Graph when you are done with this lab.

Graph Packet Loss and Recovery

If you've read this book in order from front to back, you already know how you can use the Expert Infos window to detect packet loss and recovery. You also know how to examine the TCP handshake and Duplicate ACKs to determine if SACK is in use.

In this section we will graph indications of packet loss using `tcp.analysis` filters. Then we will graph Window Size issues using the Advanced IO Graph and the TCP Stream Graph/TCP Time-Sequence Graph.

Wireshark Lab 92: Graph Packet Loss and Recovery Using TCP Analysis Filters

This trace file consists of an FTP download process.

Step 1:   Open **tr-goldengraph.pcapng**.

Step 2:   Select **Statistics | IO Graph**. In the Y Axis Unit area, select **Advanced...**

Step 3:   Set the X Axis Tick Interval to **0.1 sec**.

Step 4:   In the Graph 2 Calc area, select **COUNT FRAMES(*)** and enter `tcp.analysis.lost_segment`. Set the Style to **Line**. Click the **Graph 2** button to enable this graph.

Step 5:   In the Graph 3 Calc area, select **COUNT FRAMES(*)** and enter `tcp.analysis.duplicate_ack`. Set the Style to **Impulse**. Click the **Graph 3** button to enable this graph.

Step 6:   In the Graph 4 Calc area, select **COUNT FRAMES(*)** and enter `tcp.analysis.retransmission`. Set the Style to **Dot**. Click the **Graph 4** button to enable this graph.

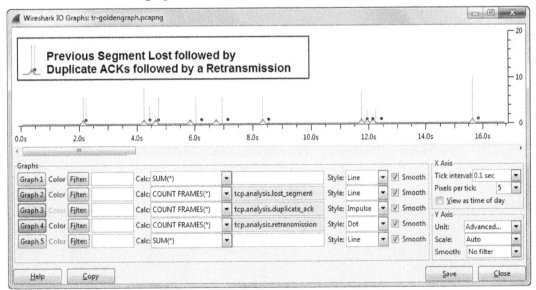

This graph clearly depicts the points in the trace where Wireshark noticed packet loss. In addition, the graph depicts the packet loss recovery process by graphing Duplicate ACKs and Retransmissions.

Remember to close the IO Graph when you are done with this lab.

Next we will use the TCP Time-Sequence graph on the same trace file to get a more detailed look at what happened in this trace file.

Wireshark Lab 93: Graph Packet Loss and Recovery Using the TCP Time-Sequence Graph

Now we will use Wireshark's TCP Stream Graph/Time-Sequence Graph to view packet loss and recovery. This graph will also depict SACK if it is in use.

Step 1:   Open **tr-goldengraph.pcapng**. Click on **Packet 27** in the Packet List pane. The TCP Time-Sequence Graph is graph is a unidirectional graph—make sure you click on a packet traveling in the same direction as the data flow before launching the graph.

Step 2:   Select **Statistics | TCP Stream Graph | Time-Sequence Graph (tcptrace)**.

Ideally, this graph would depict a straight line (created with "ɪ" markers) from the lower left corner to the upper right corner.

Step 3:   Click and drag over a **very small portion of the graphed line** at approximately the 10-second mark. (Click the Home button if you need to reset the zoom level to its original setting.)

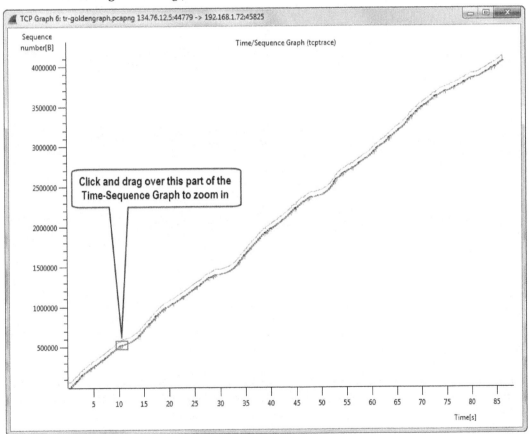

When you zoom in at this point in the trace file, you can see the following indications of packet loss and recovery:

① A blank area in the "I" bar line indicates a segment is missing.

② The first ACK requesting the missing packet is seen on the horizontal line.

③ The blue lines increase in size as the SACK right edge expands.

④ The Fast Retransmission finally appears.

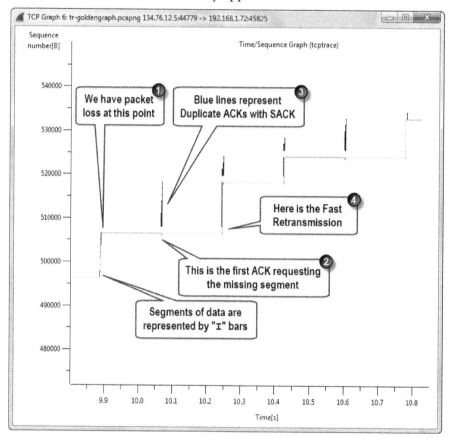

Although you can detect packet loss with a filter for `tcp.analysis.flags && !tcp.analysis.window_update` or a quick glimpse at the Expert Infos window, this Time-Sequence graph can be used to build a picture of the problem.

We've seen numerous Wireshark graphs in this Chapter. There are times when you may want to export your data for manipulation with a 3rd party graphing tool. We will look at some options for exporting and graphing in the next chapter.

Chapter 12: Export Traffic to Graph in 3rd Party Tools

Wireshark's graphing capabilities may not provide the flexibility available with third-party products such as Microsoft Excel or OpenOffice Calc.

In this section, you will learn how to export packet information and any field value in comma-separated value (CSV) format.

Chapter 12 Notes

Sometimes you need to use third-party tools to do further analysis of the traffic.

- All columns (whether hidden or visible) will be exported when you export packet dissections (Summary).

- You can easily export your packet and trace file comments to create a quick report of your analysis findings.

Export Packet List Pane Columns to CSV Format

We will start by exporting packet information and field values in comma-separated value (CSV) format. We will use our custom columns to include specific information in our exported data.

Wireshark Lab 94: Export All Columns to CSV Format

We've added numerous custom columns to our profile in this book. When we perform this export function, Wireshark will export all those columns regardless of whether the column is visible or hidden.

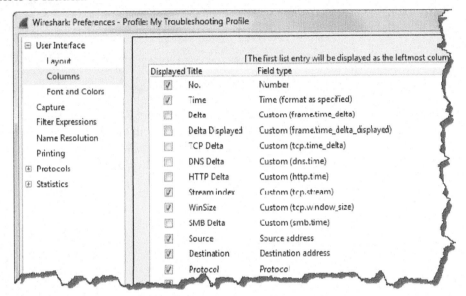

Step 1:   Open **tr-chappellu.pcapng**.

Step 2:   Select **File | Export Packet Dissections | as "CSV"** (Comma Separated Values packet summary) file…

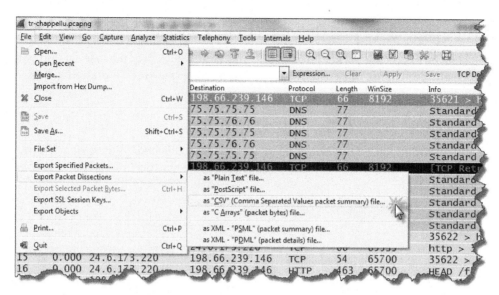

Step 3:   By default, Wireshark selects Displayed in the Packet Range area. We did not apply a display filter so the desired information on all of our packets will be exported. Check only **Packet summary line** in the Packet Format area and enter the name **tr-chappellu.csv** in the File Name area. Click **Save**.

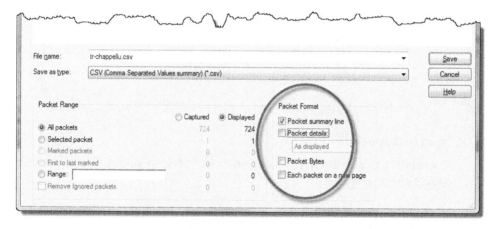

Step 4:   Open your **tr-chappellu.csv** file in a spreadsheet program. In the image that
follows we opened the file in Excel.

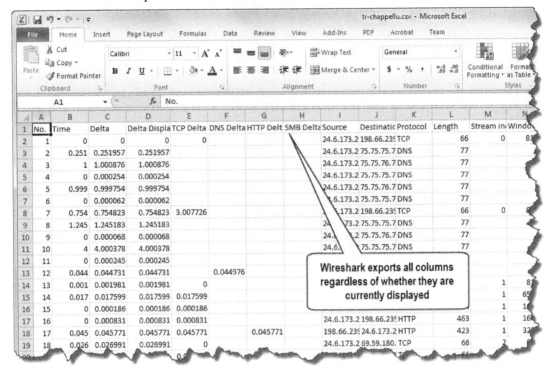

Now you can manipulate this CSV data into whatever format your spreadsheet program allows. For example, if you want to depict the total packet lengths in a 3-D graph in Excel, you can simply select the **Length** column then **Insert | Line | 3-D Line**. The image below shows the result of this process.

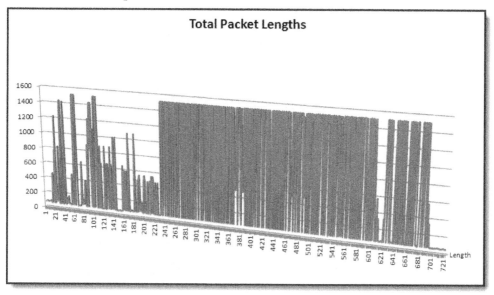

Export Your Trace File/Packet Comments Report

One of the advantages of saving trace files in .pcapng format is that this format can contain metadata about the trace file. Two of these metadata items are trace file comments and packet comments.

Adding trace file comments and packet comments can help share your trace file findings with others.

Examine the Trace File Annotation button to quickly determine if a trace file contains an annotation.

   The trace file does not contain an annotation yet (add annotation).

   The trace file does contain an annotation (view, edit annotation).

You can easily export the entire set of trace file and packet comments in ASCII format.

Wireshark Lab 95: Add and Export Trace File and Packet Comments

Step 1:   Open **tr-chappellu.pcapng**.

Step 2:   First we will add to an existing trace file comment.[43] Click the **Trace File Annotation** button on the Status Bar and add a **simple message** about this trace file before the copyright message. Click **OK**.

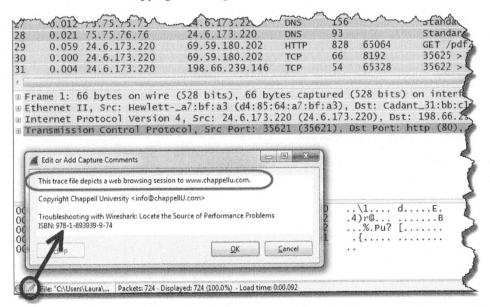

---

43   You can use these same steps to create a new trace file comment.

Step 3:   Now right-click on **Packet 11** in the Packet List pane. Select **Packet comment...** and enter a **short note** about this DNS retransmission. Click **OK**.

The Title Bar adds an asterisk before the file name to indicate the trace file has been changed. If you want to keep your trace file or packet comments you must click the **Save** button 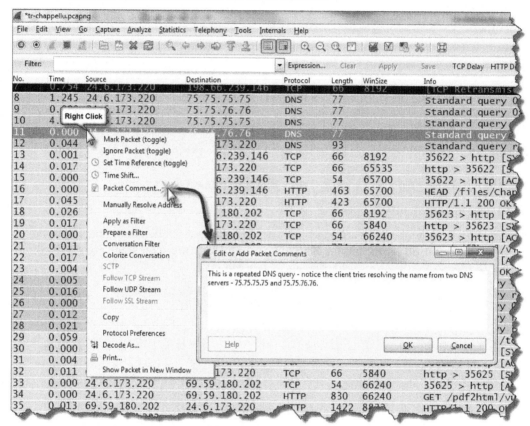 on the Main Toolbar.

Step 4:   Now we will export our trace file and packet comment. Select **Statistics |**
Comments Summary.

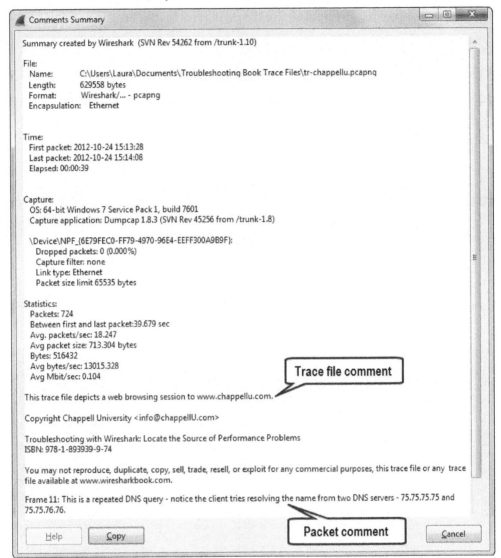

Step 5:   Click **Copy** to buffer the Comment Summary. This can now be pasted into a text
editor or word processing program. Click the **Cancel** button to close the
Comment Summary window.

Next we will export packets to .txt format.

Export Packets to TXT Format

There may be times when you want to export a single packet for use in an analysis report. Following these steps you can import one or more packets in .txt format.

Wireshark Lab 96: Export Unusual DNS Server Failures

Step 1:   Open **tr-chappellu.pcapng**.

Step 2:   Click your **DNS Errors** button (`dns.flags.rcode > 0`). Two packets (Packet 83 and Packet 84) are displayed.

Step 3:   Select Packet 83 and click the **(+)** in front of the **Domain Name System (response)** section.

Step 4:   Click the **(+)** in front of the **Answers** section.

```
⊞ Frame 83: 400 bytes on wire (3200 bits), 400 bytes captured (3200 bits) on interfac
⊞ Ethernet II, Src: Cadant_31:bb:c1 (00:01:5c:31:bb:c1), Dst: Hewlett-_a7:bf:a3 (d4:85
⊞ Internet Protocol Version 4, Src: 75.75.75.75 (75.75.75.75), Dst: 24.6.173.220 (24.6
⊞ User Datagram Protocol, Src Port: domain (53), Dst Port: 56007 (56007)
⊟ Domain Name System (response)
    [Request In: 82]
    [Time: 0.008743000 seconds]
    Transaction ID: 0xfd77
  ⊞ Flags: 0x8182 Standard query response, Server failure
    Questions: 1
    Answer RRs: 20          ┌─────────────────────────────────────┐
    Authority RRs: 0        │  Expand the Answers sections - this is the way │
    Additional RRs: 0       │  the .txt version of the packet will be expanded │
  ⊞ Queries                 └─────────────────────────────────────┘
  ⊟ Answers
    ⊞ www.nitroreader.com: type CNAME, class IN, cname cf-ss117247-protected-www.nitro
    ⊞ cf-ss117247-protected-www.nitroreader.com: type CNAME, class IN, cname direct-con
    ⊞ direct-connect.nitroreader.com: type CNAME, class IN, cname direct-connect.nitror
    ⊞ direct-connect.nitroreader.com: type CNAME, class IN, cname direct-connect.nitror
    ⊞ direct-connect.nitroreader.com: type CNAME, class IN, cname direct-connect.nitror
    ⊞ direct-connect.nitroreader.com: type CNAME, class IN, cname direct-connect.nitro
    ⊞ direct-connect.nitroreader.com: type CNAME, class IN, cname direct-connect.nitron
    ⊞ direct-connect.nitroreader.com: type CNAME, class IN, cname direct-connect.nitron
    ⊞ direct-connect.nitroreader.com: type CNAME, class IN, cname direct-connect.nitror
    ⊞ direct-connect.nitroreader.com: type CNAME, class IN, cname direct-connect.nitrop
    ⊞ direct-connect.nitroreader.com: type CNAME, class IN, cname direct-connect.nitror
    ⊞ direct-connect.nitroreader.com: type CNAME, class IN, cname direct-connect.nitror
    ⊞ direct-connect.nitroreader.com: type CNAME, class IN, cname direct-connect.nitrore
    ⊞ direct-connect.nitroreader.com: type CNAME, class IN, cname direct-connect.nitro
    ⊞ direct-connect.nitroreader.com: type CNAME, class IN, cname direct-connect.nitro
    ⊞ direct-connect.nitroreader.com: type CNAME, class IN, cname direct-connect.nitror
    ⊞ direct-connect.nitroreader.com: type CNAME, class IN, cname direct-connect.nitron
    ⊞ direct-connect.nitroreader.com: type CNAME, class IN, cname direct-connect.nitro
    ⊞ direct-connect.nitroreader.com: type CNAME, class IN, cname direct-connect.nitro
```

Step 5:   Select **File | Export Packet Dissections | as "Plain Text" file...** Again, by
            default, Wireshark will export the displayed packets only.

Step 6:   Name your file *dns-serverfailure.txt* and select only **Packet Details | As
            displayed**. Click **Save**.

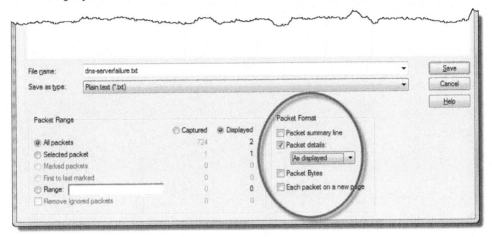

You now have a .txt file that contains the two packets formatted just as you saw them in the
Packet Details pane.

This page intentionally left blank.

Part 4: Final Tips for Troubleshooting with Wireshark

This page intentionally left blank.

CHAPTER 13: FINAL TIPS

The most difficult element of writing this book was to determine what to include and what to exclude.

On one hand, I wanted to include everything I've learned over 20 years of analyzing networks. On the other hand, I wanted the book to be less than 5,000 pages.

This chapter contains some of my final tips—items that didn't seem to fit cleanly in any other section or items that I want to call to your attention.

Laura Chappell

Chapter 13 Notes

There are many tips and tricks listed in this chapter. From tips for working with large trace files to tips for detecting 802.11 network problems.

- Check out Cascade Pilot, which was created to open large trace files, visualize traffic patterns and quickly build reports.

- Use Wireshark's file set and ring buffer capabilities to identify the cause of intermittent problems.

- Filter on 802.11 retries and watch signal strength when troubleshoooting WLAN networks.

- Visit ask.wireshark.org when you get stuck - the Wireshark community is very supportive.

Tips for Working with Large Trace Files

Wireshark performance can become degraded or Wireshark might even crash when opening very large trace files.

I try to keep my Wireshark trace files to 100 MB size maximum. As I add more columns and coloring rules, larger files load too slowly and applying filters can take too long.

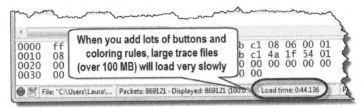

We will cover three options to consider when your trace files become too large.

Split Large Files with Editcap

Editcap is a free command-line tool that is installed in the Wireshark Program File directory during the Wireshark installation. Use the parameters **–i** to specify the seconds per file or use **–c** to specify the packets per file.

Syntax: `editcap <infile> <outfile>`

Example: `editcap –c 20000 bigfile.pcapng smallerfiles.pcapng`

Editcap will create a group of files that begin with "*smallerfiles*," contain a file number and end with a date and time stamp. When working with these files in Wireshark, select **File | File Set | List Files**.

This option is not suitable if you need to perform reassembly of traffic that will be split across multiple files.

If you want to know how many packets are in the file or how much time transpired in seconds, use Capinfos. Capinfos is another tool that is automatically installed in the Wireshark Program File directory. Simply type `capinfos <filename>` to view the trace file details.

Create a Trace File Subset with Tshark and Display Filters

Extract specific packets of interest using Tshark with display filters to create a subset with which to work.

Syntax: `tshark –r <infile> -Y "<display filter>" -w <outfile>`

Example: `tshark –r bigfile.pcapng -Y "ip.src==10.1.1.1" –w 10.pcapng`

This option may take a long time when extracting a subset from a large trace file.

It is a good idea to make a habit of using quotes around your display filters when using Tshark. The quotes are required when display filters have spaces in them.

Open Large Trace Files in Cascade Pilot (aka "Pilot")

Pilot was designed to open, visualize and export customized reports on the contents of very large trace files. In Pilot, you simply click and drag a view over a trace file to create a chart or graph.

Some of my favorite views in Pilot are circled in the following images.

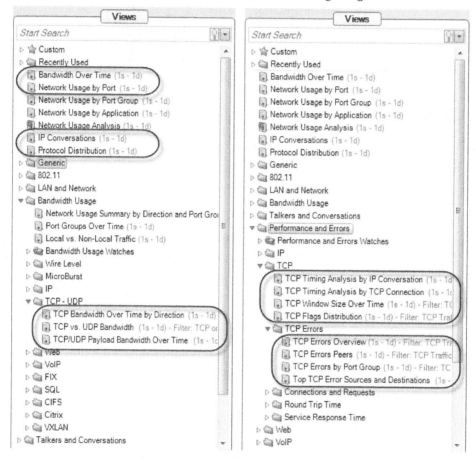

In the image that follows we opened a 1.3 GB trace file (*monsterfile.pcapng*[44]) and applied several views to the file. The TCP Flags Distribution view is in the foreground. When examining the file in Pilot we quickly found that we have some illegal TCP handshake packets in the file. We were not aware that we had a malicious host on our lab network until we opened this view.

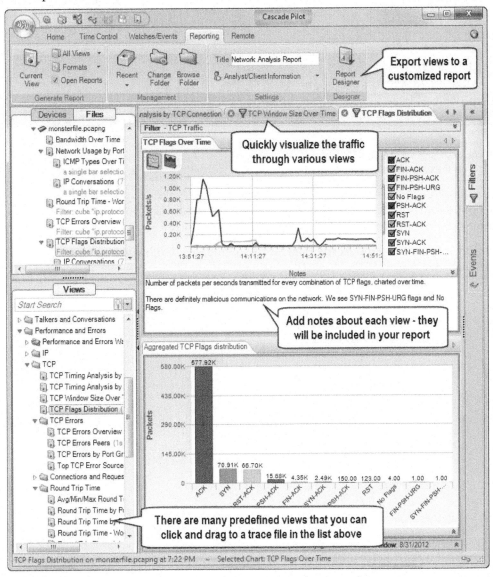

---

[44]   I did not distribute this file with the book supplements because it is too large to work with in Wireshark.

In the lower graph (Aggregated TCP Flags Distribution), we selected both unusual flag settings (No Flags and SYN-FIN-PSH…). Using right-click functionality we exported these illegal packets to Wireshark for further analysis. We identified 24.6.181.160 as the suspect machine on the network.

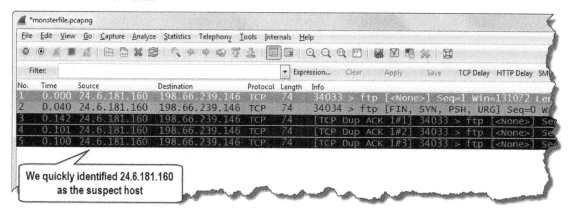

The book supplements (available at www.wiresharkbook.com/troubleshooting.html) include a sample network analysis report created with Cascade Pilot.

For more information on Cascade Pilot, or to download a demo version, visit www.riverbed.com.

Tips for Naming Your Trace Files

It is very frustrating to open a directory of trace files called *trace1.pcapng*, *trace2.pcapng*, and *trace3.pcapng*. Define a useful naming scheme for your trace files as soon as possible. Consider including capture location, capture purpose and any notes about the trace file in your trace file names.

Here are some examples of trace file names that are long, but give you an idea of what might be contained in the trace file.

- *sw1-msmith-slowsalesforce.pcapng*
- *sw1-msmith-backgroundidle.pcapng*
- *local-gspicer-slowbrowse.pcapng*
- *local-gspicer-uploadstuck.pcapng*
- *fs2-disconnects.pcapng*
- *rtr2side1-slowpath.pcapng*
- *rtr2side2-slowpath.pcapng*

You may also consider keeping a log book for your capture sessions. Enter the trace file name and a quick description of what you see. This can help when you document the troubleshooting process for management, if necessary.

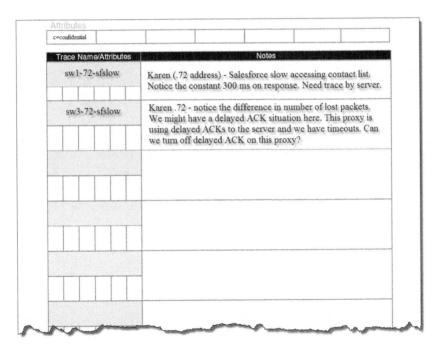

These notes can also be placed directly in your trace files using trace file annotation and packet annotation.

Tips for Detecting Security vs. Performance Issues

Keep in mind that lousy device communications may be caused by misconfigurations or possibly a compromise on the host. For example, if the entire network is being flooded with broadcasts, consider that there may be a misconfiguration leading to this problem or hosts may be compromised by malicious software that launched a network discovery process. Perhaps a bot is attempting to discover and infect other hosts on the network.

You cannot separate the task of network troubleshooting from network forensics. You should always be on the lookout for suspicious traffic patterns.

In *Open Large Trace Files in Cascade Pilot* on page 316, we were looking for the cause of poor performance, but located illegal TCP flags in the packets.

We opened the TCP Flags Distribution View of a trace file and noted TCP packets that have no TCP flags set (No Flags) and TCP packets that have illogical flags set (SYN-FIN-PSH-URG). Both of these are indications of a client that may be compromised or even a user that may be running a reconnaissance application (such as Nmap or Nessus).

If we were working with a smaller trace in Wireshark, we could apply a filter for `tcp.flags == 0x000 || tcp.flags == 0x02B` to locate these illegal TCP flag values.

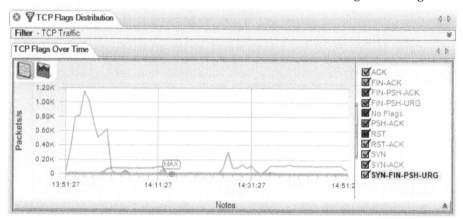

Tips for Quickly Creating the "Golden Graph"

In *Correlate Drops in Throughput with TCP Problems (the "Golden Graph")* on page 280 we created the "Golden Graph" – an IO Graph with the Bad TCP coloring rule filter string applied on Graph 2.

If you create this graph often, typing in the Bad TCP coloring rule filter string may be tedious. To speed up the process, save the Bad TCP coloring rule filter string as a display filter.

Wireshark Lab 97: Save a Bad TCP Display Filter for the Golden Graph

Step 1:   Open **tr-problemstream.pcapng**.

Step 2:   Click the **Display Filters** button 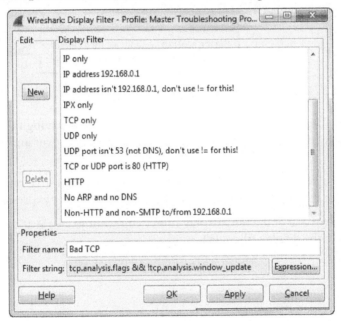 on the Main Toolbar. Click **New**.

Step 3:   Enter **Bad TCP** for the filter name and `tcp.analysis.flags &&`
`!tcp.analysis.window_update` for the filter string. Click **OK**.

Step 4:   Wireshark will automatically apply your new display filter. Click the **Clear** button.

Step 5:   Let's create the Golden Graph using this new display filer. Select **Statistics | IO Graph**.

Step 6:   Click the **Graph 2 Filter** button and select your **Bad TCP** display filter and click **OK**. Change the Style for Graph 2 to **FBar** and click the **Graph 2** button to enable the graph.

Step 7:   Change the Tick Interval to **0.1 sec**, the Y Axis Unit to **Bits/Tick**, and the Y Axis Scale to **Logarithmic**. Scroll left and right through the graph to see where the problem occurs during this file transfer.

Notice how this problem affects the throughput rate as TCP tries to recover.

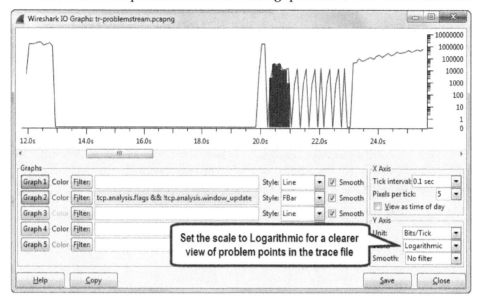

In the "olden days" (prior to Wireshark 1.8), we would focus on saving numerous display filters in the display filters list (*dfilters* file) that we want to apply over and over again to trace files.

With the creation of filter expression buttons, however, we do not save many display filters in the display filter list. Instead, we save our display filters as filter expression buttons.

This is an example of one of the few display filters you want to create and save the "old-fashioned" way, in the display filters list.

Tips for Analyzing TCP-Based Applications

TCP is a very popular transport mechanism. TCP is used for web browsing sessions, email communications, file transfer applications and more. You can troubleshoot these TCP-based communications more quickly by following these simple steps.

- ☐ Look at the TCP handshake to get a snapshot of round trip time.
  - o If capturing at the client, measure the time between the SYN and the SYN/ACK.
  - o If capturing at the server, measure the time between the SYN/ACK and ACK.
- ☐ Open SYN and SYN/ACK packets and examine TCP peer capabilities (TCP Options).
  - o Decent MSS size?
  - o SACK supported by both?
  - o Window Scaling supported by both?
  - o Decent scaling factor?
- ☐ Launch the IO Graph and look for drops in throughput.
  - o Add the Bad TCP coloring rule filter to the IO Graph to correlate drops in throughput with TCP issues (the Golden Graph).
- ☐ Open the Expert Infos to view detected problems.
  - o Focus on Errors, Warnings and Notes.
  - o Expand sections and click on packets to jump to that location in the trace file and explore further.
- ☐ View and sort the TCP Delta column (`tcp.time_delta`).
  - o Sort the column from high to low and examine delays.
  - o Do not get distracted by "normal delays" (refer to *Do not Focus on "Normal" or Acceptable Delays* on page 107).
- ☐ View and sort the Calculated window size field to look for issues.
  - o Do not worry about FIN or RST packets with Window 0 values.
  - o Look for low window size values and delays in close proximity.

Consider building on to this TCP troubleshooting checklist as you gain more experience in detecting TCP issues.

Tips for Locating the Cause of Intermittent Problems

It can be very frustrating to learn about a problem and then find that it is an intermittent problem. How do you capture the traffic during the time when the problem is occurring? Consider using a Ring Buffer during the capture process.

The Ring Buffer is a capture option that limits the number of files saved when you are automatically capturing files to disk. Use the Ring Buffer to avoid filling up a hard drive during automatic captures.

To capture intermittent problems, set up a capture machine close to one of the machines that experiences the problem. Use a tap if possible. Start capturing traffic to a file set and define the number of files to be saved by the Ring Buffer. Do not set an auto stop condition—stop the capture as soon as possible after the problem occurs.

The image below shows a possible setting to capture an intermittent problem.

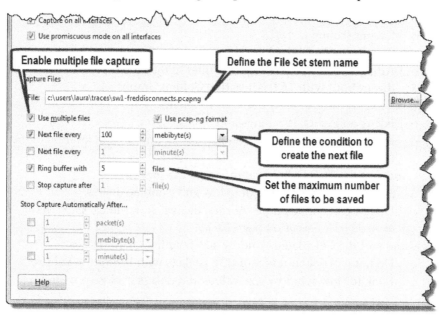

Stop the capture as soon as possible after the problem occurs. Consider asking the user to contact you when the problem occurs.

When you stop capturing the last file is displayed. Work backwards through this file and then the other files in the file set to locate the problem. Select **File | File Set | List Files** to view and navigate between files in the file set.

Tips for Detecting WLAN Problems

To troubleshoot WLAN traffic, you must capture the traffic properly. That means you need to capture the 802.11 Management, Control and Data frames, the 802.11 header, and have a pseudoheader applied — either a Radiotap header or PPI (Per Packet Information) header.

Capture Management, Control and Data Frames

Management and Control frames are necessary to identify problems with associating and authenticating to a WLAN. Data frames provide us with the actual throughput rates on a WLAN.

Prepend Radiotap or PPI Headers

Radiotap and PPI headers contain metadata on the received frame. This metadata includes the signal strength and frequency at the time of receipt. Low signal strength can be an indication of a weak transmit signal or a sender that is too far away. The frequency value tells us on what channel the packet arrived.

Capture the 802.11 Header

This may seem like an easy task, but if you use your native WLAN adapter for the capture, that adapter will likely strip off the 802.11 header. Wireshark will display an Ethernet header in its place.

The 802.11 header contains a Retry bit (`wlan.fc.retry`) setting that indicates if the packet is an 802.11 retry. This is a MAC-layer retransmission. For example, a local 802.11 device sends a data packet to the Access Point. If an 802.11 ACK is not returned within the ACK timeout, the data packet will be retransmitted with the Retry bit set to 1.

```
⊞ Frame 1: 122 bytes on wire (976 bits), 122 bytes captured
⊞ Radiotap Header v0, Length 20
⊟ IEEE 802.11 QoS Data, Flags: ....R..T.
    Type/Subtype: QoS Data (0x28)        WLAN Retries are sent then
  ⊟ Frame Control Field: 0x8809           the ACK Timeout expires
      .... ..00 = Version: 0
      .... 10.. = Type: Data frame (2)
      1000 .... = Subtype: 8
  ⊟ Flags: 0x09
      .... ..01 = DS status: Frame from STA to DS via an AP
      .... .0.. = More Fragments: This is the last fragment
    ⊞ .... 1... = Retry: Frame is being retransmitted
      ...0 .... = PWR MGT: STA will stay up
      ..0. .... = More Data: No data buffered
      .0.. .... = Protected flag: Data is not protected
      0... .... = Order flag: Not strictly ordered
```

ACK time outs may occur because the signal strength of ACKs are too weak or interference (collisions) may have corrupted the ACK packets.

Wireshark Lab 98: Filter on WLAN Retries and Examine Signal Strength

Step 1:   Open **tr-wlanissues.pcapng**.

This traffic was captured using an AirPcap adapter. The Radiotap headers are visible as are the 802.11 headers.

Step 2:   Right-click on the **IEEE 802.11 QoS Data, Flags: ....R..T** line in Packet 1 and select **Expand Subtrees**.

Step 3:   The Retry bit resides under the Flags section in the Frame Control area. Right-click on the **Retry bit** field and select **Apply as Filter | Selected**. Wireshark creates and applies a display filter for **wlan.fc.retry == 1**.

In this trace file, 1,664 packets (64.1% of the traffic) are MAC layer retransmissions. The ACK timeout value expired at the sender, so the packets needed to be resent.

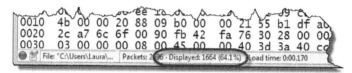

Step 4:   Notice that Packets 8, 9, and 10 are all GET requests for the same file, *sor.css*. Wireshark has marked them as TCP Retransmissions and the Retry bit is set in each packet.

Let's examine the SSI (Signal Strength Indication) Signal (dBm) value in these packets. This information is sent up from the WLAN adapter driver. A strong SSI Signal (dBm) would be closer to zero. For example, -20 dBm is a stronger signal than -70 dBm.

Right-click on the **Radiotap Header** line in Packet 8 and select **Expand Subtrees**.

Then right-click on the **SSI Signal (dBm)** line and select **Apply as Column**.

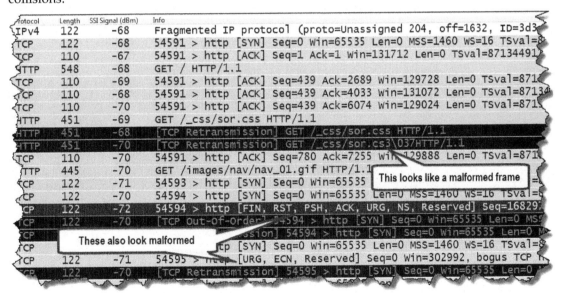

```
⊞ Frame 8: 451 bytes on wire (3608 bits), 451 bytes
⊟ Radiotap Header v0, Length 20
    Header revision: 0
    Header pad: 0
    Header length: 20
  ⊞ Present flags
  ⊞ Flags: 0x10
    Data Rate: 36.0 Mb/s
    Channel frequency: 2412 [BG 1]
  ⊞ Channel type: 802.11g (pure-g) (0x00c0)
    SSI Signal: -69 dBm          ── Watch the SSI Signal value
    SSI Noise: -100 dBm
    Signal Quality: 55
    Antenna: 0
    SSI Signal: 31 dB
⊟ IEEE 802.11 QoS Data, Flags: ....R..T.
    Type/Subtype: QoS Data (0x28)
  ⊟ Frame Control Field: 0x8809
      .... ..00 = Version: 0
      ... 10.. = Type: Data frame (2)
```

Also consider looking for malformed frames. Malformed frames appear in the Expert Infos Errors area and may be an indication of a Wireshark dissector error, a weak signal, or collisions.

Protocol	Length	SSI Signal (dBm)	Info
IPv4	122	-68	Fragmented IP protocol (proto=Unassigned 204, off=1632, ID=3d3
TCP	122	-68	54591 > http [SYN] Seq=0 Win=65535 Len=0 MSS=1460 WS=16 TSval=8
TCP	110	-67	54591 > http [ACK] Seq=1 Ack=1 Win=131712 Len=0 TSval=87134491
HTTP	548	-68	GET / HTTP/1.1
TCP	110	-69	54591 > http [ACK] Seq=439 Ack=2689 Win=129728 Len=0 TSval=871
TCP	110	-68	54591 > http [ACK] Seq=439 Ack=4033 Win=131072 Len=0 TSval=87134
TCP	110	-70	54591 > http [ACK] Seq=439 Ack=6074 Win=129024 Len=0 TSval=871
HTTP	451	-69	GET /_css/sor.css HTTP/1.1
HTTP	451	-68	[TCP Retransmission] GET /_css/sor.css HTTP/1.1
HTTP	451	-70	[TCP Retransmission] GET /_css/sor.cs3\037HTTP/1.1
TCP	110	-70	54591 > http [ACK] Seq=780 Ack=7255 Win=129888 Len=0 TSval=871
HTTP	445	-70	GET /images/nav/nav_01.gif HTTP/1.1
TCP	122	-71	54593 > http [SYN] Seq=0 Win=65535
TCP	122	-70	54594 > http [SYN] Seq=0 Win=65535 Len=0 MSS=1460 WS=16 TSval=6
TCP	122	-72	54594 > http [FIN, RST, PSH, ACK, URG, NS, Reserved] Seq=16829
TCP	122	-70	[TCP Out-Of-Order] 54594 > http [SYN] Seq=0 Win=65535 Len=0 MS
TCP			ssion] 54594 > http [SYN] Seq=0 Win=65535 Len=0 M
TCP			tp [SYN] Seq=0 Win=65535 Len=0 MSS=1460 WS=16 TSval=8
TCP	122	-71	54595 > http [URG, ECN, Reserved] Seq=0 Win=302992, bogus TCP
TCP	122	-70	[TCP Retransmission] 54595 > http [SYN] Seq=0 Win=65535 Len=0

This looks like a malformed frame

These also look malformed

This trace file shows a classic WLAN problem of packet loss. At the point of capture we see some of the client's packets are corrupt and many of the packets are retransmissions.

If we were capturing close to the Access Point, we'd move closer to the client to see if distance is the issue or when corruption appears. We'd watch for the location at which corruption does not appear and the signal strength is adequate.

If you are serious about analyzing and troubleshooting WLANs, consider investing in the Wi-Spy adapter and Chanalyzer software from MetaGeek (www.metageek.net).

Using Wireshark, we can capture the traffic and see what the packets look like, but the Wi-Spy adapter and Chanalyzer software can be used to diagnose issues with radio frequency (RF) signals.

Tips for Sanitizing Trace Files

Security rule: Never share trace files that may contain confidential information.

Now that we've set the record straight on that issue, there may be times when you must break that rule to send a trace file to a vendor or share a trace file with other Wireshark users at ask.wireshark.org. There are several ways to sanitize your trace files, but many "dedicated sanitizers" do not recognize .pcapng format, cannot work with VLAN tags, or cannot sanitize IPv6 traffic.

As of version 10.5, Wireshark still has a security flaw where it leaks name resolution information in trace files. The trace file tr-problemstream.pcapng offers an example of this information leak. This trace file was saved as a subset of a much larger trace file. If you select Statistics | Show address resolution, you will see a list of host names that are not related to this subset trace file. This problem is defined further in Wireshark bug 8349 (bugs.wireshark.org/bugzilla/show_bug.cgi?id=8349).

Edit Trace Files with a Hex Editor

You could use a hex editor (such as Hex Editor Neo, available at www.hhdsoftware.com) and perform a search and replace for specific values (such as the company or project name). This method does not recalculate any header checksums on packets that contain changes. If you enable Ethernet, IP, UDP, or TCP checksum validation these packets will generate checksum errors.

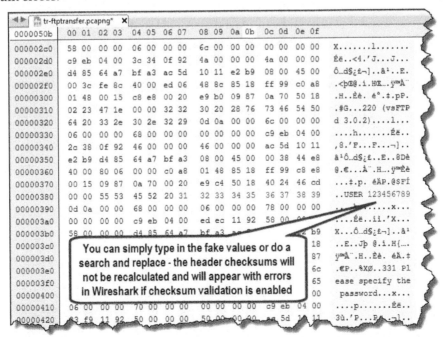

Use TraceWrangler

Jasper Bongertz, one of the Wireshark Core Developers, created TraceWrangler (available at www.tracewrangler.com), a Windows-based trace sanitization tool. TraceWrangler was created specifically to sanitize .pcapng files. You can find a video of Jasper Bongertz's Sharkfest 2013 presentation entitled "Trace File Sanitization NG" at www.lovemytool.com. TraceWrangler is a welcome addition to every analyst's toolkit.

The following image shows the TraceWrangler configuration to change all IPv4 addresses that begin with 133.24 to 10.24. The host portion of the addresses will be retained.

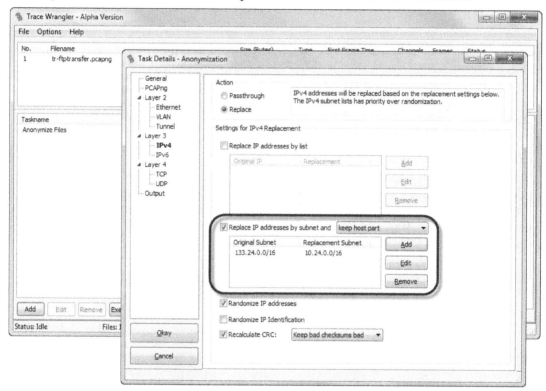

Tips for Faster Problem Detection

You need to know what is "normal" in order to spot anomalies. Baseline trace files depict traffic when things are going well.

These baselines can help you define normal behavior. For example, a baseline trace file of a login process should be created when the login procedure works well. If someone complains about the login process at a later date, you can compare the trace file of the current poor login performance to the baseline trace file. Are there large differences in the packet count? Are there errors in the newer trace file? Are there large delays in the newer trace file? A simple comparison between the two trace files can help spot where the problem lies.

The following lists some of the network traffic that you may want to baseline:

- Computer boot up sequence
- Computer shutdown sequence
- Login sequence
- Logout sequence
- Application launch sequence
- Common application tasks
- Application shutdown sequence
- Traceroute to target

Save these trace files in a special location so they do not get lost. In addition, consider creating a new baseline trace file set when you update network components, software or design.

Tips to Learn How TCP/IP Works

You must know TCP/IP well (including network, transport and application-layer elements) to spot performance problems quickly.

Analyze Your Own Traffic

One of the best ways to learn how TCP/IP and applications work is to capture and analyze your own traffic. You can do this at home or at the office (with appropriate permission, of course).

Start capturing traffic without using a capture filter. Toggle to an application, such as a web browser and visit a web site. When the main site page has loaded, toggle back to Wireshark and stop your capture. Analyze the traffic you captured.

For example, in **tr-ietfwithbackground.pcapng** we started capturing traffic on a lab machine, opened Internet Explorer and browsed to www.ietf.org.

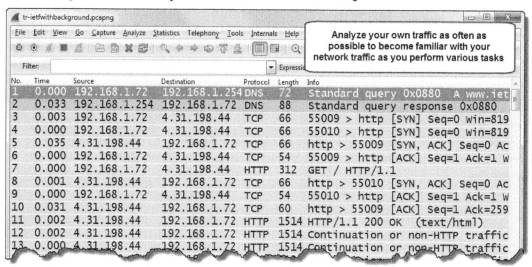

Examining **tr-ietfwithbackground.pcapng**, we notice the following characteristics:

- The client's IP address is 192.158.1.72. The client's MAC address is d4:85:64:a7:bf:a3. The OUI friendly name ("Hewlett-") indicates the client may be using an HP computer. [Packet 1]
- The DNS server is located at 192.168.1.254. [Packet 1 and Packet 2]
- The DNS server responded in approximately 33 ms. [Packet 1 and Packet 2]
- The HTTP server (www.ietf.org) is located at 4.31.198.44. [Packet 2]
- The client supports SACK and Window Scaling, with a scaling factor of 4 (shift count 2), as well as an MSS of 1,460 bytes. [Packet 3]
- The IETF server supports SACK and Window Scaling, with a scaling factor of 128 (shift count 7), as well as an MSS of 1,460 bytes. [Packet 5]

- The TCP handshake SYN-SYN/ACK indicates the round trip time is approximately 35 ms. [Packet 3 and Packet 5]
- The client is running Internet Explorer v10.0 on a Windows 64-bit host. [Packet 7]
- The IANA web server appears to be running Apache/2.2.22 (Linux/SUSE). [Packet 11]
- The client browser uses the Microsoft phishing filter (URL Reputation Service). [Packet 50 and TCP communications to/from 207.46.15.253]
- The client is running Dropbox. [Packet 151 and Packet 152]
- There is a dual-stack host at MAC address 40:61:86:3c:a9:84 that supports Zero Configuration networking (ZeroConf). [Packet 161 through Packet 166]

Try to make a habit of capturing and analyzing your own traffic as often as possible. You have control over the application, so it is often easier to spot the related traffic in the trace file.

Tips for When You Get Stuck

There will be times when the traffic just does not make sense. You have some resources available to you in these situations.

- If the question concerns a protocol, such as TCP, there are numerous educational resources on the Internet and, of course, the RFCs (www.ietf.org).
- There are also a number of resources listed at www.wiresharkbook.com/resources.html.

If you need assistance with Wireshark functionality or packet interpretation, consider asking for help at ask.wireshark.org.

Before you ask your question, enter key terms in the Search area and click the Search button to find out if anyone has asked a question about the topic. You will find that a number of the Wireshark developers, and even Gerald Combs himself, hang out at ask.wireshark.org.

APPENDIX A: CREATE A COMPLETE WIRESHARK TROUBLESHOOTING PROFILE

Wireshark is a relatively generic packet analysis tool. With the exception of a few default coloring rules and expert notifications, Wireshark is not customized for in-depth troubleshooting. It is a piece of clay—you can mold it into an ideal troubleshooting tool with very little effort.

That is exactly what you will do in this chapter.

First you have the opportunity to import a premade troubleshooting profile from the www.wiresharkbook.com web site. Consider adding further customization to that profile so it reflects your network times and traffic. For example, if you want to know if HTTP redirections are occurring, add an "HTTP Redirect" filter expression button (`http.response.code > 299 && http.response.code < 400`).

This chapter provides step-by-step instructions for creating a Troubleshooting Profile. You do not have to be a Wireshark wizard to perform these steps—you just need to set aside about 15 minutes to get it done.

You are working in a profile called "Default" when you launch a new installation of Wireshark. Unless you add new profiles, you remain working in this default state—not ideal for troubleshooting.

This page intentionally left blank.

Import Laura's Troubleshooting Profile

The profile building process should only take 15 minutes, but you may not have 15 minutes to spare right now. People are screaming at you constantly and you resort to hiding in your car at lunch to read this book.[45] In that case, this next lab walks you through the process of importing a Troubleshooting Profile that is available at the www.wiresharkbook.com web site.

Wireshark Lab 99: Import a Troubleshooting Profile

Step 1:   Visit www.wiresharkbook.com/troubleshooting.html and download the troubleshooting profile (*Troubleshooting_Book_Profile.zip*).

Step 2:   In Wireshark, select **Help | About Wireshark | Folders**. Double click on the link to your **Personal Configuration folder**.

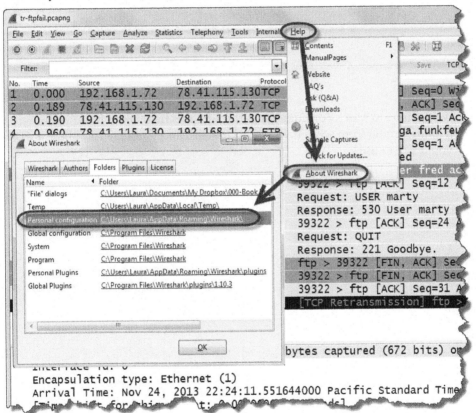

---

[45] I can relate to that. In my first real technical job I hid in my car at lunch time to read the manual on the hot new NBI master-slave system that I'd been plopped in front of. As I'd only worked on the "master" side before, I had no idea how to turn on the Slave side... I would have fired me if I didn't figure it out fast.

Step 3:   If you already have a *profiles* directory[46], copy the *Troubleshooting_Book_Profile.zip* file into that directory and unzip the file.

If you do not have a *profiles* directory, just create one. Copy the *Troubleshooting_Book_Profile.zip* file into that directory and unzip the file.

Your directory should look like the image below.

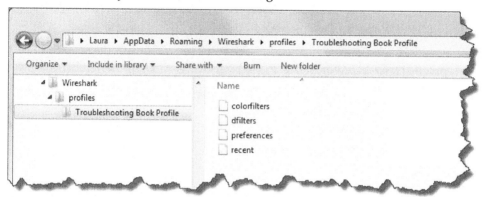

If you have the time to spare, consider going through this final lab to build your own troubleshooting profile from scratch. It is good practice and you may find there are other settings you'd like to use.

---

[46]   You will definitely have a *profiles* directory if you've followed along with the labs in this book.

Do It Yourself: Build Your New Troubleshooting Profile

Your new Troubleshooting Profile will contain all the column settings, protocol preferences, coloring rules and time values to speed up your troubleshooting processes. These settings were used in the labs throughout this book.

Wireshark Lab 100:   Create a Troubleshooting Profile

CREATE THE PROFILE

Step 1:   Right-click the **Profile** column on the Status Bar and click **New**.

Step 2:   In the Configuration Profile window, expand the **Create From** section and select **Global | Classic**. Name your new profile **My Troubleshooting Profile**. Click **OK** to close the Profile Window.

The Wireshark Status Bar now indicates that you are working in **My Troubleshooting Profile**.

SET PREFERENCES

Step 3:   Since bad checksums are typically due to task offload, we will disable Ethernet, IP, UDP and TCP checksum validation first[47]. Click the **Preferences** ⬡ button on the Main Toolbar.

Expand the **Protocols** section, select each of these protocols, and change these settings:

Ethernet	Disable *Validate the Ethernet checksum if possible*
IPv4	Disable *Validate the IPv4 checksum if possible*
UDP	Disable *Validate the UDP checksum if possible*
TCP	Disable *Validate the TCP checksum if possible*

Step 4:   Do not close the Preferences window yet. We have two more TCP settings to change:

TCP	Disable *Allow subdissector to reassemble TCP streams*
TCP	Enable *Calculate conversation timestamps*

Click **OK** to close the Preferences window.

---

[47]   The UDP and TCP checksum validation settings are disabled by default, but if you updated Wireshark and retained some older settings, they may still be enabled.

CUSTOMIZE TIME SETTINGS AND ADD A NEW TCP DELTA COLUMN

Step 5:   Now let's work with settings related to time. First, let's change the Time Column Setting.

Select **View | Time Display Format** and set the Time column to **Seconds Since Previous Displayed Packet**.

(Optional) Return to **View | Time Display Format** and set the precision to **Milliseconds: 0.123**.

Step 6:   Open **tr-chappellu.pcapng** and select Packet 16.

In the Packet Details pane, right-click on the **TCP header** section and select **Expand Subtrees**.

Right-click on the **Time since previous frame in this TCP stream: 0.000831000 seconds** line and select **Apply as Column**.

Right-click on the heading of this new column and select **Edit Column Details**. Enter **TCP Delta** in the **Title** area. Click **OK**.

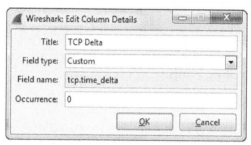

ADD OTHER COLUMNS OF INTEREST

Step 7:   Right-click on the following fields in the packets listed below and select **Apply as Column**. Right-click on the new column names, select **Edit Column Details** and rename the column as listed below.

Packet 14:   **TCP Header – Stream Index field**
Name: Stream#

Packet 14:   **TCP Header – Sequence Number field**
Name: SEQ#

Packet 14:   **TCP Header – Next Sequence Number field**
Name: NXTSEQ#

Packet 14:   **TCP Header – Acknowledgment Number field**
Name: ACK#

Packet 14:   **TCP Header – Calculated window size field**
Name: WinSize

Packet 14:   **TCP Header – Bytes in Flight (inside [SEQ/ACK Analysis]) field**
Name: Bytes in Flight

Packet 16:   **HTTP Header – HTTP Host field**
Name: HTTP Host

Packet 23:   **HTTP Header – Time Since Request field**
Name: HTTP Delta

Packet 25:   **DNS Header – Time field**
Name: DNS Delta

Step 8:   Open **tr-smb-slow.pcapng**. In this case you will create an SMB Time column twice and then edit the second column to display SMB2 time.

Packet 5:   **SMB Header – Time Since Request**
Name: SMB Time

Packet 5:   **SMB Header – Time Since Request**
Name: SMB2 Time
Field name: `smb2.time`

REALIGN AND HIDE COLUMNS

Step 9:   Right-click on the following column headings and set their alignment to **Left**:

No.
Length
Stream#
SEQ#
NXTSEQ#
ACK#
WinSize
Bytes in Flight
Host
HTTP Delta
DNS Delta
SMB Time
SMB2 Time

Step 10:   Right-click on the following columns and select **Hide**. When you want to view the columns again, right-click any column heading and select them from the **Displayed Columns** list.

> TCP Delta (created in Step 6 of this lab)
> Stream#
> SEQ#
> NXTSEQ#
> ACK#
> WinSize
> Bytes in Flight
> Host
> HTTP Delta
> DNS Delta
> SMB Time
> SMB2 Time

ADD NEW FILTER EXPRESSION BUTTONS

Step 11:   Enter the following display filter values, click **Save** and name each of these new filter expression buttons, as shown below[48]:

Name:	**TCP Delay**
Filter:	`tcp.time_delta > 1 && tcp.flags.fin==0 &&`
	`tcp.flags.reset==0 && !http.request.method=="GET"`

Name:	**HTTP Delay**
Filter:	`http.time > 1`

Name:	**SMB/SMB2 Delay**
Filter:	`smb.time > 1 || smb2.time > 1`

Name:	**DNS Delay**
Filter:	`dns.time > 1`

Name:	**Bad TCP**
Filter:	`tcp.analysis.flags && !tcp.analysis.window_update`

Name:	**DNS Errors**
Filter:	`dns.flags.rcode > 0`

Name:	**HTTP Errors**
Filter:	`http.response.code >= 400`

---

[48]   If you do not want to type all this button information separately, you could pull the **Filter Expressions** section from the *preferences* file contained in the *Troubleshooting_Book_Profile.zip* file that is available at www.wiresharkbook.com/troubleshooting.html.

Name:	**SMB/SMB2 Errors**
Filter:	`smb.nt_status > 0 || smb2.nt_status > 0`

Name:	**SIP Errors**
Filter:	`sip.Status-Code >= 400`

Name:	**FTP Errors**
Filter:	`ftp.response.code > 399`

Name:	**WLAN Retries**
Filter:	`wlan.fc.retry==1`

Great! You've done it!

If you want to share your new profile with another Wireshark user, simply select **Help | About Wireshark | Folders** and open your personal configuration directory. Navigate to the *profiles* directory.

Zip up the *My Troubleshooting Profile* directory to a file and send it to the other Wireshark user. Instruct them to unzip the file inside their *profiles* directory.

Voila! They should now see the new profile is available when they click the profiles column in the Status Bar.

This page intentionally left blank.

APPENDIX B:
TRACE FILE DESCRIPTIONS

The book web site (www.wiresharkbook.com) contains all the trace files mentioned in this book. Please note the license for use below and on the book web site.

You agree to indemnify and hold Protocol Analysis Institute and its subsidiaries, affiliates, officers, agents, employees, partners and licensors harmless from any claim or demand, including reasonable attorneys' fees, made by any third party due to or arising out of your use of the included trace files, your violation of the TOS, or your violation of any rights of another.

NO COMMERCIAL REUSE

You may not reproduce, duplicate, copy, sell, trade, resell, or exploit for any commercial purposes, any of the trace files available at www.wiresharkbook.com.

This page intentionally left blank.

tr-australia.pcapng

This trace file contains a web browsing session and was captured at the client. Pay particular attention to the RTT value between these hosts.

tr-badcapture.pcapng

This trace file was obtained using a faulty capture device. Look for the signs that the capture was not done properly — especially ACKed Unseen Segment indications.

tr-bootp.pcapng

This trace file contains traffic that indicates a DHCP server was slow in responding. For this trace file analysis, your time column(s) can be used to determine the length of the delays.

tr-chappellu.pcapng

This trace file contains a web browsing session to chappellu.com. The trace file contains some HTTP error responses and some TCP delays. What happens when the client tries to connect to 184.73.250.227?

tr-checksums.pcapng

This trace file was captured at a host that supports task offloading. If you enable Wireshark's IP checksum validation feature, all traffic from the host supporting task offload will appear colored by the Checksum Errors coloring rule.

tr-cnn.pcapng

This is a basic web browsing session to www.cnn.com. Test your filter expression buttons on this trace file. You should see TCP Delays, lots of Bad TCP packets, and an HTTP error. Look at how many DNS queries were sent out to resolve all the hosts to which the client must connect just to load the main page.

tr-delays.pcapng

This trace file has delays with separate causes. Consider creating and sorting a `tcp.time_delta` or even just a `frame.time_delta` column to locate the delays. Remember that there are some delays which are considered "normal" and shouldn't be the focus in your troubleshooting.

tr-dnserrors.pcapng

Just as the name indicates, this trace file contains DNS errors. What web addresses could not be resolved in this trace file? Can you think of an easy way to know that information using a custom column?

tr-dns-slow.pcapng

The DNS server's delays are the reason we see the ICMP packet in this trace file. By the time the DNS server sends the second response, the client has already closed the listening port for it.

tr-ftpfail.pcapng

This short trace file depicts a failed login attempt to an FTP server. You can test your FTP Errors button on this trace file.

tr-ftphttp.pcapng

This trace file contains FTP and HTTP sessions from 192.168.1.72. Do you see any delays above 1 second, FTP errors or HTTP errors in this trace file?

tr-general.pcapng

This trace file contains some general traffic. It can be used to practice creating exclusion display filters for ARP, DNS, DHCP, and more.

tr-general101d.pcapng

This trace file depicts a slow file transfer. Use your knowledge of the Wireshark Expert and maybe the Golden Graph to find out what is affecting performance.

tr-goldengraph.pcapng

This is an ideal trace file on which to build the Golden Graph. If your graph lines are too far apart, consider using a logarithmic scale for the Y Axis.

tr-httpdelta.pcapng

This trace file contains traffic to/from a user's machine that is checking for Windows updates as well as virus detection file updates. Add an `http.host` column to see with whom the client is communicating. There are also some large delays—many which are normal and some that are not.

tr-http-pcaprnet101.pcapng

This trace file also contains some serious delays. Use your troubleshooting skills to determine if the client, infrastructure or server is slowing things down.

tr-ietfwithbackground.pcapng

Someone is visiting www.ietf.org while numerous background processes run. Although the trace file appears relatively clean there is an indication of a problem with a TCP handshake.

tr-keepalives.pcapng

These keep alives are not associated with a Zero Window condition. Pay close attention to the Time column when you look for these packets. Will the connection stay "up?"

tr-localresolution.pcapng

If the resolution process doesn't complete correctly, no one is happy. In this trace you will find out that one local host can't talk with another local host. Why?

tr-malaysianairlines.pcapng

When trying to look up Malaysian Airlines flights, the user experiences numerous delays. Start by looking at the DNS response time and then identify any HTTP errors in the process.

tr-nameresolution.pcapng
The name says it all. This trace file contains name resolution issues. Test your DNS Errors button on this file. In addition, if you created the DNS Errors "butt ugly" coloring rule, look for those orange packets.

tr-noserver.pcapng
In this trace file, our client isn't even getting TCP resets from the target. Notice the time column. Follow a single TCP conversation and check out the exponential backoff process that starts at a 3 second delay when a SYN fails.

tr-notqueuing.pcapng
Compare this trace file to *tr-queuing.pcapng*. In this case we see packet loss when we zoom in closely on the IO graph.

tr-problemstream.pcapng
This trace file contains a single TCP conversation that experiences packet loss. The problem is almost invisible when we build the Golden Graph (IO Graph with the Bad TCP coloring rule applied) until we change the Y axis scale to logarithmic. This trace file also illustrates the information leak addressed in Wireshark bug 8349.

tr-queuing.pcapng
Compare this trace file to *tr-notqueuing.pcapng*. In this case we see the EKG pattern when we zoom in closely on the IO graph.

tr-reusedports.pcapng
Reused ports are usually not a problem. In this trace file, reused ports are a problem, however. Watch what happens when we hit a reused port situation in this trace file.

tr-serverresponse.pcapng
In this trace file, you will see a problem that is due to a server that is not responding to service requests. What happens after the TCP handshake?

tr-smbjoindomain.pcapng
Use this trace file to test your SMB/SMB2 Errors filter expression button. You should see two error packets in the trace.

tr-smb-slow.pcapng
Use this trace file to test graphing `smb.time` in an Advanced IO Graph. Since you are in the file, why not look at the Expert Infos window and run your filter expression buttons against the trace file?

tr-tcpdeltatime.pcapng
We looked at this trace from the perspective of the Advanced IO Graph. Plot the MAX (*) Calc value for `tcp.time_delta` to find the highest delays in the trace file.

tr-throughput.pcapng
This file transfer process is going to take a loooong time. Are we dealing with time issues, resolution problems, application errors or something else?

tr-twohosts.pcapng

This trace file contains traffic from two hosts that are using FTP to download a file called *OOo_3.3.0_Linux_x86_langpack-rpm_en-US.tar.gz*. We used a port-based filter to view the FTP data transfer connection established by 192.168.1.119. We also used this trace file and the Expressions button to walk through creating a display filter.

tr-voip-extensions.pcapng

This trace contains a VoIP call set-up and call –which did not complete successfully. Try your SIP Errors button on this trace file to quickly spot the reason for the failure.

tr-winsize.pcapng

This trace file contains a single TCP conversation. An HTTP client is downloading a large file from a web server. This trace file demonstrates the importance of looking at delays and then trying to identify any other related symptoms.

tr-winzero-print.pcapng

Printers are weird… so is the traffic to get your job printed. Take a look at the behavior of this printer as the user indicates they want to print double-sided format.

tr-wlanissues.pcapng

This trace file contains traffic from a WLAN in trouble. Try your WLAN Retries filter expression button on this trace file. Also look inside the Radiotap headers to see all the metadata included therein.

tr-youtubebad.pcapng

Use the `http.time` field to measure HTTP response time in this trace file. Where are you pointing that finger?

APPENDIX C:
NETWORK ANALYST'S GLOSSARY

Note: This Glossary defines terms as these terms relate to network analysis and Wireshark functionality.

This page intentionally left blank.

ACK—Short for Acknowledgement, this term is used to refer to the packets that are sent to acknowledge receipt of some packet on a TCP connection. For example, a handshake packet (SYN) containing an initial sequence number is acknowledged with SYN/ACK. A data packet would also be acknowledged.

Address Resolution Protocol, see *ARP*

AirPcap—This specialized wireless adapter was originally created by CACE Technologies (now owned by Riverbed) to capture wireless network traffic. Designed to work on Windows hosts, this adapter can capture traffic in promiscuous mode (capture traffic sent to all target hardware addresses, not just the local hardware address) and monitor mode (capture traffic on all wireless networks by not joining any wireless network). For more information, visit www.riverbed.com.

Annotations (aka "Comments")—Annotations, or comments, can be added to an entire trace file or to individual packets. Trace file annotations can be seen by clicking on the **Annotation** button on the Status Bar or by selecting **Statistics | Summary**. Packet annotations can be seen above the Frame section of a packet in the Packet Details pane or by opening the **Expert Infos** window and selecting the **Packet Comments** tab. The display filter `pkt_comment` will show you all packets that contain comments. Add this as a column to read all comments in the Packet List pane.

Apply as Filter—After right-clicking on a field, conversation, endpoint, or protocol/application, you can apply a display filter immediately using this option.

ARP (Address Resolution Protocol)—ARP packets are sent to determine if someone is using a particular IP address on a network (gratuitous ARP) or to locate a local host's hardware address (ARP requests/replies). Both the capture and display filters for ARP are simply `arp`.

asymmetric routing—This occurs when traffic flowing in one direction takes a different path than traffic flowing in the opposite direction. Although often not causing a problem in network performance, capturing traffic on one asymmetric path can lead to indications of Previous Segment Not Captured and ACKed Unseen Segment in Wireshark's Expert system.

background traffic—This traffic type occurs with no user-intervention. Typical background traffic may include virus detection tool updates, OS updates, and broadcasts, or multicasts from other devices on the network. Start capturing traffic on your own computer and then walk away. Let the capture run for a while to get a baseline of your machine's background traffic.

Berkeley Packet Filtering (BPF) Syntax—This is the syntax used by Wireshark capture filters. This filtering format was originally defined for tcpdump, a command-line capture tool. For more information on Wireshark capture filter syntax, see wiki.wireshark.org/CaptureFilters.

BOOTP (Bootstrap Protocol) — This protocol offered static address assignment and is the predecessor of DHCP (Dynamic Host Configuration Protocol). DHCP offers dynamic address assignment. IPv4 DHCP packets contain a BOOTP header and can be filtered on using the `bootp` display filter for DHCPv4 and `dhcpv6` for DHCPv6. Also see *DHCP*.

Bootstrap Protocol, see *BOOTP*

broadcast — Broadcast is a type of address that indicates "everyone" on this network. The Ethernet MAC-layer broadcast address is 0xFF:FF:FF:FF:FF:FF. The IPv4 broadcast address is 255.255.255.255, whereas a subnet broadcast would be 10.2.255.255, which means "everyone" on network 10.2.0.0. Broadcasts to the 255.255.255.255 address are not forwarded by routers, but broadcasts are forwarded out all switch ports. Subnet broadcasts may be forwarded by a router if that router is configured to do so.

Bytes in Flight — This tracking feature is enabled in the TCP preferences (*Track Number of Bytes in Flight*) to indicate the number of unacknowledged bytes sent in either direction between TCP peers. This is a useful column when a receiver begins advertising a Zero Window condition after not sending ACKs for a while.

Capinfos-This command-line tool is installed with Wireshark and can be used to obtain basic information about a trace file, such as file size, capture duration and checksum value. If you are going to use a trace file as evidence of a security breach, consider obtaining file checksum values immediately after saving trace files to prove the trace file has not been tampered with. The command `capinfos -H <filename>` will generate SHA1, RMD160 and MD5 checksum values only whereas `capinfos <filename>` will generate checksum values as well as all other file information.

Capture Engine-The Capture Engine is responsible for working with the link layer interfaces for packet capture. Wireshark uses dumpcap for the actual capture process.

capture filter — This is a filter that is applied during the capture process only. This filter cannot be applied to saved trace files. Use this filter type sparingly as you can't retrieve and analyze the traffic you drop with a capture filter. Use the `-f` parameter to apply capture filters with Tshark and dumpcap.

capture interface — The capture interface is the hardware device upon which you can capture traffic. To view available capture interfaces, click the **Interfaces** button on the main toolbar. If Wireshark does not see any interfaces, you cannot capture traffic. Most likely the link-layer driver (libpcap, WinPcap, or AirPcap) did not load properly.

Cascade Pilot® — The traffic visualization tool created by Loris Degioanni. Cascade Pilot can open, analyze, and visually represent very large trace files with ease. In addition, Cascade Pilot can build reports based on the charts and graphs, and export key traffic elements to Wireshark for further analysis. For more information on Cascade Pilot, see www.riverbed.com.

checksum errors — When you enable checksum validation for Ethernet, IP, UDP, or TCP in the protocol preferences area, Wireshark calculates the checksum values in each of those headers. If the checksum value is incorrect, Wireshark marks the packet with a checksum error. Since so many machines support checksum offloading, it is not uncommon to see outbound packets marked with a bad checksum because the checksum hasn't been applied yet. Turn off checksum validation and/or disable the Bad Checksum coloring rule to remove these false positives. See also *task offloading*.

CIDR (Classless Interdomain Routing) Notation — This is a way of representing the network portion of an IP address by appending a bit count value. This value indicates the number of bits that comprise the network portion of the address. For example, 130.57.3.0/24 indicates that the network portion of the address is 24-bits long (130.57.3), and is equivalent to a subnet mask of 255.255.255.0.

Classless Interdomain Routing, see *CIDR Notation*

Comma-Separated Value format, see *CSV format*

comparison operators — Comparison operators are used to look for a value in a field. For example, `ip.addr==10.2.2.2` uses the "equal" comparison operator. Other comparison operators include `>`, `>=`, `<`, `<=`, and `!=`.

Core Engine — This area of the Wireshark application is considered the "work horse" of Wireshark. Frames come into the capture engine from the Wiretap Library or from the Capture Engine. Packet dissectors, display filters, and plugins all work as part of the Core Engine.

CSV (Comma-Separated Value) format — This file format separates records with a simple comma. Saving to CSV format is available when exporting packet dissections. Using this format, Wireshark can export all Packet List pane column information for evaluation by another program, such as a spreadsheet program.

delayed ACK — Defined in *RFC 1122, "Requirements for Internet Hosts -- Communication Layers"*, delayed ACKs reduce the number of ACKs in order to increase efficiency. RFC 1122 states that ACKs should not be excessively delayed (delays must be less than .5 seconds), and when a stream of full-sized segments is received, there should be an ACK for every other segment. Note that many TCP implementations violate this rule by sending delayed ACKs less often than every other segment.

delta time (general) — This time value measures the elapsed time from the end of one packet to the end of the next packet. Set the **Time** column to this measurement using **View | Time Display Format | Seconds Since Previous Displayed Packet**. This field is inside the Frame section of the Packet Details pane (called **Time delta from previous displayed frame**).

delta time (TCP) — This time value can be enabled in TCP preferences (*Calculate conversation timestamps*) and provides a measurement from the end of one TCP packet in a stream to the end of the next TCP packet in that same stream. The field is added to the end of the TCP header in the [Timestamps] section. To filter on high TCP delta times, use `tcp.time_delta > x`, where x is a number of seconds (x.xxxxxx format is supported as well).

DHCP (Dynamic Host Configuration Protocol) — This protocol is used to dynamically assign IP addresses and other configuration parameters to IP clients. The capture filter for IPv4 DHCP traffic is `port 67` (alternately you can use `port 68`). The display filter for IPv4 DHCP traffic is `bootp`. The capture filter for DHCPv6 traffic is `port 546` (alternately you can use `port 547`). The display filter for DHCPv6 traffic is `dhcpv6`.

Differentiated Services Code Point, see *DSCP*

display filter — This filter can be applied during a live capture or to a saved trace file. Display filters can be used to focus on specific types of traffic. Wireshark's display filters use a proprietary format. Display filters are saved in a text file called *dfilters*. Use the `-R` parameter to apply display filters while using Tshark. Dumpcap does not support display filters.

dissectors — Dissectors are the Wireshark software elements that break apart applications and protocols to display their field names and interpreted values. To download the Wireshark dissectors' code, visit anonsvn.wireshark.org/viewvc/, select a Wireshark version and navigate to the *epan/dissectors* directory.

DNS (Domain Name System) — DNS is used to resolve names to IP addresses and much more. We are most familiar with hosts using DNS to obtain the IP address for a host name typed into a URL field of a browser, but DNS can provide additional information, such as the mail exchange server or canonical name (alias) information. Although most often seen over UDP, DNS can run over TCP for requests/responses and always runs over TCP for DNS zone transfers (transfer of information between DNS servers). The capture filter syntax for DNS traffic is `port 53`; the display filter syntax is simply `dns`.

Domain Name System, see *DNS*

DSCP (Differentiated Services Code Point) — This feature adds prioritization to the traffic using the DSCP fields in the IP header. To determine if DSCP is in use, apply a display filter for `ip.dsfield.dscp != 0`.

dumpcap — This command-line tool is referred to as a "pure packet capture application" and is included with Wireshark. Dumpcap is used for packet capture by Wireshark and Tshark. Type `dumpcap -h` at the command line to learn what options are available when running dumpcap alone.

Dynamic Host Configuration Protocol, see *DHCP*

Editcap — This command-line tool is included with Wireshark and is used to split trace files into file sets, remove duplicates, and alter trace file timestamps. To see the options available with Editcap, type **editcap -h** at the command prompt.

Ethereal — This is the former name of the Wireshark project. On June 7, 2006, Gerald Combs and the entire development team moved from Ethereal to the new Wireshark home. This name change was prompted by a trademark issue when Gerald Combs, the creator of Ethereal, moved to his new job at CACE Technologies.

Ethernet — Developed at Xerox PARC in 1973-1974, Ethernet defines a networking technology that consists of a physical connection to a shared medium (wire), the bit transmission mechanism, and the frame structure.

Ethernet header — This header is placed in front of the network layer header (such as IP) to get a packet from one machine to another on a local network. Once the Ethernet header is placed on the packet, we refer to it as a frame. The common Ethernet header format is Ethernet II and contains a destination hardware address (6 bytes), source hardware address (6 bytes) and Type field (2 bytes). Wireshark looks at the Type field to determine which dissector should receive the packet next. There is also an Ethernet trailer that consists of a 4-byte Frame Check Sequence field. See also *Ethernet trailer*.

Ethernet trailer — This 4-byte trailer is added to the end of a packet and consists of a Frame Check Sequence field (checksum field). Upon receipt of a frame, each device strips off the Ethernet header and trailer and performs a checksum calculation on the packet content. The receiving device compares its checksum result against the value seen in the checksum field to determine if the packet is corrupt. Most NICs strip off the Ethernet trailer before handing the frame to the computer/operating system/Wireshark.

exclusion filter — This type of filter either drops frames during the capture process (exclusion capture filter) or removes the frame from view (exclusion display filter). An example of an exclusion capture filter is **not port 80**. An example of an exclusion display filter is **!ip.addr==10.2.2.2**.

Expert Infos — This Wireshark window displays and links to various errors, warnings, notes, and additional information detected in the trace file. This window also displays packet comments. You can launch the Expert Infos window by clicking on the **Expert Infos** button on the Status Bar.

File Transfer Protocol, see *FTP*

FIN (Finish) — This bit is set by a TCP host to indicate that it is finished sending data on the connection. Once both sides of a TCP connection send a packet with the FIN bit set, each side will begin timing out the connection.

frame — The term used to define a unit of communications that consists of a packet surrounded by a MAC-layer header and trailer. Wireshark numbers each frame as it is captured or opened (in the case of a saved trace file). From that point on, however, Wireshark often refers to these frames as "packets" (**File | Export Specified Packets** for example).

FTP (File Transfer Protocol) — FTP is an established application to transfer data between devices. FTP runs over TCP using port 21 as a default for the command channel while allowing a dynamic port number to be assigned to the data channel. The capture filter for FTP command channel traffic on the default port is `port 21`. The display filter syntax is `tcp.port==21`. Although Wireshark recognizes the filter `ftp`, this filter will not display the TCP connection establishment, maintenance or tear down process.

GIMP (GNU Image Manipulation Program) Graphical Toolkit (GTK) — This is the toolkit used to present the graphical interface including the windows, dialogs, buttons, and columns.

heuristic dissector — A heuristic process can be considered "trial and error." Wireshark hands packets over to the dissectors that match the port in use (the "normal dissector"). If Wireshark does not have a normal dissector, it hands the packet off to a heuristic dissector. The heuristic dissector will look at the information received and, by trial and error, try to see if it fits within the dissector's definition of a certain protocol or application. If not, it sends an error to Wireshark which sends the packet to the next heuristic dissector.

hex — Short for hexadecimal, hex refers to the base 16 counting system, in which the digits are 0-9 and A-F. The Packet Bytes pane displays frame contents in hex format on the left and ASCII format on the right.

hosts **file** — Wireshark refers to its own *hosts* file to resolve names when network name resolution is enabled. This file is located in the Wireshark program file directory. As of Wireshark 1.9.0, you can place a *hosts* file in your profile directory and configure Wireshark's name resolution process to look at that file when resolving names.

HTTP (Hypertext Transfer Protocol) — This is the data transfer protocol used when you browse a web site. Typically seen over TCP port 80, you can create a capture filter using `tcp port 80` or a display filter using `tcp.port==80`. Although you could use an `http` display filter, that filter will not display the TCP connection establishment, maintenance or tear down process packets.

HTTPS (Hypertext Transfer Protocol Secure) — HTTPS is defined as the secure version of HTTP. In essence, HTTPS is simply HTTP running over SSL/TLS (Secure Socket Layer/Transport Layer Security), which are cryptographic protocols. The capture filter for HTTPS traffic is `port 443`, whereas the display filter is `ssl` (or `tcp.port==443` if you want to view the TCP connection establishment, maintenance or tear down process packets).

Hypertext Transfer Protocol, see *HTTP*

Hypertext Transfer Protocol Secure, see *HTTPS*

IANA (Internet Assigned Numbers Authority) — Based in Marina del Rey, California, IANA is "*responsible for the global coordination of the DNS Root, IP addressing, and other Internet protocol resources.*" For network analysts, www.iana.org is an invaluable resource for field values, assigned multicast addresses, assigned port numbers, and more.

ICMP (Internet Control Message Protocol) — This protocol is used as a messaging service on a network. Most people are familiar with the ICMP-based ping operation. ICMP communications should always be considered when you are troubleshooting network performance. The capture filter and display filter syntax for ICMP is just `icmp`.

inclusion filter — This type of filter either allows frames that match it during the capture process (inclusion capture filter) or displays the frames that match it (inclusion display filter). An example of an inclusion capture filter is `port 80`. An example of an inclusion display filter is `ip.addr==10.2.2.2`.

Internet Assigned Numbers Authority, see *IANA*

Internet Control Message Protocol, see *ICMP*

Internet Protocol (IPv4/v6) — IP is the routed protocol (not the rout*ing* protocol) used to get packets through an internetwork. The capture filter syntax for IPv4 and IPv6 are `ip` and `ip6`, respectively. The display filter syntax for IPv4 and IPv6 are `ip` and `ipv6`, respectively.

IP address — This address identifies a single host, group of hosts, or all hosts on a network. To create a capture filter based on an IPv4 address, the syntax is `host x.x.x.x`. The syntax of an IPv4 display filter is `ip.addr==x.x.x.x`. To create a capture filter based on an IPv6 address, use `host xxxx:xxxx:xxxx:xxxx:xxxx:xxxx:xxxx:xxxx`. For an IPv6 use `ipv6.addr==xxxx:xxxx:xxxx:xxxx:xxxx:xxxx:xxxx:xxxx`.

key hosts — We use the term "key hosts" to refer to the devices that are critical on the network. Key hosts may include the server that maintains the customer database or the CEO's laptop. You define which host should be tracked and analyzed as a key host.

latency — Latency is often used as a synonym for "delay." High latency times may be caused by propagation delay between hosts, switching and routing, and even buffering along a path. To measure the approximate latency times between two TCP peers we can capture at the client and measure the time from the SYN to the SYN/ACK or capture at the server and measure the time from the SYN/ACK to the ACK (the final packet of the 3-way TCP handshake).

libpcap — This is the link-layer driver used for packet capture tools, such as Wireshark. There are numerous other tools that use libpcap for packet capture. For more information, see sourceforge.net/projects/libpcap/.

link-layer driver — This is the driver that hands frames up to Wireshark. WinPcap, libpcap, and AirPcap are three link layer drivers used with Wireshark.

logical operators — These operators are used to expand filters to determine if a value is matched in some form or another. Examples of logical operators are `&&`, `and`, `||`, `or`, `!`, and `not`. An example of logical operator use is `tcp.analysis.flags && ip.addr==10.2.2.2`.

MAC (Media Access Control) address — This address is associated with a network interface card or chipset. On an Ethernet network, MAC addresses are 6 bytes long. Switches use MAC addresses to differentiate and identify devices connected to switch ports. Switches use these addresses to make forwarding decisions. To build a capture filter based on a MAC address, use the syntax `ether host 00:08:15:00:08:15`, for example. To build a display filter based on a MAC address, use `eth.addr==00:08:15:00:08:15`, for example.

manuf **file** — This Wireshark file contains a list of manufacturer OUI (Organizational Unit Identifiers) as defined by the IEEE (Institute of Electrical and Electronics Engineers). These three-byte values are used to distinguish the maker of a network interface card or chipset. In Wireshark, MAC name resolution is on by default, so you will see these OUI friendly names in the MAC addresses (such as Hewlett-_a7:bf:a3). This *manuf* file resides in the Wireshark program file directory.

Maximum Segment Size, see *MSS*

Maximum Transmission Unit, see *MTU*

Media Access Control address, see *MAC address*

Mergecap — This command-line tool is used to merge or to concatenate trace files. If you have a set of trace files, but you want to create a single IO Graph of all the communications in those trace files, consider using Mergecap to combine the files into a single file before opening an IO Graph. To identify the options available with Mergecap, type `mergecap -h`.

metadata — This is basically "extra data." In Wireshark, we see metadata in the Frame section at the top of the Packet Details pane. Using the .pcapng format, you can also add your own metadata through trace file annotations and packet annotations.

MSS (Maximum Segment Size) — This value defines how many bytes can follow a TCP header in a packet. During the TCP handshake, each side of the conversation provides their MSS value. A common MSS value on an Ethernet network is 1,460.

MTU (Maximum Transmission Unit) — The MTU defines the number of bytes that can reside within data link header (such as an Ethernet header). If a driver reduces the size of the MTU, most likely the TCP MSS will also be reduced. A common MTU value on an Ethernet network is 1500 bytes.

multicast — This is a type of address that targets a group of hosts. At the MAC layer, most multicast addresses begin with 01:00:5e while IPv4 multicasts begin with a number 224 through 239 in the first IP address byte location. An example of an IPv4 multicast is 224.0.0.2, which is targeted at all local routers. IPv6 multicasts have the preface ff00::/8 (the "8" signifying that the first 8 bits are the bits we are interested in).

name resolution — This feature is used to associate a name with a device, network interface card/chip, or port. Wireshark supports three types of name resolution: MAC name resolution, transport name resolution, and network name resolution. MAC name resolution is on by default and resolves the first three bytes of hardware addresses to a manufacturer name (such as Apple_70:66:f5). Transport name resolution is on by default and resolves port numbers to port names (such as port 80 resolved to http). Network name resolution is off by default and resolves an IP address to a host name (such as 74.125.19.106 resolving to *www.google.com*). In Wireshark, when you enable network name resolution, Wireshark may generate a series of DNS Pointer queries to obtain host names. Wireshark can be configured to look at a *hosts* file for network name resolution, rather than generating DNS Pointer queries. You can even have a separate *hosts* file for each profile.

NAT (Network Address Translation) — NAT devices alter the IP address of hosts while maintaining a master list of all the original IP addresses and the new addresses in order to forward traffic back to the correct address. NAT is often used to hide internal addresses from the outside or to enable an organization to use simple private IP addresses, such as 10.2.0.1.

NetBIOS (Network Basic Input/Output System) — This is the session-level protocol used by applications, such as SMB, to communicate among hosts on a network, typically a Microsoft-product network. In Wireshark, you can apply a display filter for **nbss** (NetBIOS Session Service) or **nbns** (NetBIOS Name Service).

Network Address Translation, see *NAT*

Network Basic Input/Output System, see *NetBIOS*

network interface card (NIC) — This card, which is typically just a chipset, offers the physical connection to the network. NICs now offer greater capability than just applying a MAC header to the packets. Some hosts now support task offloading, which relies on the NIC for various functions such as segmenting TCP data and applying IP, UDP, and TCP checksum values. See also *Task offload*.

Nmap — This network mapping tool was created by Gordon Lyons (Fyodor) to discover and characterize network hosts. For more information, visit www.nmap.org.

oversubscribed switch — Oversubscription occurs when a switch is asked to forward more traffic than the bandwidth limitations allow. When you are using switch port spanning, an oversubscribed switch will drop packets that exceed the available bandwidth on the switch port on which Wireshark is connected. In the trace file, indications of an oversubscribed switch port include ACKed Unseen Segments and the detection of Previous Segment Not Captured without any packet loss recovery process following.

packet — This is the term used to describe the elements inside a MAC frame. Once you strip off the frame, you are looking at a packet. We use this term loosely in analysis. Although Wireshark displays frames, we often refer to them as "packets".

Packet Bytes pane — This is the bottom pane displayed by default in Wireshark. The Packet Bytes pane shows the contents of the frame in both hexadecimal and ASCII formats. When you click a field in the Packet Details pane, Wireshark highlights those bytes and the related ASCII characters in the Packet Bytes pane. To toggle this pane between hidden and displayed, select **View | Packet Bytes**.

packet comments (aka packet annotations) — Right-click a packet in the Packet List pane and choose **Add or Edit Packet Comments** to add packet annotations. This feature is only supported in trace files saved in the .pcapng format. Packet comments are shown above the Frame section in the Packet Details pane. To view packet comments, open the Expert Infos window and click the **Packet Comments** tab. You can export all trace file and packet comments using **Statistics | Comments Summary | Copy**.

Packet Details Pane — This is the middle pane displayed by default in Wireshark. This pane shows the individual fields and field interpretations offered by Wireshark. When you select a frame in the Packet List pane, Wireshark displays that frame's information in the Packet Details pane. To toggle this pane between hidden and displayed, select **View | Packet Details**. This is likely a pane you will use very often in Wireshark because you can right-click on a field and quickly apply a display filter or coloring rule based on that field.

Packet List pane — This is the top pane displayed by default in Wireshark. This pane shows a summary of the individual frame values. When you select a frame in the Packet List pane, Wireshark displays that frame's information in the Packet Details pane. To toggle this pane between hidden and displayed, select **View | Packet List**. This is likely a pane you will use very often in Wireshark as you can right-click on a frame and quickly apply a conversation filter or reassemble communications using **Follow TCP stream**, **Follow UDP stream**, or **Follow SSL stream**.

.pcap **(Packet Capture)** — This trace file format is the default format for earlier versions of Wireshark (before Wireshark 1.8). This format is also referred to as the tcpdump or libpcap trace file format.

.pcapng, also *.pcap-ng* **(.pcap Next Generation)** — This trace file format is the successor to the .pcap format. This new format facilitates saving metadata, such as packet and trace file comments, local interface details, and local IP address, with a trace file. For more information about the .pcapng format, see wiki.wireshark.org/Development/PcapNg.

Per-Packet Interface, see *PPI*

Pilot, see *Cascade Pilot*

port spanning — This process is used to configure a switch to copy the traffic to and from one or more switch ports down the port to which Wireshark is connected. Not all switches support this capability. Some people refer to this as port mirroring. Note that port spanned switches will not forward corrupt packets to Wireshark. See also *Tap*.

PPI (Per-Packet Interface) — PPI is an 802.11 header specification that provides out-of-band information in a pseudoheader that is prepended to the 802.11 header. Used by AirPcap adapters, the PPI pseudoheader includes channel-frequency information, signal power, noise level, and more.

preferences **file** — This file contains the protocol preference settings, name resolution settings, column settings, and more. Each profile has its own *preferences* file, which is contained in the personal configurations folder.

Prepare a Filter — This task can be performed by right-clicking on a packet in the Packet List pane. **Prepare a Filter** creates, but does not apply, a display filter based on the selected element. See also *Apply as Filter*.

profiles — Profiles contain the customized configurations for Wireshark. There is a single profile available on a new Wireshark system — the *Default* profile. The current profile in use is displayed in the right side of the Status Bar. To switch between profiles, click the **Profile** area in the Status Bar. To create a new profile, right-click the **Profile** area.

Protocol Data Unit (PDU) — This is a set of data transferred between hosts. In Wireshark, you will see [TCP segment of a reassembled PDU] when you allow the TCP subdissector to reassemble TCP streams. In essence, these packets contain segments of a file that is being transferred.

Protocol Hierarchy window — This window breaks down the traffic according to the protocols in use and provides details regarding packet percentages and byte percentages. This window is available under the Statistics menu option. Watch for unusual protocols or applications or the dreaded "data" under TCP, UDP, or IP. This designation means that Wireshark does not recognize the traffic, which is unusual considering the number of dissectors included in Wireshark.

protocol preferences — These preferences define how Wireshark handles various protocols and applications. Protocol preferences are set by right-clicking on a protocol in the Packet Details pane, by selecting **Edit | Preferences** from the menu or by clicking the **Edit Preferences** button on the main toolbar.

proxy device — Proxy devices act on behalf of another host. In TCP/IP networking, hosts establish a TCP connection with a proxy device which, in turn, establishes a separate TCP connection with the target. If the two TCP connections do not have similar characteristics for Window Scaling and SACK, problems may occur.

QoS (Quality of Service) — This term refers to a method of prioritizing traffic as it travels through a network. QoS settings can be defined on interconnecting devices (forward web browsing traffic before email traffic, for example) or by an application. When defined by an application, the DSCP bits can be set to prioritize the traffic over other traffic. See also *DSCP*.

Quality of Service, see *QoS*

radio frequency, see *RF*

redirection — There are several types of redirection that can occur on a network. One redirection is Route Redirection (ICMP Type 5) which should be rare. Another type of redirection is an application redirection. For example, HTTP 3xx Status Codes are all redirections.

relative start (Rel.Start) — This value is shown in the Conversations window and indicates the first time this conversation was seen in the trace file. You may need to expand the Conversations window to see this column. The time is based on seconds since the first packet in the trace file.

Retransmission — Retransmissions are triggered by a receiving host that complains about missing segments or transmitting hosts that time out waiting for ACKs to data packets that have been sent. Ideally, Selective ACK (SACK) is in use to prevent excessive retransmissions on a network.

RF (Radio Frequency) — Any frequency in the electromagnetic spectrum that is associated with radio waves. Wireless networks (802.11) use RF to transmit packets between WLAN hosts and access points. A special adapter (such as an AirPcap adapter) may be required to capture packets on an RF-based network.

RST (Reset) — This bit is set by a host to terminate or refuse a TCP connection. In an established TCP connection, once this bit has been set in an outbound packet, the sender cannot send any further data on that connection. In a typical TCP connection termination process, each side of the connection sends a packet with the RST bit set and the connection is immediately closed.

Server Message Block, see *SMB*

services **file** — This file contains a list of port numbers and service names. All TCP/IP hosts have a *services* file and Wireshark has its own *services* file as well. This file resides in the Wireshark program file directory. When transport name resolution is enabled, Wireshark replaces port numbers with service names. For example, port 80 would be replaced with "http." You can edit this file if you do not like the service names displayed.

Simple Network Management Protocol, see *SNMP*

SMB (Server Message Block) — Also referred to as Common Internet File System (CIFS), SMB is an application layer protocol used to provide network access, file transfer, printing, and other functions on a Microsoft-based network.

SNMP (Simple Network Management Protocol) — This device management protocol requires that a managed device maintain a database of managed items. Managing hosts view and/or edit that database. You may see SNMP traffic flowing between network hosts and network printers, which often have SNMP enabled to track information such as ink levels, paper levels, and more. To filter on SNMP traffic use the capture filter **port 161 or port 162** or the display filter **snmp**.

Snort — Snort is a Network Intrusion Detection System (NIDS) that was created in 1998 by Martin Roesch and is currently maintained by Sourcefire. Snort relies on a set of rules to identify and generate alerts on network scans and attack traffic. For more information, see www.snort.org.

Spanning Tree Protocol (STP) — Spanning Tree is a protocol used to automatically resolve Layer 2 loops on a switched network. Spanning Tree traffic flows between switches to create a "tree" view of the network (single trunk with many branches flowing outwards) and eradicate any network switch loops that may exist.

Stream index number — This number is applied by Wireshark to each TCP conversation seen in the trace file. The first Stream index number is set at 0. When you right-click on a TCP communication in the Packet List pane and choose **Follow TCP stream**, Wireshark applies a display filter based on this Stream index number (for example, `tcp.stream==3`).

stream reassembly — This is the process of reassembling everything after the transport-layer header (TCP or UDP) enabling you to clearly read through the requests and replies in a conversation. Communications from the first host seen are colored red; communications from the second host seen are colored blue.

subdissector — This is a dissector that is called by another dissector. You will see this term when you view TCP preferences (*Allow subdissector to reassemble TCP streams*). In the case of web browsing traffic, the HTTP dissector is a subdissector of the TCP dissector.

subnet — This term defines a subset of a network and is applied by lengthening network masks. For example, if you want to create two subnets out of a single network, network 10.2.0.0/16 for example, lengthen the subnet to /24 (24-bits) and assign 10.2.1.0/24 to some hosts and 10.2.2.0/24 to other hosts. The network mask indicates that we have two networks now.

SYN (Synchronize Sequence Numbers) — This bit is set in the first two packets of the TCP handshake to synchronize the Initial Sequence Numbers (ISNs) from each TCP peer. You can use a display filter based on this bit to view the first two packets of each handshake (`tcp.flags.syn==1`) which can be used to determine the round trip time between hosts.

TAP, aka tap (Test Access Port) — These devices are used to intercept network communications and copy the traffic down a monitor port. Basic taps do not make any forwarding decisions on traffic and offer a transparent view of network communications. NetOptics is a company that makes network taps (see www.netoptics.com). See also *port spanning*.

task offloading — This process offloads numerous processes to the network interface card to free up the host's CPU for other tasks. Task offload can affect your analysis session when checksums are calculated by the network interface card on a host upon which you are running Wireshark. Since checksum values haven't been calculated yet, the checksums are incorrect at the point of capture. If you enable IP, UDP, or TCP checksum validation, or you have the Checksum Errors coloring rule enabled, you may see numerous false positives caused by task offload of the checksum calculation.

TCP/IP (Transmission Control Protocol/Internet Protocol) — This term refers to an entire suite of protocols and applications that provide connectivity among worldwide computer systems. The term "TCP/IP" refers to more than TCP and IP, it refers to UDP, ICMP, ARP, and more.

TFTP (Trivial File Transfer Protocol) — This file transfer protocol runs over UDP, offering minimal file transfer functionality. Most commonly, TFTP uses port 69, but you must keep in mind that many applications can be configured to run over non-standard port numbers. Unexpected TFTP traffic can be a symptom of a security breach on your network.

throughput — Network throughput defines the volume of bits that can travel through a network. You can use Wireshark's TCP Stream Graph – Throughput Graph or the IO Graph to examine throughput levels in a trace file.

Time to Live, see *TTL*

TLS (Transport Layer Security) — TLS is a cryptographic protocol based on Secure Socket Layer (SSL). When analyzing TLS traffic, you can look at the initial TLS handshake packets to identify connection establishment problems. To decrypt this traffic, you must have the appropriate decryption key. TLS preferences are configured under the SSL preference area in Wireshark. To capture TLS/SSL-based traffic, use a port-based capture filter, such as `port 443`. The display filter syntax for TLS/SSL-based traffic is `SSL`.

trace file — This general term refers to all files that contain network traffic, regardless of the format of the file. Wireshark currently uses the .pcapng trace file format, but it can understand most other common trace file formats. Trace files generally include a file header (which contains information about the entire trace file, including the indication of the trace file format in use) and packet headers that include metadata (such as comments) about individual packets.

TraceWrangler — Created by Jasper Bongertz, this free Windows tool can be used to sanitize trace files. TraceWrangler can be downloaded from www.tracewrangler.com.

Transport Layer Security, see *TLS*

Trivial File Transfer Protocol, see *TFTP*

Tshark — This command-line tool can be used to capture, display, and obtain basic statistics on live traffic or saved trace files. Tshark relies on dumpcap to actually capture the traffic. By far the most feature-rich version of the command-line capture tools, you can type `tshark -h` to find the list of available Tshark parameters.

TTL (Time to Live) — This IP header field is decremented by each router as the packet is forwarded along a network path. If a packet arrives at a router with a TTL value of 1, it cannot be forwarded because you cannot decrement the TTL to zero and forward the packet. The packet will be discarded.

UDP (User Datagram Protocol) — This connectionless transport protocol is used by many basic network communications, including all broadcasts, all multicasts, DHCP, DNS requests, and more. The capture filter and display filter syntax to capture UDP is `udp`.

URI (Uniform Resource Indicator) — This term defines the actual element being requested in an HTTP communication. For example, when you analyze a web browsing session, you might see a request for the "/" URI. This "/" is a request for the default page (*index.html*, for example). To build a display filter to show any packets that contain a URI, use `http.request.uri`.

User Datagram Protocol, see *UDP*

WinPcap (Windows Packet Capture) — This Windows-specific link-layer driver is used by Wireshark to capture traffic on a wired network. Originally created by Loris Degioanni. WinPcap is the industry leading utility for various network tools. For more information, see www.winpcap.org.

Wiretap Library — This library gives you the raw packet data from trace files. Wireshark's Wiretap Library understands many different trace file formats and can be seen when you select **File | Open** and click the drop-down arrow next to **Files of Type**.

WLAN (Wireless Local Area Network) — This term describes networks that rely on RF (radio frequency) media to communicate between hosts. Wireshark contains dissectors for various WLAN traffic elements. The AirPcap adapter is a great adapter for capturing WLAN traffic.

This page intentionally left blank.

INDEX

F

G

S

This page intentionally left blank.

Learn Wireshark

All Access Pass (AAP) Online Training

Register and Purchase Online
Visit https://www.lcuportal2.com to learn more about the All Access Pass.

Enroll in Classes
View available course information (including credit hours) and register for your online courses. You can enter a course immediately after registering.

My Classes
View the list of courses for which you are registered and your status (completed or in progress).

My Transcript
Print or email your training transcript (in progress and completed courses) including course CPE credits and completion dates.

AAP Special Events
Register for live AAP events or access AAP event handouts from past or upcoming events.

SAMPLE COURSE LIST

- Wireshark Jumpstart 101
- Hacked Hosts
- Analyze and Improve Throughput
- Top 10 Reasons Your Network is Slow
- TCP Analysis In-Depth
- DHCP/ARP Analysis
- Nmap Network Scanning 101
- WLAN Analysis 101
- Wireshark 201 Filtering
- New Wireshark Features
- ICMP Analysis
- Analyzing Google Secure Search

- Slow Networks - NOPs/SACK
- TCP Vulnerabilities (MS09-048)
- Packet Crafting to Test Firewalls
- Capturing Packets (Security Focus)
- Troubleshooting with Coloring
- Tshark Command-Line Capture
- Analyze the Zero Window Condition
- Trace File Analysis - Sets 1, 2 and 3
- Whiteboard Lecture Series 1
- Translate Snort Rules to Wireshark
- ...and more

We also offer customized onsite and online training. Visit www.chappellU.com for sample course outlines and more information. Contact us at info@chappellU.com if you have questions regarding your All Access Pass membership.

CPSIA information can be obtained at www.ICGtesting.com
Printed in the USA
BVOW09s1638260615

405894BV00005B/49/P